THE RULING SERVANTS

THE RULING SERVANTS

BUREAUCRACY IN RUSSIA, FRANCE
—AND BRITAIN?

E. STRAUSS

Ruskin House

GEORGE ALLEN & UNWIN LTD

MUSEUM STREET LONDON

FIRST PUBLISHED IN 1961

© *George Allen and Unwin Ltd.*, 1961

Printed in Great Britain
11 *on* 13 *pt Ehrhardt type*
by Simson Shand Ltd
London, Hertford and Harlow

PREFACE

Every generation embodies its hopes and fears in idols and monsters which assume giant size by projection on the dark screen of the future. Bureaucracy is one of the most prominent monsters of our time. Its shadow hovers over all organized efforts of modern man, but its most frightening impact is due to an intimate alliance with Leviathan itself—the State.

That our lives may be in danger of falling under the domination of large, irresponsible bureaucracies is a serious matter, even though the threat may be less than has often been claimed. This possibility is made even less palatable by the fact that the modern Leviathan is singularly lacking in grandeur and heroic stature. There is, indeed, something incongruous about it which seems to call as much for satire as for opposition, for this enormous whole consists of the combined efforts of a large number of petty agents. Like the spectacle of a Gulliver tied hand and foot by the threads of his Lilliputian captors, modern society enmeshed in the irksome bonds of bureaucratic restrictions provokes scathing taunts as well as denunciation—but all clarion calls to action have remained largely ineffective, and bureaucratic routine has proved immune to the poison of ridicule.

The following study tries to tackle its subject from a different angle. Taking for granted that bureaucracy is ridiculous, inefficient (at least in some respects) and dangerous, it looks for its roots in the soil of modern mass society and its characteristic institutions. In recent years a great deal has been done to explore the nature of large-scale organizations and the management problems arising from them, and this knowledge provides a useful starting point for a discussion of the meaning of bureaucracy and the causes of bureaucratic defects. This analysis leads to the threshold of the problem which makes bureaucracy an issue of critical importance for industrial society: the change in the balance of power between social forces and the administrators of the large organizations which these forces have found indispensable for their purposes. In favourable conditions this change has made enough progress to warrant the question whether there is a

7

genuine prospect of bureaucratic rule either at present or in the fore-seeable future.

Put in this general way, the question is not limited to the State. It applies with almost equal force to political parties, religious bodies and, above all, to the powerful institutions of the modern economy, where The Organization has assumed a life of its own in fundament-ally different economic systems: the 'Organization Man' has become a recognizable type in Soviet Russia as well as in the United States. This book, however, deals primarily with bureaucracy in the govern-ment of the State and the political parties which are its almost indis-pensable counterpart in present-day conditions. Even this limited subject cannot be covered completely in a single volume, and atten-tion has, therefore, been focused on the decisive aspect—the com-plex balance which gives rise to bureaucratic rule, and its effect on the distribution of power in political bodies.

Worthwhile conclusions about the causes and prospects of bureau-cracy as a power factor in different countries cannot be drawn in a vacuum of abstractions but need a concrete basis of solid facts. For this purpose more or less plausible illustrations taken from experi-ence, though useful and instructive in their proper place, are inade-quate, because the growth—or absence—of bureaucracy is rooted far too deeply in the history of each individual country to be understood in isolation. The only practicable alternative was an attempt to sup-ply historical outlines of the development of a few selected countries, concentrating on the interaction of social forces and political insti-tutions. The longer half of the book, therefore, consists of surveys of the political evolution of Russia, France and Great Britain, with special emphasis on the machinery of the State and the organization of the party system.

To review in such a compass the problems of a huge bureaucratic dictatorship, a more or less democratic bureaucracy and a parlia-mentary democracy is obviously a difficult undertaking, for the sub-ject matter of each of these chapters would not be exhausted by as many separate volumes. The inevitable limitation of space affects not only the presentation of the material, for the sacrifice of detail tends to reduce chains of argument to bald assertions. But with all its imperfections, this method provides at least the essential facts for a reasonably balanced view of the main issue—the conditions of bureaucratic rule in countries where it has been successfully established, such as Russia and France, and its chances of victory in countries such as Britain which have so far remained largely free from it.

At the same time, insight into the bureaucratic tendencies of political institutions ought to broaden the understanding of their problems and operation. Russia past and present, and only to a slightly lesser extent France, cannot be properly understood while ignoring the part played by the bureaucracy at the most critical historical moments; and while it would be an exaggeration to claim a similar pivotal importance for the British Civil Service, its role in the direction of government policy, though imperfectly known, is probably greater than frequently assumed.

Last but not least, this approach illustrates, however incompletely, the close link between modern government and the structure of the party system, as a rule the only way through which the ordinary citizen may hope to exert a systematic influence on public affairs. This extension of the political horizon may not reveal a more hopeful vista of the future, but it may help to clarify the real functions of party organizations which are sometimes very different from their ostensible aims.

E. S.

CONTENTS

PART I

CHAPTER ONE

THE AGE OF MASS ORGANIZATION

The inevitable starting point of any enquiry into the problems of modern society is a fundamental common place—the increase in the size of its characteristic organizations, political, economic, military and cultural. At first sight, this is simply a reflection of an apparently still more fundamental process, the increase in population in almost all countries of the modern world.

This increase in numbers is plainly one of the outstanding features of modern society, but it is less the cause than the effect of the social forces which dominate the life of growing numbers—the forces of modern industrialism, organized in its classical form by capitalist entrepreneurs, but more recently ever more prominently by the State.

Population growth has not been confined to the industrialized countries, for the contact of modern capitalism was usually sufficient to undermine the existing barriers to population increase in backward communities, and its progress has invariably been accompanied by a rapid rise in the number of people. At the same time as population increased, the social structure was changed by the familiar effects of industrialization, flight from the land, concentration of large numbers in the towns, etc. Against this background, the State itself was transformed by reform or revolution from a backward, corrupt and inefficient parasite on society into its regulating and directing organ. As an essential part of this process, the administrative machine has grown in size, while the centralization of power has made tremendous advances, above all in the English-speaking countries, where the traditional independence of local self-government has declined in favour of the central authorities.

Where a century ago the number of public officials in important Ministries may have been counted in hundreds or even dozens, it now amounts to thousands or tens of thousands. New departments of State have been created in order to cope with problems, or to satisfy needs, which in earlier days did not even exist (such as mechanical transport by road or air, or the application of atomic energy), or which were commonly regarded as outside the scope of government and its functions (such as care for public health or provision for old age, sickness and unemployment). In particular, each of the Great Wars of the first half of the twentieth century brought in its train a previously undreamed-of extension in the size of the organs of government which was never completely reversed after the return to peace-time conditions.

These wars were 'total' wars involving the use of huge armies of combatants, while practically the whole civilian population in the rear had to contribute in one way or another to the war effort. The war-time functions of the State thus broadened into the co-ordination and direction of the whole life of the community in the service of one over-riding purpose, and the growth of the organs of government followed inevitably from the gigantic effort required, This extreme situation may have been relatively short-lived, but it was preceded by massive war preparations and followed by a slow and painful process of reconversion and recovery which in many countries lasted rather longer than the wars themselves—and even in peace-time the armed forces of most great and not-so-great powers remain formidable mass organizations differing not only in size but also in kind from the armies which fought the Crimean War of 1854 and the Boer War of 1899.

The growth in the number of officials thus reflects the increase in the functions of governments in the modern world and their growing complexity. It is paralleled by the development of party machines which have become an essential part of the political life of practically all modern countries. Political cliques and factions have a respectable historical pedigree, particularly in a parliamentary system such as the British or a political democracy like that of the United States, but parties in the modern sense of organized electoral machines are a product of the recent past. Their creation, or at least their evolution from pressure groups or currents of opinion into organized forces, forms part of a broad social process whose supporters describe it as the democratization of political life, while its enemies denounce it as the corruption of government by the irruption of the masses.

The extension to the adult male population of the right to vote during the second part of the nineteenth century, followed by the enfranchisement of women in most modern countries since the first World War, has made it impossible to ignore the political importance of the masses for the process of government. This fact has been recognized by all political tendencies, and the establishment of national or even international political parties with distinctive programmes and, above all, separate party organizations for the purpose of gaining and keeping the allegiance of the largest possible part of the electorate bears eloquent witness to its importance.

On a different plane, the rise of dictatorships in countries like Russia, Germany and Italy has mainly been the work of political parties, and even well entrenched authoritarian regimes find it necessary to use similar organizations in order to keep the support of the masses, or at least in order to prevent the growth of opposition movements.

The radical transformation in body and spirit of political life in most or all modern countries thus reflects and reinforces the changes in social and economic structure introduced by the rise of industrial capitalism. This reorganization of the political system in all its branches went hand in hand with equally spectacular changes in the structure and organization of the economy. In the middle of the nineteenth century, the typical form of private enterprise was a single unit under the personal control of the proprietor or a few partners, employing a mere handful of men; joint stock companies were carefully restricted by legislation and confined to a few selected fields such as banking, railways, etc. Since then, the technical and economic forces at work within the system have transformed trade and industry even more thoroughly than the parallel social and political forces revolutionized the State and the party system.

On the technical side, the palpable advantages of mass production methods requiring large-scale capital investment in plant and buildings resulted in enormously increased productive units employing hundreds or thousands of men instead of a few dozens. The application of new scientific and technical knowledge to the technique of production and plant organization replaced the single boss assisted by a few overseers by a complicated system of technical experts in charge of different phases of the productive process, and the artisan by a no less complex system of skilled engineers, semi-skilled workers and unskilled 'hands'. Many of the most important modern industries, such as the construction of planes and motor cars, the petrochemical and electronic industries or the production of atomic energy, were, indeed, unknown a comparatively short time ago, and most of these new industries are by technical necessity concentrated in large-scale productive and economic units.

In this development the constant pressure of economic power has been at least as important as technical change. Productive units have grown in size and simultaneously a concentration within the most important industries has resulted in the rise of economic empires dominating and controlling their output and marketing policies. In exceptional cases, a single firm may thus become responsible for a large proportion of the productive power of a whole industry, like Ford in the American motor industry or Krupp and Skoda amongst the German and Czech armament firms; but it is more in keeping with modern trends that such positions should be held by combines resulting from the merger of a number of individual firms, like General Motors in the United States, Imperial Chemical Industries in Britain, or the *I. G. Farben* and the *Vereinigte Stahlwerke* in pre-1945 Germany. Through trusts, holding companies or interlocking directorates the power of a small group or clique may spread through a broad cross-section of the economy of a modern industrial nation, and the co-operation of a few large concerns may dominate a major industry throughout the (non-Communist) world.

Attempts to curb the power of private monopolies through the establishment of publicly owned organizations, and particularly through nationalization, are likely to intensify the trend towards bigger productive and economic units. The (temporary) nationalization of the British road transport industry involved the establishment of British Road Services replacing the activities of thousands of private road hauliers, and the nationalization of the British coal mines substituted a single National Coal Board for hundreds of separate colliery undertakings. However, the outstanding example of nationalization is not the tame and half-hearted application of socialist principles to British practice in the form of public authorities but the Soviet economic system. For the present purpose it is less remarkable for its allegedly socialist inspiration than for its administrative problems which are reflected in the feverish organizational changes which its institutions undergo periodically. In this giant laboratory of social experimentation, 'group management' was discarded in favour of 'personal management', centralization followed decentralization, unitary administration replaced federalism in succession, only to be succeeded by new combinations, when the preceding panacea turned out to be nothing but a counter-revolutionary heresy.

This continuous critique of organizational devices is not unknown in other large organizations—and the history of the British Imperial Chemical Industries provides illuminating examples of the same tendency—but in the Soviet Union it has assumed an importance all its own. It is an essential part of the *mystique* of the Soviet system that the justification for diverging or conflicting interests has disappeared with the overthrow of capitalism; hence social tension or internal friction frequently finds expression in differences of opinion on questions or organization which thus assume critical and symptomatic importance in all branches of Russian life, in the structure of State and government as well as in the economic system with its State industry and its complex agriculture.

This may be one of the reasons why the criticism of 'bureaucracy' is nowhere more vocal than in the Soviet Union, not even in the United States. The almost ritual condemnation of bureaucracy coupled with the existence of powerful bureaucratic tendencies is, indeed, one of the most striking similarities between the two countries, although its American enemies stigmatize it as creeping communism, while its Russian critics attack it as a pernicious remnant of capitalism.

The relative justification as well as the practical limitations of this attitude can be properly understood only against the background of concentration of economic and political power in mass organizations. Such organizations exert a tremendous, if sometimes ill-defined, influence over the peoples of all modern countries in their capacities as citizens, producers and consumers, and not even the professed enemies of this trend can reverse it, when they are in control of all the resources of the government. The State enforces its policies on all members of the community without caring for their opinions about the justice or injustice of these policies—except, perhaps, at election times. The exercise of active political rights is almost invariably monopolized by political mass parties acting on behalf of powerful pressure groups and by no means necessarily with the approval of the majority of their nominal supporters. The citizen as a producer is in nine cases out of ten an employee of a large company which does not consult or even effectively inform him about its broad policy; even if he is a small independent business man, he works within the framework set by the activities of a small number of large corporations, and in general his independence is further circumscribed by manufacturers' price maintenance, trade association rules, cartel restrictions, and similar more or less voluntary but very stringent regulations. The consumer in his turn, though the subject of a good deal of formal homage by the business community, is in fact largely dependent on the existing organization of the economy in trying to make use of his vaunted 'freedom of choice', and further conditioned in his reactions by the all-pervading influence of mass publicity.

Most people as individuals as well as powerful group interests are in some ways adversely affected by some of these trends, and their dissatisfaction is becoming more and more vocal. The growth of mammoth organizations may not be the root cause of the defects of present-day society but only one of its symptoms, but such distinctions are too subtle for the man in the street and his more articulate spokesmen. His analytical powers are not sharpened but blunted by the force of emotional discontent which is the normal stimulus inducing him to look beyond his personal affairs and to take part in the discussion of public issues. Evil tendencies must be embodied in palpable facts or, better still, in clearly indentifiable human beings whose peculiar traits or functions may qualify them for the part of theatrical villains in the drama of modern life. The traditional scapegoat of continental European history, the Jew, has never been cast for this role in the Western world, but in recent years the bureaucrat has been frequently chosen for this unenviable part.

Without a doubt, bureaucracy stands high on the list of modern discontents. Fear of bureaucracy has been growing at least since the beginning of the present century, and public protests against its advance have found strident, and sometimes hysterical, expression after each of the last two wars. During the *laissez faire* epoch, the absence of bureaucracy seemed to be one of the characteristic features of life in the English-speaking countries, and its power on the Continent of Europe was generally regarded as an expression of backwardness. But so far from succumbing to the march of progress, the bureaucratic system of government has outlasted social revolution in Russia, Fascism in Germany and Italy and defeat, occupation and liberation in France, while its numerous opponents claim that it is daily making headway in the United States, Great Britain and the British Commonwealth at the expense of the traditional liberty of the subject.

Such statements must be taken seriously, not because they are necessarily true, but because their wide acceptance reflects deep-seated misgivings about the trends of modern society. Nor is this attitude confined to critics of the central government and its administration; in recent years, the study of political parties and comparable mass organizations, like the trade unions, has made great strides in depth as well as in breadth, and it is remarkable that attention has been focused much less on their professed aims than on their structure. Such studies have thrown much valuable light on the internal balance of power of these bodies and explained the influence of their organizational arrangements on their choice of leaders and policies. The expression 'party bureaucracy' reflects the connection in the mind of the public between these developments and the parallel changes in the working of the modern State.

Side by side with this growing preoccupation with the structure and mechanism of modern government, a substantial body of literature has been devoted to the problem of organization as such. Its smaller part is abstract in method and general in conception, although perhaps not sufficiently so as to make good its claim to independent scientific status, but the bulk of these writings is more limited in scope and practical in purpose and deals mainly with the technical problems for the business executive which the growth of the modern corporation has brought to the fore. It is, therefore, not surprising that a large proportion of this literature and many of its characteristic ideas originated in the United States and it may, indeed, be regarded as the intellectual counterpart to the rise of the Corporation to its present position as the main repository of economic power in America.

The direct influence of this development on the study of politics has been more limited than it deserves, although it can be traced in the emerging theory of public administration and the rudimentary efforts to apply it to practical problems of government, which owe a considerable debt to 'scientific management'. It is still a very imperfect tool for the analysis of political organizations and at present hardly more than a promising method of approach, more useful for putting the right questions than for providing definite answers. Even in its own sphere of business administration, it is usually more successful in its warnings against popular fallacies than in its positive precepts, and its canon of so-called principles is rarely more than a collection of rather trite semi-technical maxims.

Nevertheless, it is of considerable interest for the understanding of modern political institutions, because a good many of its problems are common to all large organizations, public as well as private, political as well as economic. One of these is the problem bureaucracy which is surrounded with a host of tiresome but persistent irrelevancies which have to be removed before the real issue can be properly brought into focus.

To describe and even to explain bureaucracy, however difficult, can only provide a diagnosis and not a patent medicine for a cure. In this field, the step from theory to practice is not only difficult but risky, for no sooner has it been taken than the enquirer finds himself translated to a sphere where politics is not the subject of theory but of practical interest—and the unfolding analysis will make it clear why this is bound to happen.

CHAPTER TWO

THE NATURE OF
LARGE-SCALE ORGANIZATION

Modern mass organizations are only established by important interests as instruments of social action on a large scale, although once they are successfully launched, they may continue to grow by their own impetus. The setting up of such organizations involves a sustained effort of considerable magnitude and the deployment of large resources which is not undertaken without compelling reason. Every large organization, therefore presents a fascinating problem of its own.

Basis and Purpose
The interests willing and able to create large organizations may be called their 'primary social force'; the social action at which it aims may be called the 'purpose' of the organization. Both can be as varied as human society, always provided that its material development has been sufficient to make the necessary resources available for such an undertaking.

The primary social force behind really large organizations is normally a social group or an economic class, but it is not impossible that it may be represented by individuals in certain social key positions; in modern times, they happen to be typically those of the economic empire builder, particularly in the heroic stage of capitalism—the Carnegies, Fords, Levers, Krupps or Tatas. The identification of the primary social force is vital for the understanding of the purpose and functioning of an organization, but in the case of old-established organizations it may not always be a simple matter.

The purposes pursued by large organizations must not be confused with the motives of their founders, wherever these can be identified. The actions of broad social forces often play havoc with the intentions of the individuals involved in their course, and their consequences are not infrequently incompatible with the motives of their human agents. However fascinating for the psychologist, these are therefore best discarded in attempting to define the real purposes pursued by large organizations and their relation to the interests of their primary social forces.

The ultimate purpose of all strictly *political* organizations is power or, at least, influence. Their primary objective is control of the machinery of the State which is the organization with a legal monopoly of the use of power in its most palpable forms. The State is not the only organization capable of laying down rules of conduct for its 'members' and of prescribing sanctions for the breach of these rules. Its distinctive character is its universality, which enables it to apply these rules to all persons satisfying the condition of citizenship or even residence, and the finality of its most drastic sanctions. It is, therefore, the political organization *par excellence*, and no group or person wishing to obtain political power can afford to ignore it.

For this reason the activities of political parties centre on the control of the State machine or, if this is impossible, at least on ways and means of influencing the exercise of governmental power. The primary social forces of the parties generally determine the purposes for which the power of the State is to be used. Even revolutionary parties aiming at the destruction of the existing machinery of government must in the first place aim at obtaining power, and this goes some way to explain the similarities in structure and strategy between parties with opposed aims.

The purposes of modern *economic* organizations may cause more difficulty. Historically, the typical company or corporation is part and parcel of the development of modern capitalism and it is, therefore, generally easy enough to single out the primary social force and to recognize the profit motive as the fundamental purpose of the organization. Yet it is not its only purpose, for as a rule profits cannot be earned without satisfying human needs in the process; as the profit motive has lost some of its original repute as a result of persistent attacks by the critics of the capitalist system, it is tempting to play it down in favour of the subsidiary purpose of 'service': 'In an industrial organization the purpose is the production of goods and services. The purpose is not profit, notwithstanding that business men, economists, ecclesiastics, politicians, labour unions persistently mis-state the purpose. Profit may be essential to having a supply of inducements to satisfy the motives of that class of contributors usually called owners or investors whose contributions in turn are essential to the supply of other classes of contributors . . . but the objective purpose of no organization is profit but services.'[1]

Such abstract distinctions between 'profit' and 'services' are quite unrealistic, because they ignore the basic division of interests inherent in private enterprise. In the words of another equally distinguished American writer on the subject, 'certain individuals, primarily the customers, contribute to the organization because of the service it provides; others, the entrepreneurs, because of the profits they may derive'.[2] The search for an abstract purpose of modern business is plainly fruitless, for such purposes have real meaning only in relation to social interests. Now it is true that a business organization could not exist without customers, but it is not the customers who take the decision to establish and maintain it; hence it is not they who are its primary social force, but the owners and managers.

Economic associations which play such an important part in modern economic life, such as cartels, trade associations, employers' federations, etc., may be traced back at one remove to the same primary forces and the same basic purposes, for they are founded and maintained by their constituent bodies, the business firms which form their membership. It is, however, much more difficult to identify such a clear-cut relationship in bodies like the nationalized industries in predominantly non-socialist countries such as Great Britain, France and the Scandinavian States. The British Coal or Gas Boards behave practically in the same way as private business firms, but

[1] C. I. Barnard, *The Functions of the Executive* (Harvard, 1951 edn.), p. 154.
[2] H. A. Simon, *Administrative Behaviour* (New York, 1951 edn.), p. 113.

their primary force is not that of capital, and their purpose is not the making of profits, although their position is further complicated by their obligation to pay interest on the large sums paid out as compensation to their previous owners.

The transformation of profit-making business enterprises into public services, however admirable in social purpose, has undoubtedly weakened the nexus between the primary social force and the organization established in its service, and thereby magnified the difficulties inherent in the size of the newly created bodies. The fact that even in private business firms this control is becoming less and less effective, at least as far as it is exercised by the shareholders, does not solve this peculiar difficulty, though it may help to put it into its proper perspective. Yet some important question marks remain: To whom are the managers of these giant corporations responsible for their decisions? Is parliamentary control of broad issues of policy enough to safeguard the public interest, or is there a case for closer scrutiny of their administration? Should the employees of a nationalized industry be more closely associated with its management than in private industry? Such questions, and a host of others, reflect the uncertainty caused by the partial dethronement of the primary social force of capital and the replacement of the brutal but clear purpose of the profit motive by the criterion of public service in a society where this principle is not recognized throughout the major part of the economic system.

Another important form of large organizations which is extremely difficult to analyse satisfactorily is that of *religious* communities. The Roman Catholic Church is certainly the most ancient and one of the most majestic bodies, and although no other religious group can equal it in outward power or intrinsic interest, there are many remarkable organizations amongst them with a long history and an outstanding record of stability. The balance of dogma and organization, of spiritual and material power, differs widely in different denominations, but matters of Church government, i.e. organization, play a prominent part in most of them and usually contribute to the frequent schisms in which a large number of sects originated.

The definition of the primary force or the purpose of a religious community is a highly delicate question. It is easy enough to point out the material, social or political factors involved in the growth and decline of most churches or sects, nor does it present much difficulty to show that the claims of their leaders to sanctity are less convincing to the dispassionate onlooker than to the faithful, but the issue is not settled by mere 'debunking'. Solutions will vary from case to case but will probably include in most instances a historical element in the shape of the situation in which the religious body originated. Broadly speaking, religious belief may become a powerful motive force of social action in certain historical conditions, and its adherents tend to establish organizations for the defence or propagation of their creed and for the proper celebration of religious ceremonies. Non-religious interests exert a strong, and sometimes fateful, influence on most religious bodies, particularly after the conditions responsible for their birth have disappeared, but the real problem is not the decline of their spiritual element but their survival as religious organizations for centuries after the end of their evangelistic youth.

Although the purposes of large organizations are determined by the social interests responsible for their establishment, they need not be freely accepted, or even clearly understood, by all individuals to whom the influence of the organization extends. 'Membership' in many important organizations is, indeed, involuntary. Citizenship is acquired by birth, and not every unwilling citizen is able to renounce his citizenship, i.e. his membership in a State, even by flight. In a number of countries, the same applies also to membership in religious organizations. For many people, 'membership' in the firm for which they work, though not absolutely compulsory except in emergencies, is by no means voluntary in the true sense of the word which implies the possibility of a choice. If the position of the customer of a monopolistic business is regarded as a form of membership (and there is good authority for this procedure), it need not be truly voluntary any more than that of the worker in the coal mine which provides the only opportunity of employment in the neighbourhood.

Thus it is perfectly possible for an organization to exist and thrive, although many of its members are in ignorance of its purposes or disagree with them. It is even less essential for the functioning of an organization that all its members should be able to influence its policy: democracy is not the rule but the exception in the government of large organizations, and still more in the determination of their purposes. As long as these purposes are, in fact, laid down and controlled by its primary social force, an organization will have an adequate basis and a sound standard for measuring its practical success.

Structure

That the first part of management is man is true of all organizations, however different in purpose, size and structure, because they all consist of men. They are designed for the end of making people act in concert in the interests of the primary social force. In other words, the operation of large organizations is a technique for achieving social purposes on a scale requiring the co-operation of large numbers of human beings. No such organization can rely on instinctive harmony between the actions of its members, which is the outstanding feature of insect society, or at least of our conception of it, however complete the agreement between their wishes and its aims. In practice, such agreement is in any case more the exception than the rule.

The 'constitutions' of small and simple organizations may consist of little more than an informal, common-sense understanding between a handful of persons to behave in an agreed manner: every action may be directly fashioned by the primary purpose of the organization, and this connection may be so clear and unmistakable that every problem can be solved either by a few fixed rules or by improvisation. Penalties for failure to conform to the rules will be imposed by the group as a whole and will follow swiftly on the offence. Primitive communities of the type known as 'squatter democracy' come close to this description, although they usually develop a simple system of functional differentiation for special purposes which may be the starting point for more formal arrangements. On a different level, a small private business firm whose purpose is directly represented by its individual owner, belongs to a similar category.

Conditions are very different in typical modern organizations which owe their existence to the size and complexity of industrial society; the larger the area they cover and the more complex their activities, the greater is the need of a permanent system for the direction of their members and for regular communication between them.

Large size may be due either to the 'reduplication of units of one and the same type of activity or to the agglomeration of many units of different activities',[1] although in practice both factors are usually found in combination. Examples of essentially simple activities which require elaborate organization only because they occur on a very large scale are political parties marshalling their supporters in order to achieve the maximum 'turn-out' at elections, religious communities organizing worship, the post office collecting and delivering letters day after day in town and village, or insurance companies covering large areas by resident agents. Such *extensive* organizations have a structure shaped like a pyramid which is rather more elaborate than the simplicity of their purposes might suggest.

The base of the organizational pyramid consists of all persons with whom the organization is habitually in contact and who need not belong to it in any formal way, e.g. the electors or the public of potential policy-holders. This social environment forms an essential part of the organization, but from the point of view of the organizers its role is quite passive and may be ignored at this stage. Its main function consists in being organized in various ways by the local representatives of the organization who are entrusted with the task of carrying out its 'purposes'.

In mainly extensive organizations this task, however simple, requires the services of large numbers of people, because the area of the organization has a large number of geographical subdivisions such as constituencies, parishes, blocks of streets, etc. The more frequent and regular the contact between the organization and its social environment, the smaller the size of the basic geographical unit. A postman with two deliveries per day to every other house cannot be expected to cover the same number of households as an insurance agent; similar considerations govern the geographical radius of the units of more honorific and powerful extensive organizations.

[1] Sir C. Renold in *Large Scale Organization*, edited by G. E. Milward (1950), p. 216.

Super-imposed on this basic layer of local representatives is a structure of officials who are as a rule not in direct and continuous contact with the social environment of the organization and whose main concern is with the local agents and the problems to which their activities tend to give rise. According to circumstances, this structure may consist of a number of tiers culminating in a narrow apex of one or more persons who exercise control of the organization as a whole. Thus the London Prudential Assurance Company employs about 13,000 agents throughout Britain. These are organized in groups of five to seven under a section superintendent; three to five sections form a district in charge of a district manager; forty to sixty districts constitute a division under a divisional inspector, of whom there are fourteen, and who are supervised by seven divisional managers at the head office of the Company.[1]

The officials in charge of larger areas are invariably in a position of authority over those in charge of smaller areas, which implies that they have the power of making decisions concerning the behaviour of their subordinates in the expectation of being obeyed by them. It depends on the constitution of the organization whether this authority is general, in which case the actions of subordinate officials are entirely governed by their superiors (centralized organizations), or whether it is limited to certain more or less clearly defined matters which exclude purely local affairs for which the subordinate officials bear themselves the responsibility (decentralized organizations).

In all such bodies there is a double chain linking each level with the one above and the one below, a chain of authority from the apex to the base of the pyramid and a chain of responsibility from the base to the apex. Even in organizations with a substantial measure of decentralization, such as the Roman Catholic Church, there is a clear line of authority from the Pope and the College of Cardinals via archbishops with supervisory functions over a number of dioceses and bishops to the parish priest in charge of a congregation, and the relations between these dignitaries are regulated by a legal system of great subtlety. In the well-organized political mass parties of Britain

[1] K. A. Usherwood in Milward, loc. cit., pp. 88 ff.

and its Dominions and many European countries, there is a corresponding arrangement, although in deference to the democratic theory behind modern mass parties it is usually viewed in the opposite direction, from ward organizations and constituency parties to regional and national headquarters. This form of organization is particularly well developed in the Communist party whose system is described as 'democratic centralism', although the latter feature is much more in evidence than the former. Thus the French Communist party, which is one of the largest in non-Communist countries, is organized in cells, sections and federations, with the Central Committee and its political bureau at the apex of the pyramid.[1] Trade unions and other voluntary mass organizations are modelled on the same scheme as political parties, though with wide variations in practice which reflect differences in environment, functions or policy.

Although the officers on the higher levels of the pyramid usually have their own contacts with the social environment of the organization, a large part of their official existence consists of the direction and control of other parts of the organization and of decisions on the ways and means of giving effect to the purposes of the organization. On the lower and middle levels of the pyramid the task of direct supervision of the work of subordinate officials tends to preponderate, while the top-ranking officials are mainly concerned with policy-making.

The most commonly used illustration of such an organization is that of an army, and in some respects it is a classical case of a complete chain of command and obedience, because its grim purpose makes absolute reliability an essential condition of the success, or even the survival, of the organization as a whole. The typical army formation is divided into clear-cut units (army corps, divisions, brigades, regiments, battalions, companies, platoons, sections) whose commanding officers are linked by an equally definite chain of authority ensuring, as far as humanly possible, the accurate and speedy execution of orders given at the top.

The distinctive feature of this form of extensive organization is the

[1] M. Duverger, *Political Parties* (English trans., 1954), p. 48.

existence of a single line of authority, and it is, therefore, technically known as a 'line' or 'linear' organization; alternatively, it has been compared with a ladder and given the name of 'scalar' organization. It is the simplest form of a large organization, and in practice few perfect specimens survive. The army, even before the revolution in technique caused by the development of the internal combustion engine and its use in tanks and aircraft, in its simple nineteenth-century form of infantry, cavalry and artillery, with sappers, commissariat, etc., was a much more complex affair than the straight line of authority from general to corporal may suggest. Each of its individual components formed (and forms) a parallel but independent structure. There is, indeed, a clear line of command within each branch, but this is coupled with a rigid division between the separate branches, with each member of any one branch responsible only to his own superior officers and not to those of any other branch.

This strict division may help to ensure the efficient performance of their duties by all parts of the military machine, but it makes it even more difficult to establish the effective co-ordination between the work of these parts on which the success of the organization above all depends. For this purpose the device of a 'staff' has been employed, and this institution is now widely used in spheres far removed from the armed forces. Staffs charged with the duty of preparing policies and the measures required for carrying them out may exist at various levels of authority. Those operating at the top level are mainly concerned with policy matters and the 'grand strategy', for instance in the army with that of a campaign as a whole, while the staff officers attached to lower levels are mainly concerned with the detailed movements of different bodies whose operations are necessary in order to carry out the policy laid down by the higher authorities.

The work of outlining policy and preparing the measures for giving effect to it thus forms a separate function of groups of men who are standing outside the line of authority. The orders for putting the necessary measures into effect, on the other hand, are given and supervised by the executive organs. 'Staff' devices are indispensable in all large organizations, from the government as a whole, and a good many of its departments, to every large business firm. Even where the primary purposes of an organization are relatively simple, the complex conditions of modern society ask for ever more ingenious methods of putting them into effect, and the 'line-and-staff' form of organization supplies the appropriate technique for using thorough-going specialization without losing track of the specialists.

In a small organization, every member is of necessity a Jack of all trades. Specialists need scope for the development of their special skill; when they are given full scope within an organization large enough to employ them, they soon prove their superiority over the 'good all-rounder' in their own sphere. Specialization is superficially similar to the 'division of labour' with which it is frequently confused, but the difference between the two processes goes very deep. In modern conditions, the division of labour involves the breaking down of complete operations into their simplest parts by purely technical analysis; the result is a system in which individuals only too often have to carry out work which is not only monotonous but meaningless, if viewed in isolation from the process as a whole. The specialist, on the other hand, performs a significant and coherent function of often absorbing interest, and in a large organization such tasks may occupy him (and usually many like him) throughout his working life. As far as he is concerned, his immediate purpose frequently tends to overshadow the general purpose of the whole organization: 'The primary aspect of specialization is the analysis of purpose or general ends into intermediate or detailed ends which are means to the more remote ends.'[1] In contrast to the operative who becomes indifferent to the apparently senseless work to which he is condemned, the specialist is inclined to suffer from myopia induced by excessive concentration on partial purposes.

In linear organizations, specialization is mainly geographical; in more complex bodies it is functional, and the structure of the whole organization becomes *departmental*. The technical advantages of this system are massive, but it is, nevertheless, not an unmixed blessing. The efficiency of each specialist in his own sphere is purchased by the atrophy of his other abilities, some of which are also required for

[1] Chester I. Barnard, op. cit., p. 132.

C   33

the success of the organization and become the duty of other specialists. Many large organizations thus tend to become agglomerations of special functions carried out by specialists organized in different departments and comparatively indifferent to the purposes of the organization as a whole and to the interests of its primary social force.

Developments of this kind are by no means confined to large organizations; they are, indeed, characteristic of modern society in many spheres, including that of science. The difference between the old family doctor and the complex modern procedure of a 'check-up' carried out by half a dozen specialists, is just as wide as that between the old family business and the modern corporation. But an organization must preserve its unity of action and purpose in day-to-day life much more closely than a civilization can ever hope to do; the penalty may be defeat and losses which are much more tangible, though not necessarily more vital, than social losses incurred by society as a whole or its members.

Hence specialization must be pushed to its logical conclusion in the creation of a specialized organ charged with the function of maintaining the fundamental unity of the purpose of the organization in spite of the proliferation of specialized departments. This function involves the co-ordination of the activities of all the specialists, and the direction of their work in the interests of the organization as a whole: 'In the process of dividing activities into a number of component organization parts and decentralizing responsibility to a high degree and within each unit encouraging delegation to the maximum extent; there is created a problem of co-ordination and the need to bring the parts together again in proper relationship, to ensure that all the activities and all the functions are inter-related and harmonized to achieve the purposes for which the undertaking exists. Successful co-ordination is sometimes the keystone to an efficient organization.'[1]

The organ charged with the responsibility of co-ordinating the work of all departments and of directing it in the service of the purposes of the organization as a whole is obviously the most responsible

[1] J. R. Simpson in Milward, loc. cit., pp. 11 f.

34

and powerful part of the whole structure. In commercial enterprise, it is usually called its 'management' or 'top management', but whatever its name, it is distinguished by the fact that it represents the unity of the whole organization in its diversity and is, therefore, the central repository of its authority. Its task is the interpretation of the purpose of the organization in practical terms which includes all measures required for putting it into operation. Thus it is both policy-making and executive and it will be seen that this twin function may become the source of very grave difficulties.

The translation of a general purpose into systematic action requires a special technique which may be called *administrative*, and the whole organization, if viewed from this point of view, becomes an *administration*. The difference between these terms is, therefore, not a difference between different things but between different ways of looking at the same thing.

From this it follows that administration does not exist apart from the organization to which it is applied and cannot divorce itself from its facts: the only way in which it can fulfil its purpose is through the existing organizational arrangements or, if need be, through a change in these arrangements if they are no longer suitable for their purpose.

Administrative Problems

Co-ordination and direction are so vital to the success of large organizations that they must pervade all their activities from the highest to the lowest, and the technique of administration consists, by and large, in the creation and application of suitable methods to achieve this aim. The most authoritative summary of the technical requirements is given in the opening pages of the Hoover Report on the machinery of government in the United States which bears throughout the stamp of thought of the industrial consultant: 'Responsibility and accountability are impossible without authority—the power to direct. The exercise of authority is impossible without a clear line of command from the top to the bottom and a return line of responsibility and authority from the bottom to the top. The wise exercise of authority is impossible without the aids which staff institutions can provide to assemble facts and recommendations upon which judgment may be made and to supervise and report upon the execution of decisions.'[1]

However practical in intention, this statement is so abstract, and in this form inevitably question-begging, that it is more a succinct expression of administrative hopes than a reliable guide to effective action. The idea of a 'clear line of command from the top to the bottom' may bear a close relation to the facts in a primitive linear organization where it may be possible to speak with some degree of simplification of *one* line of command from the commander-in-chief to the private or from the Pope to every faithful Catholic. In departmental organizations, however, there can be no question of a single line of command but of any number of such lines, and all that can be expected is proper provision that these lines should not cross each other. The managing director or president of a large corporation can issue orders which will be obeyed throughout the whole organization, but it would be impracticable and intolerable if every order had to emanate from the top. In real life, the 'unity of command' has to be combined with the parellelism of departments whose actions are coordinated at varying levels by officials whose authority extends to some departments and not to others.

The Hoover Commission's conception of the 'return line of responsibility and authority from the bottom to the top' is also a rather jejune reflection of real administrative problems. These arise even in simple linear organizations as a result of their large scale of operations. Its local agents are by definition limited to a very narrow field, and the normal counterpart of this limitation is a parochial outlook which cannot do full justice to the over-all interests of the organization. The interplay of forces in a large organization is such that this humdrum fact may seriously affect the policy of the whole body.

Local patriotism is, of course, a force to be reckoned with in politics, where the heat engendered by the selection of a candidate for local office may be much greater than that provoked by reputedly 'burning' issues of national or international significance, but it plays its part in all large organizations. Its most obvious effect is the dis-

[1] *The Hoover Commission Report on Organization of the Executive Branch of Government* (New York, 1949), p. 3.

tortion of the information which the local representatives of the organization pass on to their superiors in the shape of reports on local conditions and requests for instructions. This stream of information moving from the bottom of the administrative ladder towards its top is one of the crucial administrative facts which exercises a surprising influence on the day-to-day activities of almost every large organization and ultimately on its basic policy. Higher officials spend much of their time reading reports and use them as raw material for decisions and the formulation of policy.

Policies wholly or partly determined on this basis are applied in detail in the shape of instructions. These may issue in response to requests from the lower levels of the organization or as the result of reports from below. The larger the organization, the longer as a rule the chain of command and the greater the distance between its representatives in the field and the policy-making officials at headquarters. This fact inevitably produces distortions in the emphasis, and even the contents, of the information reaching the higher levels, and corresponding mistakes in the appraisal of the situation on which they base their decisions and the instructions for action which they hand down to their subordinates.

The complex departmental organizations of practical life suffer, in addition, from other problems peculiar to themselves for which the maxims of modern management have no effective cures to offer. Many of the top administrators in each department are at the same time specialists in their own field, and their constant pre-occupation with their special subject inevitably increases its significance in their own imagination. Hence they invariably tend to exaggerate not only their own importance but also that of their departments in relation to the primary purpose of the organization, and correspondingly resent and reject outside interference either by the specialists of other departments or by highly-placed 'laymen'.

The task of co-ordination and direction in departmental organizations is thus much more complex and difficult than the conception of a clear line of command would seem to suggest. Each department is to a considerable extent autonomous in carrying out its special tasks, particularly if these are technical and for outsiders difficult to understand in detail. The art of the administrator does not consist in the issuing of orders to the heads of department for transmission to their own subordinates but in dovetailing the activities of a number of departments in the light of over-all policy, and in the resolution of inter-departmental differences. As such differences reflect by and large the one-sided approach of specialists in different fields to problems affecting them in different ways, they are inherent in the very nature of large-scale organizations and their solution is a permanent task. The technique most frequently adopted for this purpose is that of 'group management' operating with the help of conferences and committees.

Conferences may range from full-dress meetings of departmental chiefs under the chairmanship of the highest dignitaries in the administrative hierarchy to informal discussions between the specialists directly concerned, who are usually of similar status as officials and have to report back for approval to their departmental superiors. The *Committee* is a special form of conference organized frequently on a semi-permanent basis; it is usually smaller than the conference and, therefore, more suitable for thrashing out differences and agreeing plans for action. It sometimes carries out 'staff' functions without giving rise to the awkward complications introduced by the appointment of separate 'staff' officers whose activities are frequently resented by their colleagues of the 'line'.

Where conflicts between different departments cannot be resolved by such means, they have to be decided at a higher level, ultimately by the head of the administration, and in many cases such conflicts may not be unwelcome to him: 'As a matter of fact, jurisdictional disputes are an important means of bringing to the top Administrator significant issues of policy, and of preventing these from being decided on lower levels without his knowledge. . . . Certainly, the technique of "playing one against the other" is used by top administrators so often that it cannot be casually dismissed as poor administration.'[1]

It is, however, significant that in a growing number of important organizations there is no personal top administrator and that his place

[1] H. A. Simon, op. cit., p. 145.

has been taken by a permanent Committee or Board. This may consist of a few individuals without departmental responsibility, but usually the heads of the most important departments or divisions of the organization are represented on it. This is the logical conclusion of the process of departmentalization and as such it has obvious dangers. This type of group management has the advantage of bringing inter-departmental friction into the open, but it suffers from the corresponding disadvantage of involving top-level administrators in problems which ought to have been resolved on a lower level. Thus it may tend to produce a situation of permanent stalemate and lead to dangerous rigidity in the direction of an organization. Similarly, the advantage of educating departmental heads in the broader issues involved may in practice turn into the dangerous habit of putting policy decisions affecting the primary purpose of the organization into the hands of specialists who are better fitted, and more inclined, to deal with the application of policy to their own problems.

CHAPTER THREE

BUREAUCRATIC DEFECTS

The dominant organization of the medieval western world, the Roman Catholic Church, has left its imprint in the very name of the orderly structure of large-scale administration, whose ladder of authority is still commonly described as a 'hierarchy'. The outstanding organization of modern society, the centralized State, is not concerned with eternal salvation but with temporal government, and in its classical French form it has provided most languages with the word 'bureaucracy'. However ill-defined in daily usage, this term is normally employed as an unflattering description of a badly functioning or otherwise reprehensible administrative system.

This meaning of bureaucracy, which coincides with the popular sense of the word, must not be confused with another use of the same word in a somewhat different context. Some important writers on the subject of social organization, above all the German economist and social philosopher Max Weber, have employed it primarily as a description of a rational system of administration in general.[1] Max Weber's rudimentary theory has exerted a strong influence on the American literature on the subject, and his terminology has, therefore, been accepted by a number of other writers,[2] frequently with confusing results.

The disadvantages of the application of the words 'bureaucracy' and 'bureaucratic' to the normal structure of modern administration,

---

[1] Max Weber, *Wirtschaft und Gesellschaft*, part iii, chap. 6, translated in Max Weber, *Essays in Sociology*, edited by H. H. Gerth and C. Wright Mills (1948), pp. 196 ff.

[2] See the symposium in *Reader in Bureaucracy*, edited by Robert K. Merton and others (Glencoe, Ill., 1952) and among later books A. W. Gouldner's *Patterns of Industrial Bureaucracy* (1955) which applies Weber's terminology to industrial relations.

as well as to its perversion, are an unnecessary ambiguity and a partial, but incomplete, break with every-day usage which is only justified, if it leads to a clarification of ideas and not to their confusion. Weber's sketch of the nature of large-scale administration and its methods, which he categorically describes as 'bureaucratic', is a compact and highly suggestive outline of the whole subject; in particular, he was fully alive to the importance of bureaucracy as a social power, and his indiscriminate use of the term 'bureaucracy' was, therefore, particularly unfortunate.

From a radically different angle to Weber's, Lenin got involved in an even more puzzling difficulty which was, indeed, much more than a matter of mere terminology. Like every Russian, he was painfully aware of the crucial importance of bureaucracy in the system of Russian government, both before and after the Soviet revolution, but unlike most Russians he was a convinced and untiring, though not a very effective, critic of bureaucracy under the new regime. It is, therefore, particularly interesting, that on an important occasion Lenin waged an impassioned and successful campaign for the adoption of 'bureaucratic methods' in political and economic administration, meaning management by individual administrators personally responsible for their departments in contrast to management by boards. In fact, this apparently technical dispute was closely connected with the struggle for power within the Russian Communist Party.[1]

These illustrations underline the need for a clear and consistent use of terms in a field where tradition, popular polemics and the abstractions of theorists meet with perplexing results. In the following analysis, the word 'bureaucracy' will be reserved for the many imperfections in the structure and functioning of big organizations. It is not surprising that such organizations have more than their fair share of such faults, for they have been established in order to cope with difficult tasks, and in the common run of things difficult problems are solved with only indifferent success. Some of their defects are the inevitable consequence of their intricate structure and com-

---

[1] E. Strauss, *Soviet Russia* (1941), p. 72, Julian Towster, *Political Power in the USSR*, 1917-1947 (New York, 1948), pp. 288 ff.

plex operations, though their specific faults vary with their size, purpose and environment. Other weaknesses are dependent on certain social conditions and are therefore less universal, though frequently more spectacular.

This distinction between *technical* bureaucratic defects and *social* bureaucratic weaknesses is vital both as a starting point and as a clue for a realistic interpretation of the vaguely assorted facts lumped together under the general condemnation of bureaucracy.

Technical bureaucratic defects are inherent in the structure and operations of big organizations and are, therefore, to some extent inevitable, though they vary in form and intensity from one organization to another. However, this does not mean that such defects have to be accepted without ameliorative action, and the chances of such action will be greatly enhanced by a clear idea of their origin and nature.

Nor does it imply that all features of large-scale organization which have come under criticism in recent years are necessarily to be regarded as defects from the point of view of the organization itself. The strong reaction against the dreary and hum-drum mass character of modern industrial civilization has fastened on the large organization as the perfect embodiment of anonymous and irresistible power which tends to crush the individual. However significant from the social point of view, this criticism of the large organization is irrelevant to its real nature and problems. In a differently organized society with smaller units, simpler needs and less artificial means for their satisfaction, large-scale bodies of the kind which occupy an increasingly important place in modern life might well be unnecessary and a host of other problems would never arise. But with industrial society being what it is, such organizations exist and are, in fact, indispensable—provided they really fulfil their primary social purposes.

This is the ultimate standard by which every organizational action and institution must be judged. The typical modern mass organizations are large and intricate arrangements for the achievement of definite social aims. Every detail in their structure and operation which is required for their purpose is thereby justified from a practical, though not necessarily from a moral, point of view. It may well provoke strong hostility from all those who are not in agreement with the aims pursued by the organization, but this is no reason to criticize its arrangements as technically defective. On the other hand, features which do not contribute anything to the realization of the purpose of the organization, and still more those which actually conflict with it, must be regarded as 'bureaucratic defects'.

The Bureaucratic Mind

The bureaucratic defects of large organizations may arise either from the effects of administrative duties on the behaviour of the individual official or from the structure and processes of the administrative system. They are naturally most prominent in the government service; the public official, civil servant, *fonctionnaire* or *Beamter*, for this reason looms overwhelmingly large in the popular picture of the bureaucrat, but many of his characteristic traits can also be discovered amongst the professional administrators of other large bodies.

A useful summary of the every-day criticisms of the bureaucratic official was given towards the end of the second World War by a British parliamentary committee on the training of civil servants, and it undoubtedly forms an impressive catalogue: 'The faults most frequently enumerated are over-devotion to precedent; remoteness from the rest of the community, inaccessibility and faulty handling of the general public; lack of initiative and imagination; ineffective organization and waste of manpower; procrastination and unwillingness to take responsibility or to give decisions.'[1]

With the exception of ineffective organization and waste of manpower, which are defects of the administrative system, all the faults mentioned relate to the individual official and his behaviour. They are not all due to the same circumstances, nor are they equally important in all types of organization or in all countries. 'Remoteness from the rest of the community' is more characteristic of the public official than of the employee of a trade union or corporation, and perhaps more typical of the English civil servant and the German *Beamter* than of their American counterpart. Nevertheless it is com-

[1] *Report of the Committee on the Training of Civil Servants* (May 1944), Cmd. 6525.

paratively easy to see the extent to which these faults reflect the position of administrative officials and are, therefore, to some extent inherent in their work, but the logical sequence is somewhat different from the order in which the public, and the parliamentary committee of inquiry, tends to look at them.

The typical administrative official is a professional who devotes most of his time and energy to his employment, and public administration in particular is normally a life-time 'career'. The difference between success in a profession and in a career is the existence of a definite organizational framework for the latter. In the professions, success may at least to some extent be measured by technical achievement. Professional eminence may be associated with outward rank, but this is not invariably the case, and the two are by no means necessarily indentical. It is, to say the least, possible to be a great lawyer without being a Lord Chancellor, or a great divine without being an Archbishop, and *vice versa*. Even in the armed forces, acknowledged greatness is not necessarily identical with highest rank— the greatest genius produced by the British navy died as a Vice Admiral. In an administrative career, on the other hand, success is identical with promotion: there is no 'great' junior clerk. It is a career in the sense of an obstacle race, where success is measured entirely by the official position attained within the hierarchy, with promotion the key to higher rank, greater power and bigger income. The chances and effects of promotion are, therefore, of overriding importance for the individual official and influence his outlook to an extent which can hardly be exaggerated.

The individual official may only be a small cog, but he forms part of a very large wheel, and his modest share in the power wielded by the organization as a whole tends to colour his attitude towards all outsiders who have no part in his great mystery. If he is in the service of the government, the consciousness of belonging to the paramount organization of the country naturally intensifies this attitude, but every large organization has its full-time staff, with its scale of ranks, its promotion system and its material rewards. This setting is the primary and decisive fact which conditions the daily life and outlook of the individual official. He is, therefore, inevitably somewhat removed from the rough-and-tumble of the outside world and primarily concerned with the official world to which he belongs, with its rules of procedure and conduct, its chances of promotion and its gossip, which is of absorbing interest to the initiate, however fatuous it may appear to the outsider.

Although inherent in the position of the administrative official, and therefore to some extent inevitable, this aloofness is a definite drawback to the proper functioning of the organization. There are many routine jobs within a large organization whose holders have little or no contact with the outside world, but the body as a whole is not a self-contained and self-regulating mechanism but an instrument for the furtherance of specific social interests, and therefore intimately concerned with the world at large and its problems. Its officials, therefore, have to maintain contact with the outside world, and the ability to respond quickly and correctly to changes in the social environment is vital for the success, or even for the survival, of the whole organization.

The administrative official thus belongs to two worlds, and has to perform the difficult task of balancing their requirements in his daily work. One of the symptoms of failure consists in 'faulty handling of the general public'. This defect is most acute at the base of the administrative pyramid, where routine officials are in daily contact with the public. In the higher ranks of the administration different problems arise, and the 'remoteness from the rest of the community' with which many higher officials are charged is largely due to the insulating effect of a number of administrative layers between themselves and the outside world. Although the senior official usually has his own outside contacts and deals directly with important problems or personalities, the bulk of his duties normally consists of official matters reaching him at the second or third remove through the administrative chain.

'Overdevotion to precedent', combined with 'lack of initiative and imagination . . . procrastination and unwillingness to take responsibility or to give decisions' are closely related bureaucratic defects, due in the last resort to the hierarchic structure of large-scale administration. The ordinary official is far below the policy-making level, where the primary purposes of the organization are transformed into a scheme of administrative action. For him, policy consists of definite, though not unalterable, instructions governing his behaviour in typical circumstances and supplemented by rulings on special cases which he obtains in case of need from his superiors.

While he is dealing only with matters adequately covered by his instructions, the routine work will run smoothly, but social life is essentially a changeable and unruly element, and sooner or later the official will be confronted by an unexpected combination of circumstances, because the policy of the organization and the instructions given from the top are based on past experience and have not caught up with the march of time. When this happens, the subordinate official may have to choose between different courses: either to apply his rules to a case which they do not properly fit, or to deviate from his orders and make an independent decision, or to do nothing and ask for new instructions.

The attempt to force changing facts to fit the established policy of the organization, though always made by routine officials, cannot be indefinitely kept up, because sooner or later it is bound to end in failure. The disregarding of official rules by junior officials is for very good reasons discouraged in every large organization, for it is incompatible with orderly administration. More important from the point of view of the individual, it may have serious repercussions for the culprit, and 'disobeying orders' is, therefore, one of the gravest steps a subordinate official can take.[1] Barring acute emergencies, a display of independence is neither expected from a junior official, nor would it be countenanced by authority.

The decision of administrative cases by precedent is, therefore, deeply routed in the structure of the whole system, and where precedent is lacking, or where its application is resisted by powerful outside interests, the official will not feel entitled to give a decision on the spot and thereby accept a responsibility which the rules of the administration withhold from him. He will instead refer the matter

[1] A characteristically illogical recognition of the inherent dilemma was to be found in the Order of Maria Theresa in the Imperial Austrian army (cr. 1757), which could be obtained by successful action by an officer in disregard of orders—with the court martial as penalty for failure.

to his superior, and if the case is unusually difficult it may slowly travel along the 'return line of responsibility', until a decision is made at top level, whence it will return to the starting point in the form of an instruction, after an exasperating time lag.

Red Tape

The peculiar habits or failings of the official mind have their counterpart in the cumbersome procedure of the administrative machine which goes by the name of Red Tape. In a racy American definition, this includes 'delay, buck-passing, pigeon-holing, indecision and other phenomena which contribute to, and end in, inaction'.[1]

(i) *Procrastination* or delay is the most obvious form of administrative inefficiency, and widely regarded as the archetype of bureaucratic incompetence. However simple the service required of an organization, if it has to be rendered on a sufficiently large scale, it cannot be performed at all without a regular procedure. What is criticized as 'red tape' or 'procrastination' may, therefore, simply be the legitimate time needed by the organization for doing its work. As in many instances the services undertaken by such organizations are far from simple, and may require reference to a number of different departments for their proper performance, delay need not be identical with culpable procrastination. But popular insistence on this point is too strong to be dismissed as a common prejudice, and there are good reasons for it.

By and large, the operations of every organization may be divided into 'routine matters' and problems raising 'policy issues'. The working procedure laid down for the latter must be flexible, that for the former must be detailed, specific and fairly rigid. Without a certain measure of rigidity it might, indeed, be impossible to cope with the flood of routine operations which form a large part of the day-to-day work of most large organizations, but a price has to be paid for this convenience in the form of a certain lack of consideration for individual circumstances. In addition, even if the working procedure governing the routine operations is intrinsically sound at the time it

[1] J. M. Juran, *Bureaucracy* (*A Challenge to Better Management*) (New York, 1944), p. 38.

is laid down, it may be rendered wholly or partly obsolete by changing conditions. This applies particularly to large government departments whose rules must be determined in advance in considerable detail, thereby frequently being too rigid in practice, particularly in times of quick social changes.

Sometimes the only remedy is a change in the law; thus an Income Tax Code which may be perfectly adequate for dealing with a small number of well-to-do taxpayers may become hopelessly inadequate when applied to the mass of the wage-earning population. Similarly, an inflationary rise in income levels may compel the revenue authorities to tax large numbers of small wage earners for trivial sums at an excessive collection cost, but only an alteration of the law can provide relief.

On other occasions, the excessive rigidity of the administration may well be the cause of the trouble. Thus it has been argued that the 'disease of making no errors at all costs' involved the American government during the last war in disproportionate expenses through the detailed checking of comparatively trivial travelling expenses of huge numbers of officials, with the result that 'the total money disallowed is much less than the salaries of the auditors. Not only that, the amount of money disallowed is for the most part less than the cost of keeping it.'[1] This may not be an adequate standard for passing final judgment on the issue, but it is a good illustration of the different outlook of the official and the outsider.

Financially much more important was the state of the American government system for purchasing goods from the commercial world: 'A maze of laws and regulations surrounds the whole process with unnecessary red tape. The emphasis of the laws is not on promoting efficiency and economy but on preventing fraud. Over-regulation encourages routine buying and prevents economy and the exercise of initiative. Purchasing is consumed in red tape. It is estimated that, on over half of the three million purchase orders issued by civilian administrations, the cost of paper work exceeded the cost of the items purchased.'[2] There is no reason to believe that these de-

[1] Juran, op. cit., p. 44.
[2] *Hoover Commission Report*, p. 97.

fects are confined to the United States, although it is unusual to see them pilloried with such admirable clarity.

Where administration is completely governed by public law, there is little room for administrative ingenuity, but this is rarely the case, and in general working routines may be rigid or elastic, out-of-date and hidebound, or alive and forward-looking over a fairly wide field. A typical cause of unjustified delay is the processing of simple routine matters through an excessively complex procedure, and this is particularly characteristic of money claims against large organizations, licence applications, etc.

Broadly speaking, an administrator confronted with a sharp rise in the volume of work in his department will demand more staff to carry out the prescribed routine operations on every case or document; the correct reaction might well be a new survey of the whole problem leading to changes in routine, with different methods for cases of different importance. However, the need to keep administrative procedure under constant review in the light of changing circumstances must be balanced against the need for administrative stability. The technical efficiency of the whole system, and of its individual servants, depends to a great extent on the smoooth application of an established drill by trained staff. In this tug-of-war between the ideal and reality, the result is more often than not excessive adherence to tried and trusted methods.

Only when the disadvantages of a routine become patent and cause considerable public dissatisfaction, will it be supplanted by another system less out of step with the demands of the time—but destined to grow obsolete in turn with the next substantial change in conditions. Administrative reform, therefore, proceeds comparatively rarely by small and more or less automatic adjustments to gradual changes in conditions but by large and jerky steps intended to bring the whole machine into line with changed circumstances.

Delay in the settlement of 'policy issues' is due in many instances to the limited authority of the individual official who must refer certain matters to his superiors; however much this may be criticized by justly impatient outside interests, it is inevitable that such issues should occur from time to time. The limitation of the junior official to the handling of a definite working routine may however narrow his field of vision so much that he fears and resents the need to use his own judgment even where this forms part of his duties. Delay may, therefore, arise because the official prefers to deal with the simple cases first and intentionally defers tackling more complicated jobs, thus combining procrastination with indecision. This is a well-known tendency, and an efficient administrative system will provide adequate safeguards against its harmful effects, if it wants to avoid the charge of bureaucracy.

(ii) *Forms*. Another popular bugbear is the use of forms. As a device for simplifying and speeding up the work of an organization, forms are an essential part of a regular administrative routine, but their abuse may easily defeat their ends.

Standardized forms for accounting, reporting and record purposes are indispensable within the administrative system, but their use in the relations between an organization and the outside public may become contentious. Outsiders frequently resent them as little short of an affront, because they compel them to express their individual requirements, wishes and complaints in the way in which the administrators want them presented for their own convenience, and not according to the individual's judgment of their relevance and order of priorities.

Wherever administrative operations of a simple type have to be carried out very frequently, e.g. in the issue of driving licences or passports, forms are undoubtedly necessary. In their absence, each letter from each individual applicant would have to be scrutinized in detail for the essential information, ignoring superfluous verbiage and frequently following up for missing data. In other words, information obtained in this way would have to be used for the construction of 'forms'. To employ ready-made forms for work of this kind is not simply a saving of time, but the necessary condition of the efficient handling of routine matters on the required scale; to this extent the sacrifice of the free expression of individual personality involved in their use is inevitable. 'The abolition of forms would make most administrative processes excessively expensive and in some cases too cumbersome to be practicable.'[1]

There are, however, two types of abuse to which the employment of forms may lead in the relations between the government and the public. They undeniably express the growing ascendancy of official-dom and its success in adapting the facts of the outside world to the needs of the administrative process. This may ultimately induce the official designers of forms to elicit information from the public which has nothing to do with the ostensible purpose of the form. The more harmless type of this abuse would tend to exploit forms for in-trinsically useful purposes like the collection of statistical information, while its more virulent type would transform them into a sort of trap for extracting particulars designed to increase official control over the individual by back-door methods.

Such practices are open to serious abuse and their social dangers far outweigh their administrative advantages. At least in democratic countries, they are less frequent than the incomprehensible form, which is a bureaucratic defect of a less dangerous kind. As a rule, forms are designed by officials for the convenience of officials who usually have a fairly clear idea of the purpose for which they need the information provided by the form, but who are much less familiar with the outlook of the private individual who has to complete it. Forms which make insufficient allowance for the lack of expertise on the part of the general public cause unnecessary queries and errors; if the point of view of the user is completely subordinated to admini-strative comfort, the result may be unintelligible forms, and mistakes in their completion will increase to such an extent that they will be-come a source of friction and delay instead of a means of eliminating waste and speeding-up routine.

(iii) *Buck-passing*. The study of a recent American President is said to have been decorated with the categorical inscription: 'The Buck Stops Here'. As the President occupies the apex of the admini-strative pyramid of the American government, this statement was both lapidary and true.[2]

[1] E. N. Gladden, *The Essentials of Public Administration* (1953), p. 180.
[2] D. W. Brogan, *An Introduction to American Politics* (1954), p. 278.

Where failure to give final decisions is due to the inefficiency of the officials concerned, cases are bound to travel upwards from one administrative level to the next, until the top of the machine is reached. Such lack of moral courage is, however, much more frequent amongst juniors than amongst senior officials who are, indeed, more often accused of an inordinate lust for power, except in instances where decisions are 'charged with political dynamite'. The normal course of 'buck-passing' is, therefore, not vertical but horizontal; its usual cause is not the refusal of the competent official to make a decision but lack of functional competence, although both factors may occur in combination.

As a rule, the irritating migration of cases and files from one official to another reflects not so much the hierarchical structure of the administration as its functional division into a number of separate departments. Usually the process is set in motion through the approach of an outsider without detailed knowledge of the organization with which he is dealing—typically a department of the national government. If he contacts its nearest local representative, he may be referred to a different department which, in the opinion of the local official, may be better able to deal with his problem; if he addresses himself to headquarters, his request may not be properly formulated or it may be misunderstood, and in either case it is likely to take some time and effort until the proper pigeon-hole is discovered. Being hazy about the technicalities of his case the claimant will express himself clumsily and it may only be after protracted correspondence that an official comes to the conclusion that the case is, after all, not within his competence. However infuriating for the victim, such difficulties may occasionally arise without malice or even without palpable inefficiency on the part of the administrator as an unfortunate by-product of the complicated process of large-scale administration.

The subdivision of authority between different departments and between different officials of the same department often leads to unwelcome complications even in the hands of experts. In the *cause célèbre* of British bureaucracy, the Crichel Down case, a critical stage in the confused proceedings was reached, when the objecting party obtained the assistance of the local member of parliament who personally intervened with the Parliamentary Secretary of the Ministry of Agriculture. The result was a request for an authoritative report for the personal attention of the ministerial chiefs of the government department concerned.

Although it might be expected that particular care would be taken in such a case, this did not prevent it from being passed on from one official to another: 'So Mr Nugent (Parliamentary Secretary, Ministry of Agriculture) wanted a report. He asked Mr Payne (Assistant Secretary, Ministry of Agriculture), who asked Mr Smith (Secretary of the Land Commission), who asked Mr Hole (Provincial Land Commissioner at Bristol), who asked Mr Lofthouse (District Land Commissioner at Taunton). At that point, it might be supposed, there would have been action. So indeed, there would have been but for the unfortunate fact that Mr Lofthouse, when he received the request on July 17, was about to go on holiday. Mr Lofthouse deputed the work to Mr Brown, his assistant working at Taunton . . .'[1]

The movement of the file in this case was comparatively simple, for it consisted of one vertical step followed by one horizontal and three vertical steps. It commenced near the very top of the pyramid and was backed by the authority and expertise of some of the highest civil servants in their own department. Nevertheless, the transfer of the file from hand to hand so strongly distorted the purpose and meaning of the original request that the final report was seriously inaccurate and misleading, although 'no blame whatever' for its defects attached to the official who finally dealt with it, because he had received faulty instructions for carrying out his work.[2]

The criticism of the results of 'buck-passing' may, therefore, be justified even where the organization of the administrative machine leaves the official without any choice in the matter. In practice, officials sometimes indulge in this far from harmless pastime, because the lines of responsibility are not clearly drawn or because they want to economize their own efforts at the expense of some other department, and of the efficiency of the organization which they are sup-

[1] R. Douglas Brown, *The Battle of Crichel Down* (1955), p. 44. The explanatory descriptions within brackets are not in the original quotation.

[2] *Report of the Public Enquiry into the disposal of land at Crichel Down* (1954), Cmd. 9176, pp. 8 ff, 27.

posed to serve. The dividing line between administrative necessity and bureaucratic defect may thus be perilously narrow.

(iv) *Duplication.* Specialization of functions and the resulting multiplicity of departments is the cause of a host of other bureaucratic defects which reduce the working efficiency of an administrative system and lead to a good deal of friction with outside interests. A typical case in point is duplication of efforts by different departments.

Although servants of the same organization, the officials of different departments look at the same events from varying angles, and consequently find it difficult to agree with each other on the proper weight attributable to the facts with which they are dealing. In most large organizations, certain basic records enter into the work of a number of departments and must be accessible to various officials for their different purposes. Almost invariably, the same arrangement does not suit all of them equally well, and the difficulty is solved, wherever possible, by the duplication in a number of departments of near-identical records with slight variations, irrespective of the fact that the bulk of this information is already available elsewhere.

The Hoover Commission found that in 1947 'about ten thousand five hundred employees in some fifty different civilian agencies of the (US) Government were engaged in statistical work at a cost of about $43m'.[1] As a result of this proliferation of small service units, there was hardly a crime against the principles of sound statistics which was not committed by the departmental statisticians. Apart from defective training, the Commission criticized 'incomplete co-ordination, overlapping of functions, jurisdictional conflicts, lack of comparability, lack of standard concepts, definitions and classifications. There are conflicts between reports, faulty coverage in various areas and gaps in the statistics assembled.'[2] This is one of the most commonplace examples of duplication of effort. A rarer illustration from a very different field is provided by the statement that 'more than half of the departments and administrations of the Federal Government conduct medical or health activities. These administrations

[1] *Report*, p. 47.
[2] *Ibid.*, p. 48.

Bureaucratic Defects

compete for doctors and other technical personnel, and for funds. There is no central supervision of their activities; and they operate under diverse policies with respect to quality of treatment, types of beneficiaries served, types of research, and areas of authority.'[1]

Duplication becomes a scandal and a public nuisance, when it leaves the privacy of official buildings and occurs in the relations between the administration and its public. It is bad enough for different departments of the same organization to approach the public with identical demands, requests or even advice, but the mischief rarely ends there: as no two experts ever agree on the same question, their disagreement becomes even more blatant, when the experts come from different departments with different tasks. To the layman a problem may appear single and indivisible, but to the specialist it reveals subtle differences which prevent him from working with the existing information of another department and compel him to issue yet another questionnaire, return or set of instructions.

Examples of this tendency abound in the public administration of most modern countries. In Great Britain, a war-time parliamentary committee established that as many as nine different official investigations in one and the same household could occur, resulting 'from the numerous forms in which enquiries are made before social assistance, dependent on a means test, or relief from taxation is granted'.[2] In the United States, 'forty-seven employees attached to seven districts and separate field services of the Department of Agriculture in one cotton-producing county in Georgia were working with fifteen hundred farmers; a fruit and grazing county in the State of Washington has 184 employees of separate field services working with some six thousand seven hundred farmers. . . . Farmers are confused and irritated, as climaxed in one Missouri county, where a farmer recently received from five different administrations varying advice on the application of fertilizer to his farm.'[3]

This failure of a service intended exclusively for the benefit of a section of the community is less serious than corresponding failures

[1] *Report*, p. 339.
[2] Sel. Comm. on National Expenditure, *16th Report* (H. of C. 120, 1941/42), pp. 35 f.
[3] *Hoover Commission Report*, pp. 244 f.

55

of the machinery of the State in its regulative functions. Thus in wartime Britain, the official arrangements for the supply and welfare of workers involved 'the inspection of each firm by officers of at least two departments, and where, as is often the case, the firm is working for three departments, it may be visited for the same purpose by four inspectors. . . . The Labour Division of the Ministry of Supply and the Directorate of Labour of the Ministry of Aircraft Production duplicate to a considerable extent the work on labour supply and welfare of the Ministry of Labour. There is in consequence both waste of effort and failure to cover properly the *whole* field.'[1]

Departmentalism

Departmentalism is the most serious bureaucratic defect and invariably indicates a serious deterioration in the efficiency of the administrative system as a whole. The symptom of this disease is a decay of the consciousness of an overriding common purpose between different departments and a corresponding decline in the authority of the central leadership. Its result is the replacement of co-operation between different departments in the service of common aims by chronic friction which may flare up into acute inter-departmental warfare.

A common and comparatively harmless form of this disease follows the sudden expansion of existing organizations. Where new purposes have to be carried out with insufficient preparation, the administrative centre of gravity moves away from its traditional place, and new men may dispute the authority of the established leaders. The sudden growth of the administrative machine may affect its balance and overtax the technical abilities of the administrators, and a few important departments may attempt to supplant the aims of the whole organization by their own interests.

In great emergencies the dividing line between legitimate ruthlessness and departmental megalomania is difficult to lay down and still more difficult to observe; admirers of the methods used by Lord Beaverbrook as British Minister of Aircraft Production during the second World War will probably never be able to agree with his

[1] Sel. Comm. on National Expenditure, *7th Report* (H. of C. 75, 1941/42), pp. 31ff.

critics on this point. However, healthy organizations may survive even gross excesses without permanent damage, provided the emergency does not last so long as to destroy the existing balance between the primary purpose of the organization and its institutions.

In *politics*, the classical modern illustration of rampant departmentalism in a comparatively healthy environment is, curiously enough, the United States government of the New Deal and the second World War with its aftermath. The number of new federal organs, departments and agencies, among them the notorious 'alphabetical' agencies, created between 1933 and 1943 reached the fantastic total of 195, including not only the special New Deal departments but also the massive block of war-time emergency organizations.[1] Thus it is not surprising and hardly even shocking that the great inquest carried out by the Hoover Commission on the structure of American Government after fifteen years of almost uninterrupted expansion brought in a general verdict of departmental anarchy: 'Instead of being unified organizations, many departments and agencies are but loose federations of bureaus and sub-divisions, each jealously defending its own jurisdiction.'[2]

In this 'chaos of bureaus and sub-divisions', the National Security Organization held, perhaps, pride of place, because its growth had been particularly precipitate, and the Commission found 'continuous disharmony and lack of unified planning, extravagance in military budgets and waste in military expenditure'.[3] The Veterans' Administration was taken to task for the excessive number of its staff officers and the complexity of its structure, with its 88 different manuals, 665 varieties of technical bulletins and over 400 circulars of various kinds, adding up to a wealth of 'instructions on internal methods and procedures which defy intelligent execution'.[4]

The co-existence of the manifold departments of the American Government, whether old or new, was and is by no means always peaceful. The outstanding example of inter-departmental rivalry in the civilian field is an administrative heirloom going back well before

---

[1] L. Sullivan, *Bureaucracy runs Amuck* (New York, 1944), pp. 304-10 gives a complete list.
[2] *Report*, p. 6. [3] *Ibid.*, p. 17. [4] *Ibid.*, p. 361.

the origin of the New Deal. It concerns the soil conservation services of the Departments of the Interior and of Agriculture, and particularly the Forestry Service. Their vendetta warfare went well beyond official levels, and at times the Forestry Service was lobbying against a Bill put before Congress by the Department of the Interior,[1] while the latter submitted programmes to Congress without even informing the Secretary of Agriculture.[2] More recently, such breaches of decorum have been completely eclipsed by the notorious wrangling between different branches of the armed forces which show a remarkable latitude in their interpretation of military discipline and the constitutional proprieties.

Not even the severest critics of the American system of government would describe it as a fully-fledged bureaucracy, however alarming some of these recent manifestations. The growth of departmentalism, though spectacular like all things American, has so far not gone unchecked, but if it is allowed to proceed without the self-assertion of the top leadership which is the guardian of the conscience of the organization as a whole, such processes may reach the point of non-return.

Soviet Russia provides unsurpassed illustrations of these tendencies, particularly in the *economic* field. The economic bureaucracies of capitalist countries function in the discreet seclusion of private enterprise, but in the Soviet Union glimpses at the way in which things are done, or remain undone, may be obtained as a by-product of official 'self-criticism' on the occasion of changes in policy. Thus it was at least one of the purposes of the great Massacre of the Ministries carried out in the summer of 1957 under Khrushchev's leadership to break the stranglehold of central departments on the operation of industry.

In his speech in May 1957, Khrushchev complained: 'It is very difficult indeed to carry through specialization and co-operation in production where there are so many ministries and departments, because the departmental interests of the numerous ministries and cen-

---

[1] *The Secret Diary of Harold L. Ickes: The First Thousand Days, 1933-1936* (New York, 1953), pp. 598 ff.

[2] *Hoover Commission Report*, p. 249.

tral boards raise obstacles in the way.'[1] The meaning of this general statement was made clear with the help of everyday illustrations, of which there was obviously no shortage: 'Often enterprises that are closely linked with one another and situated side by side operate as independent units, because they are managed by different central boards of one and the same ministry. . . . The directors of those enterprises copy the methods of the central boards in seeking to shut themselves off from each other as best they can. Comrade Maximov, who heads the Zhdanov coke and by-products plant, being intent on upholding his "sovereignty", had a slag stone wall 915 metres (3,000 feet) long and $2\frac{1}{2}$ metres (over 8 feet) high built to shut off the Azovstal works, spending about 200,000 roubles on this useless idea.'[2]

The next example is less naïve and much more serious, because it emphasizes the threat of departmentalism to administrative efficiency. It concerns a cement works and an asbestos and slate plant occupying the same premises and processing the cement produced by the former: 'The two enterprises are virtually one. But see how the bureaucratic practices prevailing in some departments deform industry. The Ministry of the Building Materials Industry has artificially divided that single production unit into two independent ones under two different central boards—the Glavzapadsement and the Glavasboshifer respectively. The result is two directors, two chief engineers, two independent accounts departments and other departments that are duplicating each other's work . . . and in Moscow there are two central departments in charge of the twin enterprises, and hence if there are any differences between the two departments, the matter can only be settled by the top level executives of the ministry.'[3]

With an acute sense for the intrinsic logic of this process, Khrushchev finally quotes the following result of the division of responsibility for the Moscow electrical works between three ministries: 'What used to be factory shops have been turned into three different plants with three independent managements and the corresponding staffs.'[4]

---

[1] N. S. Khrushchev, *Improvement of Industrial Management in the USSR* (London, 1957), p. 28.
[2] *Ibid.* [3] *Ibid.*, p. 29. [4] *Ibid.*

Large departmentalized organizations tend to reproduce bureaucratic defects on a much bigger scale; whole departments behave like individual officials, and departmental inertia, refusal to make decisions and other forms of procrastination are added to, and intensify, parallel tendencies amongst individuals. The acknowledged impotence of the private person faced by the lack of sympathy of a bureaucratic machine may then be matched by the helplessness of one department in obtaining the necessary co-operation of other departments.

This state of affairs is, perhaps, more characteristic of old-established administrations whose efficiency has been allowed to run down than of new mushroom organizations like the 'alphabetical' agencies of the New Deal in America. There is more than a suspicion that something of this kind occurred in the British government service during the 1930s. This was at least the experience of a somewhat unorthodox British diplomat of the period, Sir Walford Selby, who attributed a good deal of the responsibility for the unsatisfactory diplomatic policy of the British Government 'to the seeming inability of the Foreign Office to obtain decisions of any kind from other departments of Government'.[1] This agrees well enough with the impressions of an experienced politician like Dr Dalton who reflected on the vagaries of the 'Whitehall obstacle race—of trying to push or pull some piece of policy over, or through a long series of obstacles. This included in this case [an amendment to the Statute of Arbitration of the International Court of Justice] first, some of our own officials in the Foreign Office; second, some other Departments, particularly the Service Departments; third, some members of the Cabinet; fourth, some of the Dominion Governments.'[2]

Unchecked departmentalism does not exhaust itself in protestations of one's own good intentions and protests against unsympathetic and, therefore, ignorant critics. Every department easily convinces itself that it cannot carry out its functions (which are invariably interpreted in the most liberal manner and may include a growing amount of duplication) without bigger and better staff, and

[1] Sir Walford Selby, *Diplomatic Twilight* (1953), p. 98.
[2] Hugh Dalton, *Call Back Yesterday* (1953), p. 238.

is thus firmly set on the way towards carving out its own empire. In this virulent stage of the disease of departmentalism, self-aggrandizement becomes the main principle of every department, either on its own or in temporary coalition with others. At this point the original purposes of the organization are in imminent danger of losing their creative and guiding function, although they may still be evoked as formulae. It will depend on the vitality of the primary organization whether such dangerous tendencies can be curbed by a reform regime, or whether the whole administrative system degenerates into a jungle of jarring and warring departmental factions.

This is the watershed between bureaucratic defects, which arise in the common soil of technical difficulties, and the great social evil of bureaucratic degeneration.

CHAPTER FOUR

REMEDIES AGAINST
BUREAUCRATIC DEFECTS

The weaknesses described in the previous chapter are deeply rooted in the profession of administration and the structure of the administrative machine. They belong, therefore, to the facts of life which have to be reckoned with by all types of large-scale administration. This is, of course, no reason for meekly accepting them without any attempts at alleviation or cure. On the contrary, the difference between good and bad administration consists precisely in the steps taken to keep bureaucratic defects under control and to counteract their insidious tendencies.

Staff Management

The first line of defence against bureaucracy is the establishment and maintenance of an efficient staff, capable of carrying out the fundamental purposes of the organization and alert to any symptoms of bureaucratic deterioration. This is more easily said than done, for such a policy may conflict with the power of tradition and with strong vested interests benefiting from its perpetuation, particularly in the government service.

If public officials are not to remain aloof from the public and its problems, they must not form a privileged group living in a world of their own and motivated by interests which may conflict with those of the society to which they belong. In most countries, public service was at one time or another a valuable property which enabled its owners or tenants to enrich themselves at the expense of the people, either by direct exploitation or through the enjoyment of excessive fees and salaries for negligible services.

With the progress of democracy, sinecures in public administration were swept away more or less thoroughly and the public service was put on a truly professional basis by the restriction of patronage and the more plebeian spoils system in its various forms. Perhaps the most important material privilege retained by most civil services at this stage was the fairly universal grant of pensions at a time, when provision for old age was not generally conceded as a right to the rest of the population. At present, the progress of social services and the growing scope of private pension schemes has gone a long way to transforming this one-time privilege into a still valuable but by no means unique right.

Such pensions are as a rule based on contributions by the beneficiary, with corresponding contributions by the employer and sometimes by the State. The non-contributory character of the British civil service pension is an interesting and characteristic relic from a past in which the prospect of a pension was not a right but a favour. For this reason, the replacement of the non-contributory pension 'granted' by the State by a contributory pension right accruing to the civil servant year by year—and preferably transferable on change of employment—would obviously be a step in the direction of narrowing the psychological gap between the public and the civil servant by making him less a servant of the State and more a servant of the public.

The other distinctive feature of civil-service status is its far-reaching security of tenure. The virtual certainty of employment throughout the whole working life during good behaviour is, again, less a right than a privilege, although it is not enjoyed exclusively by civil servants. Administrative employment in any large organization is inevitably more secure than manual work, which is much more exposed to the vagaries of booms and slumps, or employment in any capacity with a small firm whose existence may be short-lived, while that of a large corporation is virtually unlimited. It is only right and proper that such bodies, and in particular the government, should not discard their servants at short notice on the whim of a highly-placed individual, but this is a very different matter from security of tenure without reference to efficiency.

There may be strong arguments for the permanence of judges *quamdiu se bene gesserint* in order to ensure their impartiality, although in this case equal care should naturally be taken to ensure a no less impartial method of selection, but there is no good reason why the civil servant, like the trade union official in Bernard Shaw's *Apple Cart*, should be safer in his job than any king: 'There is only one thing that can get him sacked; and that is drink. Not even that, as long as he doesn't actually fall down.' Where inefficiency is due to the early decay of mental powers, premature retirement on a lower pension may be advisable, and the British Foreign Service makes provision for this possibility amongst the highest grades; in general, however, the only adequate solution of the problem consists in the dismissal of unsuitable officials, preferably at an early stage in their career. At present this is generally so difficult as to be almost impracticable, even in the civil service of the United States, where 'the separation of inefficient and unnecessary employees has been surrounded with so much red tape as to inhibit action. . . . When an employee receives an efficiency rating of "unsatisfactory" and his discharge is proposed, he often has three appeals. . . . Supervising officials are compelled to produce a documented bill of particulars at great trouble and loss of time. In consequence, there are very few ratings less than "fair", and there is a resulting apathy in connection with weeding out the inefficient. In two administrations examined, fewer than three in a thousand employees were marked "unsatisfactory" over a year . . .'[1]

The abolition of special privileges for members of the government service and their replacement by rights similar to those enjoyed by other members of the population in roughly corresponding conditions is an essentially negative form of remedial action. In order to overcome irresolution, lack of initiative and similar bureaucratic defects and to get administrators of really high calibre, more positive steps are needed; these include, above all, the proper selection, training and promotion of suitable candidates.

[1] *Hoover Commission Report*, pp. 121, 127. For a similar, though less hard-hitting, criticism of English conditions see W. J. M. Mackenzie and J. W. Grove, *Central Administration in Britain* (1957), p. 150.

The selection of the higher civil servants is, of course, as much a social as a technical problem. At one time the social element was regarded as paramount, and this was reflected in the ample use of patronage. In Great Britain, patronage was replaced by the separate recruitment of officials of different rank groups as a subtle and effective way of combining a certain level of technical competence with social reliability of the top ranks of the administration. Although far from conclusive, selection by examination is on the whole superior to most other methods of selection and less liable to bias in favour of individual competitors, though not necessarily unbiased as between groups.[1] Its main value, which is substantial, is largely negative, for although examination success is an inadequate proof of ability, examination failure may well indicate a lack of essential qualities.

One of the most serious defects of separate recruitment for different grades of an administrative system is the creation of a promotion barrier which constitutes a deterrent for the ablest men in the lower ranks of the service. Senior positions are invariably few in relation to lower posts, and if a substantial proportion of such positions is habitually filled from outside sources, the ablest members of the lower grades are bound to suffer from resentment and frustration. *La carrière ouverte aux talents* is not the panacea hoped for by its original advocates, but where the 'junior' officials know for certain that no amount of ability, knowledge or industry can gain them promotion beyond a certain point, this is bound to kill their enthusiasm and deters from the administrative career men of initiative and imagination but without the external advantages which might gain them quick access to the leading positions.

Promotion prospects are the most absorbing subject for administrative officials everywhere. The grievances of the lower ranks on this subject are often justified, but their favourite remedy is of very doubtful value, for they and their trade unions or professional bodies show, on the whole, a strong bias in favour of promotion by seniority and are more or less critical of promotion by merit.

Seniority is an unambiguous and objective standard which can be reached on even terms by all competitors by the mere effluxion of

[1] R. K. Kelsall, *Higher Civil Servants in Great Britain* (1955), pp. 61 f., 66 ff.

time. In addition, long service gives an undeniable claim to preferential treatment in some respects, for instance in pension rights or in case of redundancy, where the principle of 'last in, first out' is generally accepted as the fairest basis for making invidious decisions. Merit, on the other hand, though theoretically acknowledged as the best standard for promotion, is rarely sufficiently transcendent to be recognized by disappointed rivals who may regard it as little better than a disguised form of favouritism.

Promotion by seniority will go as a rule to the most experienced official of junior grade, and in his eyes this may be a sufficient claim even by the standard of a selection by merit: 'Merit itself may be adequately measured by seniority in the more routine tasks.'[1] Yet such a claim is little more than a rationalization of interest. The value of experience, loyalty and long service ought to be recognized by increments on the same grade of a salary scale, though even in this respect the device of an 'efficiency bar' at a certain level has a good deal in its favour. Promotion, on the other hand, normally involves a change in duties, and seniority in routine tasks is no measure of merit in the sense of adaptability to new functions. On the contrary, it may be a handicap, because extended application to routine work may cause the atrophy of faculties needed in positions making greater demands on foresight and initiative: 'A lengthy service in the Second Division on routine work, far from brightening a man's wits and intellect, was likely to stunt the growth of his abilities.'[2] As Professor Parkinson remarks from a slightly different angle: 'The man who is denied the opportunity of taking decisions of importance begins to regard as important the decisions he is allowed to take.'[3] The use of seniority as the main standard in making promotions will act like a promotion barrier through separate recruitment in the natural selection of candidates for administrative career service. Men of initiative and resolution are in any case not likely to be attracted by the very moderate financial rewards of subordinate officials, and particularly liable to fall foul of established authority. If promotion comes more or less

[1] H. Finer, *The British Civil Service* (1937), p. 148. See also E. N. Gladden, op. cit., p. 97.
[2] Quoted by Kelsall, op. cit., p. 38.
[3] *Parkinson's Law* (1958), p. 112.

automatically to those patient enough to wait for it, provided they manage to keep out of trouble, the higher ranks of the administrative system will consist of colourless and indecisive persons instead of men of drive and energy who are unwilling to wait for dead men's shoes and lacking in the negative qualities necessary for success in this game. 'An inexorable senority system is security at its worst. It disregards individual superiorities, unusual combinations of skill, superior effort, all the springs of capacity which keep enterprise from ossifying and finally dying by inches.'[1]

However strong the case against promotion by seniority, the measurement of merit remains difficult and its appraisal largely arbitrary. Even acknowledged and demonstrable merit in the sense of exemplary performance of the duties of a lower rank is no reliable guide to performance on a higher level, for an excellent routine worker may, and often does, make a poor supervisor and an execrable policy-maker. Impersonal tests, like examinations, are of greater value in grading the knowledge and ability of new entrants than the competence of experienced officials. Finally, the recruitment of administrative top officials by promotion from lower grades almost invariably puts the direction of the administrative machine into the hands of elderly or old men, for most of whom routine operations have become an end in themselves. This may be quite acceptable in traditional organizations like churches, but it has frequently been the cause of military catastrophes, and its results may be just as dangerous, though usually less spectacular, in the civil service or in the modern business corporation.

For all these reasons, promotion policy is one of the most difficult problems of staff management in all large organizations and it has to be settled with very little guidance from theory. The only important practical advance in fairly general use is the increasing popularity of training schemes. These serve the double purpose of improving the performance of the present duties carried out by the trainees and of spotting promising candidates for future promotion by testing their attitude towards problems outside their practical experience. Such

[1] Marshall E. Dimock, *Bureaucracy self-examined*, in *Reader in Bureaucracy*, op. cit., p. 400.

schemes may vary in scope from simple refresher courses to extended study periods at elaborate Staff Colleges, where officials on various levels may come to grips with questions of principle and their application to the operations of the organization.

It is only natural that special attention should have been paid to measures for improving the efficiency of top-rank administrators whose calibre has an obvious bearing on the efficiency of the whole organization. It has been said that 'a complete change of environment or an opportunity to stand back from one's job and to shake oneself free from the daily routine is most desirable in order to gain a broader vision and some fresh experience'.[1] This unexceptionable sentiment applies in theory even more strongly to subordinate officials than to their superiors, although in practice only a small minority could ever be given the chance of benefiting from this advice, or from such recommendations as opportunities for outside study and research, or even temporary transfers to other branches of related organizations. Nevertheless, it is at the routine level of administration that the de-humanizing and de-vitalizing forces of mass organizations are exerting their full pressure. The policy-making functions of the top administrators and even the supervisory tasks of the middle layers of officials are sufficiently varied, interesting and stimulating to counteract most of the harmful influences to which they are exposed.

The provision of suitable promotion channels for the most talented junior officials is essential for the health of large-scale organizations. The need for preventing the rank-and-file from succumbing to the deadening effects of permanent routine work is just as great but much less widely accepted. Training schemes in the ordinary sense, and still less sabbatical leave and similar measures suitable for a small *élite* may not be applicable to them, although short refresher courses could be extended to them with good results. The only officially envisaged measure is the transfer from one department to another. This policy is sound as far as it goes, and most officials and their performance might be the better for an upper time limit for the performance of each individual official. But this problem is so important that a

[1] *Report of the Committee on Training of Civil Servants*, l.c., p. 31.

conscious effort should be made to improve the relations between the leaders of large organizations and their subordinates.

It is the almost inevitable consequence of the administrative heirarchy that the routine of all large organizations, including the public service, tends to overstress the 'formal system of communications'[1] which regards the subordinate official simply as a tool for the execution of decisions in which he has no share and which he is supposed to carry out without asking any questions. Lack of initiative and resolution at the lower levels is the reverse of an authoritarian use of their formidable powers by the leaders of the administration. The need for 'built-in' correctives, for organizational devices for giving the subordinate officials fuller inside knowledge of the motive forces of official policy and organized means of expressing their own reactions to the working of the machine and its policy, is directly proportionate to the temptation to use the organization simply as a piece of machinery for the transmission of orders.

Yet even in the most progressive organizations there is barely a trace of a movement in this direction, and where it exists it is not regarded as an essential measure for the maintenance of administrative efficiency but as a kind of extended welfare service or an exercise in 'internal public relations'. The growth of joint consultative committees and similar devices in industry presents a parallel, but in the administrative sphere there is actually far wider scope for such arrangements, because the functions of all members of the administrative system are much more closely related to each other and the advantages of the fullest possible exchange of ideas and information correspondingly greater.

Scientific Management

The correct deployment of human resources is the first and foremost task of the good administrator. His second task is the arrangement of these activities in their most efficient form.

Most large organizations have developed in a haphazard and empirical way without much regard for theoretical principles, and their growth, particularly during the hectic last few decades, has in many

[1] Simon, op. cit., chap. viii.

cases outstripped their resources of management. This has been responsible for the rise of the modern profession of management consultant which specializes in the logical analysis of the frequently illogical administrative structures of large business corporations, and in the preparation of blueprints for stream-lining and modernizing them in accordance with the needs of the time. From this point it was only a short step, at least in theory, to the more ambitious attempt of applying the same technique to the reform of public administration.

The so-called 'principles' evolved by writers on management and followed by management experts in the service of private or public organizations, reflect closely the analysis of the formal structure of large modern organizations, and include items likely to improve the working of the organizational hierarchy organized on the 'linear' or 'scalar' model, the distinction between the functions of different departments in more complex bodies, the allocation of duties between 'line' and 'staff' officials and the best devices for co-ordination. Administrators and their consultants have been taught in the hard school of experience a series of 'maxims', e.g. that every official should have only one direct superior ('line of command') and only a limited number of direct subordinates ('span of control'), and similar rules of recognized practical value.

There can be no doubt about the primacy of the United States in the theory and practice of this new profession. In Great Britain, the structure and functions of the machinery of government have been repeatedly reviewed by royal commissions or parliamentary committees; in the United States, similar tasks are either carried out through congressional investigations or entrusted to specialists whose approach is normally closely akin to that of the private management consultant. This efficient, if limited, outlook has found its perfect expression in the early reports of the Hoover Commission, with their impatience of time-honoured but expensive administrative anomalies and their clear-cut recipes for a rational administrative system: 'We have urged in our first report that the foundation of good departmental administration is that the Secretary shall have authority from the Congress to organize and control his organization, and that separate authorities be eliminated. Under our recommendations elsewhere we propose a new form of "performance" budget. We propose that the Department will keep its own administrative accounts as prescribed by the Accountant General in the Treasury.... The Commission also recommends that personnel recruitment be performed by the Department (except possibly in the lower grades), subject to standards and methods of merit selection to be proposed by the Department, but with the approval and enforcement of the Civil Service Commission. The Commission likewise recommends elsewhere that procurement of supplies should be decentralized into the Department with the exception of items of common use to all Departments. ... Further, we propose that the Department should strengthen its management research unit, working in co-operation with a comparable staff unit under the Office of the Budget.'[1]

The value of these proposals—and it is by no means insignificant —can almost be summed up in one word: decentralization. This is, indeed, the only 'management principle' worthy of the name, because it provides a reasonably reliable guide for action in practically every specific case.

Decentralization

Even a well-managed big organization is a clumsy piece of social machinery, operating with high running expenses, liable to bureaucratic defects and tending to concentrate too much power in the hands of its leaders. This tendency is commonly known as centralization.

To a certain extent, this is inherent in the very structure and operation of large-scale organizations, and a centralized organization has certain important technical advantages. Chief amongst these are its efficiency as an instrument for the transmission and execution of orders and, therefore, for the application of policy, and the full utilization of specialized staff services. But these and similar advantages are more than balanced by the formidable weaknesses of centralization: it stifles the initiative of the subordinate official, swells the number of supervisors, clogs the channels of communication and

[1] *Hoover Commission Report*, p. 239.

overburdens the heads of the administrative system. Thus it tends to inflate the whole organization and creates increasingly complex problems of co-ordination. It is inflexible, leads to delays in the settlement of all but the simplest cases and is particularly prone to all the bureaucratic defects in the calendar. The avoidance of complete centralization is, therefore, important for the health and vitality of every large organization; more positively, decentralization of functions is desirable, wherever it is possible.

In a decentralized organization, the official in direct contact with a problem is empowered, within fairly wide limits, to use his own discretion in solving it. His discretion does not extend to the substance of policy, which is laid down by the top management or the policy-making authorities of the organization, but it is nevertheless considerable. The possibility of decentralization varies therefore with the extent to which the application of policy can be delegated in different organizations. The simpler their purposes, the easier it will be to entrust relatively junior members of the administration with this task without frequent reference to superior authority for instructions before action is taken.

Alternatively, decentralization may be applied only to activities of mainly local significance, while reserving more important cases for the decision of the central authority. The greater the advantage of quick action to an organization in order to grasp fleeting opportunities or to avoid unforeseeable losses, the greater is the advantage of decentralization.

For this reason, business corporations are particularly interested in the widest possible decentralization, and their primary purpose, the profit motive, is capable of quantitative expression. Thus it provides both a standard and a measure of the success of administrative action which thereby becomes as nearly self-regulating as its nature permits. The modern business firm is, therefore, the field where decentralization can be pushed to the limit compatible with technical efficiency and the proper utilization of expert staff services—and sometimes it may well 'pay' to accept some inefficiency in these respects for the sake of the practical advantages of far-reaching decentralization.

In the giant combines of modern business, like General Motors in the United States and the Unilever concern of Great Britain and the Netherlands, with their world-wide ramifications, decentralization is almost a condition of survival, because in such cases the 'parent company' is little more than a framework constructed generally for reasons of finance and business strategy, in control of a whole agglomeration of previously independent business enterprises. In organizations of this kind, decentralization in the relations between the central body and its operating companies is normally the only possible method.

In the Unilever organization, for instance, the function of central management, assisted by an economic 'staff', is usually confined to three control devices: '(1) Annual operating plans. (2) Annual expenditure budgets. (3) Selection and annual review of remuneration of top management.'[1] The system operated by General Motors, though outwardly similar, indicates a rather tighter hold of Head Office over the subsidiary companies. The central management sets the goals for each division, determines the authority of the divisional managers whom it appoints, takes complete responsibility for all financial matters and provides service staffs for the division—as well as keeping a 'constant check on divisional problems and progress'.[2] To speak of 'decentralization' in such a system is probably a misnomer, as it stands more than half-way between the semi-decentralization of Unilever and the dualism of functional and operational control favoured by Imperial Chemical Industries.[3]

The problems of fully-fledged public services or nationalized industries, such as the British Transport Commission or Coal Board and industry in Soviet Russia and other Communist countries, reflect a different facet of the need for decentralization. The planned administration of a whole sector of the national economy involves the substitution of new purposes for the simple aim of making as much money as possible by keeping costs low and selling for what the traffic will bear. The great economic advantages of nationalization,

---

[1] Lord Heyworth, 'Lever Bros. and Unilever Ltd'., in *Large Scale Organization, etc.*, p. 171.

[2] P. Drucker, *Big Business* (1947), pp. 51 ff.

[3] *Large Scale Organization*, pp. 153 ff.

like the cutting-out of duplication, the possibility—which is by no means always matched by practical performance—of reducing overheads, the provision of adequate research facilities and the planning of new development on a national scale, however important in themselves, are not the only objectives of nationalization; though economic considerations are not eliminated, they must be co-ordinated with, or even subordinated to the pursuit of new social aims. Such a combination of purposes is obviously difficult, and the achievement of a new balance may elude the planners for a considerable time. Yet in all the diversities of social and political problems there remains one constant factor: the management of the constituent productive units must remain the central point for the solutions of day-to-day problems, if the whole structure is not to be overloaded to the point of breakdown. For this reason, efficient operation imperatively demands thorough-going decentralization. The solution of the administrative problems of nationalized industries must involve a combination of operational decentralization with the provision of central staff services and over-all planning and direction.

The difficulties of decentralization increase with the complexity of the primary aims of the organization and with the prevalence of administrative acts directly connected with policy matters. Decentralization is therefore extremely difficult to apply in the national government service, except in routine departments dealing with straightforward rules and regulations on a massive scale, such as the British Ministry of Pensions and National Insurance or the Employment Service of the Ministry of Labour. In such departments, 'public administration tends to divide into two layers, comprising a headquarters organization, whose functions are regulatory and concentrated round the chief policy-making authority, and a series of field organizations, which are mainly executive'.[1]

The creation of field organizations does not necessarily involve decentralization except in the geographical sense and is quite compatible with strict centralization of power and decisions. The existence of a network of subordinate officials throughout the whole area of operations of an organization may, indeed, be an important ele-

[1] E. N. Gladden, op. cit., p. 77.

ment in its internal balance of power and may add tremendously to the effective authority of the leaders in charge of this part of the official 'machine'.

Decentralization in the true sense of the term is achieved only by a genuine division of authority which involves a limitation on the power of the central management in favour of the autonomy of lower officials within their own area (which need not be geographical), as opposed to the complete subordination of such officials to the will of their superiors in all their activities, which is characteristic of the fully centralized organization. Viewed from this angle, decentralization is no longer a technical device for the smooth transaction of routine business and for the achievement of administrative flexibility but an element in the balance of power within large organizations.

CHAPTER FIVE

BUREAUCRATIC DEGENERATION

The administrative pyramid leads up to a narrow apex of top administrators whose position is one of formidable power. They are in charge of the resources of the whole organization whose activities they co-ordinate and direct with an authority demanding unquestioning obedience from their subordinates. At the same time they are charged with the duty, and therefore vested with the right, of formulating the policy of the organization, or its course of action in specific circumstances. Its primary purpose is laid down only in general terms, or often not at all, in the form of constitutions and similar documents which must be translated into directives for specific action, and this is one of the most important tasks of the top-level management of an organization.

Administration and Leadership
The twin power of authority over the functioning of the organization and of practical interpretation of its primary purpose endows the administrators with important functions of management and control but not with exclusive leadership. Sociologists have distinguished different types of leadership, most of which are of a more fundamental kind than theirs and not necessarily dependent on the existence of large scale organizations. They include the 'traditional' leadership of the hereditary ruler, the 'charismatic' leadership (Max Weber) of the great individual whose followers regard him as the embodiment of superior powers, and the 'representative' leadership obtained by election or equivalent methods for the purpose of furthering the interests of the group as a whole. Most leaders, however constituted, have to carry out some administrative tasks and the

distinction between them and the professional administrators is, therefore, less clear-cut in practice than in theory, but it is nevertheless important.

All primary forms of leadership are based on a direct nexus between the leaders and the social group whose aims and interests they represent. The 'charismatic' leader is barely distinguishable from the group purpose and this identity may take the form of proclaiming his personal rule as the purpose of the group as a whole, which is characteristic of Fascism. The 'traditional' leader, though not normally surrounded personally by the same supernatural glamour, has a kind of proprietary interest in the organization created by the group: the monarchs of the *ancien régime* claimed supernatural authority not as individuals but as representatives of an institution established by the Grace of God. Later on this was toned down into the principle of 'legitimacy', just as Louis XIV's claim to be the State was toned down into Frederick II's more subtle claim to be its first servant. 'Representative' leadership is more limited in scope and duration, but its exponents for the time being are the characteristic rulers of modern society as the authorized spokesmen of their constituents; such is the relationship between presidents or legislators and voters in democratic government, leaders and members in political parties, trade unions and other mass organizations, or directors and shareholders in private business. Leaders of these types invariably express the primary social force of the organization, and formulate and, if necessary, modify policy in accordance with its interests.

Administrative leadership, on the other hand, is a secondary product of the growth of large-scale organization and in principle subordinate to the direct representatives of the primary social force. In democratic countries, elected presidents or governments responsible to parliament are put in charge of the permanent Civil Service, and this relationship may be formally emphasized by the principle of ministerial responsibility for the acts of administrative staffs. In trade unions, as well as in most political parties, there is an elaborate hierarchy of elected leaders charged with the duty of supervising the staff of appointed employees, instructing them on all policy matters, and even of dismissing them, if they prove unsatisfactory. The

Boards of Directors of business corporations have invariably almost complete power over all members of the staff whom they can 'hire and fire'.

There are, nevertheless, some organizations where this controlling power is either much less in evidence or even completely missing. In many countries, such as pre-war Germany or Japan and all military dictatorships, the leadership of the armed forces is a self-governing and self-perpetuating body. Religious communities show an even greater variety, from the democratic constitution of many Protestant sects to the different types of established State Churches and the Roman Catholic Church.

In such bodies, the men in charge of the 'machine' are to all intents and purposes independent of outside control, and therefore the sole judges of the interests and policies of their organizations. Their characteristic form of leadership is an oligarchy presided over by a prominent but by no means absolute head, like the Pope and the College of Cardinals in the Catholic Church or an officers' clique in most military regimes. Such leading groups consist of men who have reached their position by virtue of their special abilities and who combine technical competence with the exercise of administrative functions.

As a rule, however, the leadership functions of even the highest-ranking administrators are incomplete and lacking in independence. Indispensable, influential, they find their proper sphere in the efficient preparation and execution of policies—briefing ministers for a Cabinet meeting or in attendance in the Board room—but in the last resort they are governed by decisions taken by other men. In principle their power, however substantial, is purely functional and their leadership is not primary but derivative: it is not due to what they are but to their place at the helm of a piece of social machinery for the translation of social purposes into administrative action.

There is, however, a reverse to this medal. In modern society with its conflicts of interests and its uneasy balance of divergent forces, large and intricate organizations are formidable concentrations of power. Although differing widely in purpose and technical structure, they all have similar administrative problems and need capable administrators for their solution. The ubiquity of their functions and the growing demand for their services have combined to give the administrators in practice a much stronger position than in theory. Even more important, the growth of mass organizations tends to blur the dividing line between administrative functions and primary social power by emphasizing the administrative qualities of the leaders, sometimes at the expense of more fundamental requirements.

New organizations need 'charismatic' leaders with great determination and powerful vision much more than able administrators: new religious movements are led by prophets or missionaries, crusading armies by generals of genius, political mass movements by great orators whose personal magnetism gives them unquestioned power over their followers—the letters patent of a Mohammed or Calvin, Cromwell or Napoleon, Jefferson or Bebel. In old-established organizations 'the bases of elite recruitment shift'[1] and personal brilliance or technical virtuosity may count for less than administrative skill.

In normal times, administrative ability is frequently regarded as an indispensable qualification for high office in many fields, even though this is usually expressed less crudely than by Henri Fayol, one of the pioneers of 'scientific management', who claimed that 'the Prime Minister should above all things be a good administrator'.[2] The growing power of the 'machine' in modern political parties and mass organizations such as trade unions is a commonplace of modern society, and corresponding developments in business life have been sufficiently striking to find expression in the popular idea of a 'managerial revolution'.

It is nevertheless mistaken to conclude from these facts that a complete separation between primary social forces and administrators or 'managers' has taken place. The men in charge of the administrative machine are almost invariably unconditionally devoted to the purposes of their organizations as well as technically competent: at the top level, administrative calibre is based no only on professional but

---

[1] H. D. Lasswell and A. Kaplan, *Power and Society* (1952), p. 281.
[2] *Papers on the Science of Administration* (New York, 1937), p. 108. Even more intriguing is the enthusiasm of M. Fayol's socialist compatriot, Léon Blum, for 'a method Taylor of government and administration'. *La Réforme gouvernementale* (Paris, 1936 edn.), p. 206.

also on social qualifications which give the administrative personnel of most important organizations a certain representative character. Conversely, social unreliability is an absolute disqualification for high administrative office, however brilliant a man's purely professional ability.

The highest civil servants need not necessarily agree with the party politics of the government of the day, but they must be unquestioningly loyal to 'the State' in its existing form. Such loyalty is perfectly compatible with a completely 'unpolitical' system of selection, like that of open competition. In modern business, the original identity of social and administrative functions in the person of the owner-manager is a thing of the past, but it may still be said, though with some qualifications, that the management of large corporations rests securely in the hands of the agents of the power of capital.

The choice of socially reliable persons as leaders of the administrative hierarchy may assure that the organization will not fall into the hands of anatagonistic social interests, but it is no permanent positive guarantee of the achievement of its primary purposes. These may be threatened from within the organization, if the administrators use their steadily growing power in their own interests and not in those of the primary social force. This tendency is the direct result of a gradual shift in the balance of power characteristic of old-established organizations.

Bureaucratic Power

Compared with natural science, the social sciences still form a labyrinth, with the problem of power at its centre. It affects every social relationship, though it exhausts few, and the just appreciation of the distribution and balance of power and of the factors responsible for its changes distinguishes the realistic observer from the romantic. A strong instinct for the balance of power is, indeed, hardly less essential for the student of society than for the practical politician.

Power has an irresistible attraction for the moralizer, but the moralistic approach to social problems, though undoubtedly impressive, is generally sterile. Lord Acton's famous *dictum* about the corrupting effect of power may be true, but it is irrelevant to the understanding of the course of history and the predominant trends of social development. To stipulate lust for power or ambition in general as the source of all that is evil in social life obscures the essential facts instead of explaining them, There is no need to deny the reality of psycholigical motives of human action in society, but it is more important to demonstrate, and thereby to understand, how men act according to the inner logic of the positions which they occupy, even though they may not be fully aware of their relentless influence.

Modern organizations, or at least the more important amongst them, are above all means of influencing the distribution of power in the interests of their primary social forces, either by extending their sphere of influence or by protecting them against hostile forces. The usefulness of an organization depends on its efficiency as a servant of its primary group, but its existence introduces a new, and potentially dangerous, element: the organization itself may exert an independent influence on the social balance of power. Instead of serving its primary interests, it may develop interests of its own and use its resources in its own service and for its own benefit. Put in the simplest terms, organizations may change from being means to an end into ends in themselves.

This transformation may affect both the relations between the organization and its primary social force and the internal character of the organization. In the beginning, it is the servant and the primary social force the master; this relationship involves the existence of a controlling organ directly representing the primary social group which is independent of the administrative machine and sufficiently strong to impose its will on the organization. The effectiveness of this political leadership is important not only for the over-all direction of the administrative machine but also for its technical efficiency. All large organizations are prone to bureaucratic defects, but these are either invisible to the top-level administrators or appear to them much less serious than they are; sometimes they may even be regarded by them as positive advantages unfairly criticized by ignorant outsiders.

High-ranking civil servants, party secretaries or business executives, though by no means without direct contacts with the outside world, receive the bulk of their official information from subordinates who have generally fewer outside contacts and whose outlook is almost entirely conditioned by the routine of the organization, the superiors from whom they receive their orders and the subordinates to whom they pass them on. Although not all top-level administrators share this outlook, and some may even try to correct it, they are in the nature of things rarely able to free themselves from its pervasive influence. In matters relating to the operation of the administrative machine they are, therefore, strongly imbued by the official mind with its aloofness from the rough and tumble of social life and its respect for precedent, its emphasis on orderly procedure and its lack of sympathy with public outcries about delays and procrastination. They know that the complex business of their organizations can only be carried out by meticulous division of functions between separate departments and they remain unimpressed by complaints that the outside world is inconvenienced by the official routine for dealing with affairs which may appear simple to the uninitiated but which are actually very intricate.

The propensity to bureaucratic defects thus affects the administrative pyramid from top to bottom, and if they are to be kept within reasonable limits, action must come from the political leaders who represent the primary social force of the organization: they, and they alone, can tell the officials to mend their ways and to overcome their natural reluctance, if necessary on pain of dismissal.

This relationship introduces an element of inevitable tension between politicians and officials. The experts may have a low opinion of the politicians in the seats of power, and their feelings will not be made any friendlier by the criticisms levied against them from that quarter with an air of natural authority. They would be more than human, if they did not find this dependence irksome and incompatible with the efficient performance of their duties, because they think that they are the best judges in this matter.

In most old-established organizations, the influence of the political leadership tends to weaken in time and that of the officials to increase correspondingly. This change in the balance of power goes farthest in the strictly administrative sphere, where the professional

82

administrators generally get their way, and 'outside interference' declines, provided that certain minimum standards of efficiency are maintained.

However, the process is unlikely to stop at this point, for the hard-and-fast distinction between 'administration' as the sphere of the officials and 'policy' as that of the politicians is increasingly difficult to maintain in practice, because policies cannot be framed without detailed preparation which must be left to the administrators and their staffs.

The political leadership may retain the right of taking final decisions, but it must choose between alternative courses of action which have usually been mapped out by the experts. Its choice is, therefore, often more formal than real, because the facts may have been selected in such a manner that it can only give one answer to the respectful questions put by its advisers. It thus tends to become an oracle managed by its priests. In practice the official administrators do not confine themselves to the preparation of materials, they also submit their advice on the conclusions to be drawn from them—a development of the greatest importance, although it is in some cases, e.g. in the British Foreign Service, of remarkably recent origin. By preparing policy decisions and tendering expert advice on them, the top-level officials exercise a strong, and sometimes irresistible, influence on the political leadership.

Once policy decisions have been taken, the heads of the administration have a wide measure of flexibility in their execution, because it is impossible to lay down tactics far in advance except in the broadest terms. The chief executives must be allowed to choose the right moment for putting the agreed policy into effect, to concentrate on measures favoured by circumstances and to delay (which in practice may well mean to discard) others for which conditions are less propitious. These functions have a strong political bias, although they belong properly to the administrative sphere, and the dividing line between policy-makers and administrators is consequently blurred in favour of the latter: 'It is the cumulative force of administrative acts which are at the heart of the modern State. The principles behind these acts are, of course, of prime importance. But principles may be invalidated by the method of their application and it is governments which have the actual application of them.'[1] This observation is just as true of political parties, public Boards and large business corporations as of the modern State—and in all cases the 'governments' wielding this formidable power are advised and guided by full-time administrators.

The growing power of the administrators over the policy of their organizations, however inevitable in the modern world, may involve even healthy and strongly-led organizations in serious difficulties. Their opinion of what is happening in the world and what ought to be done in the best interests of their principals is coloured by their experience as administrators and they will be strongly tempted to confuse administrative requirements with social interests. As practical men of affairs they may, indeed, refuse to recognize the possibility of any cleavage between the two and insist that what is good for the one must be good for the other; but however sensible such an attitude may seem to other practical men, it is rarely adequate to ensure the healthy development of large organizations caught up in the cross-currents of divergent and therefore antagonistic social forces, and may not even ensure their survival.

The administrative hierarchy cushions its high-priests against the full impact of such forces and thus misleads them about their intensity and sometimes even about their trend. The heads of the administration are, therefore, in important respects ill-qualified for advising the political leadership on matters of first-rate consequence. Their very position makes them unfit to form an unbiased opinion of the balance of social forces and its effects on the organization which they serve with ability and devotion. If serious setbacks are to be prevented, they must be precluded from obtaining the decisive voice on this crucial matter, because only the political leadership can be expected to know 'who gets what, when and how'. This facet of the relationship between administrators and politicians was well expressed in Sir William Harcourt's famous saying that it is the job of the minister to tell his civil servants what the public will not stand.

In broader terms, every important organization is a nucleus of

[1] H. J. Laski, *A Grammar of Politics* (1926 edn.), p. 145.

social power confronted by other powers; its aims and policy must be decided by its political leadership and cannot be left with impunity to its administrative servants.

Bureaucratic Rule

The power of the administration has increased, is increasing and, in spite of all fulminations, is likely to go on increasing, wherever conditions favour the growth of big organizations: 'The decisive reason for the advance of bureaucratic organization has always been its purely technical superiority over any other form of organization. The fully developed bureaucratic mechanism compares with other organizations exactly as does the machine with the non-mechanical modes of production, Precision, speed, unambiguity, knowledge of the files, continuity, discretion, unity, strict subordination, reduction of friction and of material and personal costs—these are raised to the optimum point in the strictly bureaucratic administration, and especially in its monocratic form.'[1] Where this change in the balance of power within an organization removes the outside control over the activities of the administration, its chiefs assume full authority to run the organization and to determine its policy.

This transformation of an administrative system into a ruling bureaucracy may be called, in a telling phrase coined by Trotsky about Stalin's Russia, its 'bureaucratic degeneration'. Its result is the establishment of the bureaucracy as a hierarchical system, unfettered by dependence on outside forces, commanded by leaders owing their power to their position at the top of the bureaucracy and following a policy determined primarily by its own interests. *Bureaucratic defects* are technical weaknesses of administration on a large scale and may, therefore, be regarded as to some extent inevitable, *bureaucratic degeneration* is a complex social process dependent on specific historical conditions.

In the polemical literature on the subject of bureaucracy a good deal of confusion has arisen from the identification of distant possibilities with accomplished facts. It is easy enough to focus attention

[1] M. Weber, chapter Bureaucracy in *Wirtschaft and Gesellschaft*, in *Essays in Sociology* (Gerth-Mills), (1948), p. 214.

on the undeniable growth of bureaucracy to the exclusion of all other factors, and on this basis to proclaim its complete victory as inevitable, or even as already accomplished, but such sensationalism is just as unconvincing in semi-scientific garb as in the daily press. The fact is that pure bureaucracies, organizations ruled entirely by their administrators who owe their position exclusively to their administrative functions, are not easy to discover in history or in contemporary life. They are not the rule but the exception, and their future is necessarily highly speculative.

The idea of a ruling bureaucracy is, of course, pre-eminently connected with that of a despotic central government with '. . . a vast body of officials, wielding great power, imbued with so definite and particular a tradition and view of their calling that it separates them from, and makes their ways of thought and behaviour strange and alien to the rest of society. We imagine that bureaucracy is exactly what the word itself implies—government by officials; that these act, as a general rule, upon principles which they alone predominantly create; that they form a special caste or estate. . . .'[1] But there is no need to confine this conception entirely to the field of government. It may also be applied to the management of political parties, and its criticism in political mass organizations has a long tradition. The growth of bureaucracy in modern business has been traced in the factual New Deal Study on *Bureaucracy and Trusteeship in Large Corporations*[2] and, more sweepingly, in Mr James Burnham's well-known book on the *Managerial Revolution*, which its author practically identified with a bureaucratic revolution.

It is not necessary to accept any of these theories in order to agree that a reversal of the original balance of power within large organizations in favour of the administrative machine is more than a second-rate technical problem and constitutes one of the crucial issues of modern society. It is unlikely that any set of abstractions will provide a complete key to the understanding of this process, but it may be useful to construct a kind of working model, an 'ideal type' of a completely bureaucratic organization—not as a realistic picture of

[1] H. Finer, *The British Civil Service* (1937), pp. 15 ff.
[2] TNEC Monograph No 11, Washington (1940).

actual conditions, but as a simplified standard of comparison for the measurement of the bureaucratic features of real-life bodies.

(1) In a healthy organization, the interests of the primary social force constitute the end, and the administration is the means for serving its interests in the most effective manner. In a perfect bureaucracy, the administration serves only itself. Its *purpose* is no longer prescribed from outside but arises from its own operation. It is the maintenance or expansion of its power and material strength in the interests of the rulers of the administrative machine.

(2) This radical change in functions is reflected in the *structure* of the organization. In normal circumstances, the administrative officials are controlled by the representatives of the primary power. In a bureaucracy, the organs of independent outside control suffer partial or complete atrophy. In extreme cases they may be abolished, but it is more in line with the nature of bureaucratic degeneration to permit their survival as impotent ceremonial figureheads.

The corollary to this removal of independent outside control is the concentration of power in the hands of the central leadership, for bureaucracy in this sense of the term is inconceivable without a high degree of centralization. In a ruling bureaucracy, the top bureaucrats are the absolute masters of the organization, and therefore of the fate of their subordinates. The line of authority becomes a chain weighing heavily on the lower ranks of the bureaucracy: uncontrolled administrative power means their complete subordination to the orders, or even the whims, of their superiors. The individual official knows that his advancement depends entirely on the sense of justice or the prejudices of his superior, and as he does not dare to run any risk by relying on the former, he flatters the latter. For this permanent humiliation he tries to indemnify himself by the treatment which he metes out to his own subordinates, for whom he reserves the same contempt with which he is regarded by those above him in the official hierarchy.

The excessive dependence of the individual official on the discretion of his departmental head strengthens the centrifugal tendencies inherent in the system of departmental large-scale organization, as soon as the common bond of the primary purpose is weakend or removed. Every member of the bureaucracy depends in the first place on his own superior and on the leaders of his own department; directly or indirectly, he is their henchman. The head of the department is his 'boss' and the position, as well as the material rewards, of his subordinates depend to some extent on his power in relation to that of other bureaucratic dignitaries. The bureaucracy thus tends to split up into different sections under the leadership of more or less prominent 'bosses', with disastrous effects on the cohesion and effectiveness of the organization as a whole. Departmental and divisional heads engage in 'empire building' in order to buttress their position, either on their own account, if they are sufficiently strong, or in coalition with others in order to balance the power of stronger rivals. This 'inter-departmental tribal warfare'[1] is normally not confined to the highest departmental level and may extend far down the hierarchy which thus becomes a jungle of warring factions.

Another important influence on the structure of a bureaucratic organization is the change in its relations with the outside world. Administration involves the application of firm rules to changing conditions in the service of certain basic purposes. If the bureaucratic machine has emancipated itself from the necessity of following a policy laid down by an outside power and has amassed sufficient power of its own to follow its separate interests, it may try to adapt its social environment to its own convenience, instead of having to adapt its activities to changes in circumstances.

In the short run, this may well produce the illusion of increased administrative efficiency, because it reduces the troublesome friction between the administration and the outside world, but in the long run a heavy price is exacted for this apparent advantage. The removal of *technical friction* is obtained at the expense of the interests with which the bureaucracy comes into close contact, and the invariable result is a sharp increase in *social tension* between the bureaucracy and its environment. Such tension may result at first in increased resistance to the bureaucracy and ultimately in a threat to its dominating position. When this stage is reached, the bureaucracy must create new repressive organs, although these may be superfluous or

---

[1] L. Urwick, *Management of Tomorrow* (1933), p. 161.

even dangerous from the point of view of the original purpose of the organization.

(3) With these changes in purpose and structure of the bureaucratic body, the *process of administration* takes on a different character. To begin with, bureaucratic defects luxuriate in the absence of independent outside control. The aloofness of the bureaucrat from the rest of the community takes the form of arrogant superciliousness, the faulty handling of the general public proceeds unchecked to the callous subordination of its interests to the needs of bureaucratic routine, delays tend to multiply with the growing centralization of power and with the refusal of local officials to jeopardize their official existence for the sake of obliging the public.

Objectionable as this may be, it is far less important from the point of view of the bureaucracy itself than the subtle change in the system of formal communications within the administration which constitutes the most important link between different administrative levels and which is particularly exposed to bureaucratic defects in the form of undue complacency at the top and insufficient integrity at the bottom of the administrative pyramid: 'The temptation to tell a Chief in a great position the things he most likes to hear is one of the commonest explanations of mistaken policy. An emperor, a commander-in-chief, even a Prime Minister in peace or war, is in the main surrounded by smiling and respectful faces. Most people who come into contact with him in times of strain feel honoured by contact with so much power or in sympathy with the bearer of such heavy burdens. They are often prompted to use smooth processes, to mention some favourable item, to leave unsaid some ugly misgiving or some awkward contradiction. Thus the outlook of the leader on whose decision fateful events depend, is usually far more sanguine than brutal facts admit.'[1] In less powerful organizations or further down the line humbler but just as effective forces are at work: '. . . information tends to be submitted upward in the organization only if (1) its transmission will not have unpleasant consequences for the transmitter, or (2) the superior will hear of it anyway from other channels, and it is better to tell him first, or (3) it is information that

[1] W. S. Churchill, *The World Crisis* 1916-8, Part I (1927), pp. 193 f.

the superior needs in his dealings with his own superiors, and he will be displeased if he is caught without it.'[1]

In a ruling bureaucracy, the system of upward communications is thoroughly biased in favour of a facile optimism nourished by a general conspiracy against all dangerous or subversive news. The information about outside conditions collected by the rank-and-file and submitted to the leaders of the bureaucracy is almost invariably untrustworthy, because it is not only coloured by the inevitable local patriotism and parochialism of the junior official but also tainted by his eagerness to curry favour with his superiors and to avoid mentioning anything likely to antagonize them.

(4) For a ruling bureaucracy, the possession of power is the highest goal, and to keep and strengthen its power is the paramount aim of its *policy*. The chiefs of the bureaucracy are by nature, or become by experience, hard-boiled realists and practical men of affairs of a distinctive type, technically efficient in their own sphere but shortsighted and narrow-minded and, above all, suspicious. They have reached the top by playing the bureaucratic game better than their competitors and know its rules so well that they have become second nature to them. The essence of this 'game' is the correct appraisal of the balance of power within the organization, the choice of the right boss and, if necessary, a judicious change of masters in order to remain always on the winning side in the inevitable internal trials of strength. Having reached the top, they have to exercise the same technique which has already proved its value in getting them there, without undue squeamishness and without being deflected from their main purpose by moral qualms or intellectual doubts.

As the ruling bureaucracy has shaken off all subservience to the interests of its primary social group, it must rely for its survival in its usurped place on its 'purely technical superiority over any other form of organization'.[2] Where the hostility towards this usurpation assumes dangerous forms, the bureaucracy keeps control of the situation through special coercive organs capable of eliminating active opposition. In the short run, this policy is frequently successful, but

[1] H. Simon, op. cit., p. 163.
[2] Max Weber, chapter on Bureaucracy, loc. cit., p. 214.

its success usually contains the seeds of future troubles: the bureaucracy fails to distinguish between the suppression of symptoms and the elimination of their causes, and usually believes it has done the one, when it has only managed to accomplish the other. The success in dealing with articulate forms of opposition will give it a false sense of security which ignores the accumulation of underground discontent up to the very moment of its eruption.

Thus the chiefs of a ruling bureaucracy are specialists in power politics suffering from a chronic lack of reliable information about shifts in the balance of power outside the artificial world of their own machine; they are the prisoners of their own position. Hence it is not only possible but almost inevitable that the administrative machine may run smoothly without giving any indication of trouble, although there may be a formidable volume of discontent with its operation in the outside world. By ignoring facts not in harmony with official routine, by glossing over awkward events and exaggerating every scrap of favourable information, an atmosphere of artificial optimism may persist even in times of crisis and threatening catastrophe. Small irregularities will be smoothed out at the expense of ignoring radical changes in external conditions, thereby falsifying their rhythm and even their trend, until the machine is brought up, often without warning, against an outside obstacle too big to be crushed by its weight and too dangerous to be by-passed. This may be the first indication to the chiefs of the bureaucracy that their previous policy was dangerously wrong, and in order to cope with the new situation the whole complex machine may have to be thrown into reverse. A ruling bureaucracy has to move by fits and starts, because it has lost the ability to make small adjustments or gradual changes of course as and when the need for them arises.

(5) The *survival* of a fully-fledged bureaucratic regime is, therefore, problematical; it depends only partly on its own strength and mainly on the character of its environment. Its very existence demonstrates its ability to gain power, and in the absence of material changes in the balance of social forces it may consolidate its position and maintain itself for quite a long time: 'A dead, inactive, agricultural country may be governed by an unalterable bureau for years and

years, and no harm come of it. If a wise man arranged the bureau rightly in the beginning, it may run rightly a long time. But if the country be a progressive, eager, changing one, soon the bureau will either cramp improvement, or be destroyed itself.'[1]

A ruling bureaucracy is static by nature and adapted only to static conditions, and in a modern society these are very much the exception. If the social and political balance undergoes sudden and violent changes, the rigidity and lack of foresight of the bureaucracy make it entirely dependent on the strength of its coercive machinery, which may be defeated in the end, after scoring a few Pyrrhic victories, or succeed too well and pursue the path of all Janissaries.

A bureaucracy is, therefore, fundamentally in a precarious position, although it may be all-powerful in appearance. In theory it continues to 'serve' an organization, while in practice it follows a selfishly independent policy. Thus it is bound to antagonize its original backers, without necessarily gaining allies or making friends in other quarters. Thus it may find itself in a cross-fire of hostile elements, and may have to seek safety in balancing these opposing forces. Faced on one side by the outraged supporters of the original aims of the organization, confronted on the other side by frankly hostile social forces which find the power of the bureaucracy incompatible with their own interests and development, the bureaucracy may either resort to force and establish itself as a new ruling power, or collapse amidst the ruins of the administrative machine and the primary organization.

The preceding outline of a model bureaucracy may demonstrate that such a system is possible, but it does not prove that ruling bureaucracies actually exist, nor does it explain the necessary conditions for their development. For this purpose abstract analysis must be supplemented by a closer approach to the facts. Although bureaucratic deterioration is not confined to any one type of organization, it is first and foremost a political reality, and the modern State and its parties present a bewildering range of material for a study of the social conditions of bureaucracy and the extent of its practical influence in modern life.

[1] W. Bagehot, *The English Constitution* (1898 edn.), p. 200.

CHAPTER SIX

BUREAUCRACY AND THE STATE

The State is the most powerful of all organizations, and the exercise of power is its characteristic purpose. Beyond this fact there is an almost complete lack of agreement about the aims which the State ought to serve, and political thinkers as well as practical politicians hold violently opposed opinions on the subject. These differences form the stuff of political controversy.

The purpose of the State cannot be established once for all by philosophical speculation but must be found in every case by careful analysis, because it does not exist independently of the purposes pursued by various social groups. In order to be generally acceptable, many definitions of the State have, therefore, ignored this disputed, if crucial, point and confined themselves to the obvious fact that it is 'a human community that (successfully) claims the *monopoly of the legitimate use of force* within a given territory';[1] more pithily, and without the circular reasoning implied in the use of the word 'legitimate', the State has been simply described as 'a sovereign territorial group'.[2]

The price paid for the harmlessness of such definitions is their emptiness. As they must be compatible with all kinds of States, they can say very little about any of them. Yet, both in practice and in theory, almost everything depends on the nature of the 'human community' which has succeeded in monopolizing the use of force within the frontiers of the State. It may vary from a tiny minority of military conquerors, such as the Norman invaders of England, to the

---

[1] Max Weber, 'Politics as a Vocation' in *Essays in Sociology* (edited by Gerth and Mills), p. 78.

[2] H. D. Lasswell and A. Kaplan, *Power and Society* (1952), p. 181.

Jesuit rulers of Paraguay, and from the sovereign people of the revolutionary United States of America in 1776 to the Chinese Communist party.

This 'community' need not, and frequently will not, be identical with the whole population living within the State. In the past, the division between rulers and ruled was often harsh and complete, and even at present, when it is usual to pay lip service to the principle of popular sovereignty, there is often a wide gulf between democratic theory and oligarchic or dictatorial practice. In the terms employed in this study, the primary social force of the State need not be its population as a whole but may be a caste, a distinct group or a more or less clearly defined social class. But whatever its characteristics, if it has established the monopoly of legitimate force over its territory through its domination of the State, it wields political power and is the repository of legal sovereignty which endows it with authority for its actions.

The modern State in almost all its forms derives its character from two main influences—the needs of an industrial society and its own historical development.

Industrial Society and the State

Although the results of modern industrialism vary according to the social, economic and political circumstances of its environment, its basic needs and requirements are the same everywhere. It is incompatible with the system of primitive subsistence farming which keeps the bulk of the population tied to the land, either by legal compulsion or by economic pressure. One of its most important conditions and effects is, therefore, a social revolution in the countryside which is stimulated either by the growing demands of the towns for food and raw materials or by the development of a lucrative export market for agricultural produce. At the same time, the development of industry transforms the towns from centres of consumption by the upper classes or sleepy market places into huge workshops responsible for a steadily growing proportion of the national income. Thus it creates for the first time a genuinely national, and in some aspects even an international, economic system in which every part is affected by the fate of all others. It sucks the mass of the people into the vortex of modern capitalism, with its cycles of prosperity and depression and its contrasts of expansion for some interests and decay for others.

This revolution in economic conditions extends to all other spheres of social life, and in particular to the State. Industrial progress depends on a favourable political climate. Trade and industry demand an efficient system of land communications. The provision of a network of roads (supplemented where necessary by inland water ways) was well beyond the resources of the inefficient local government system of pre-capitalist society and required action by the State, or generous government assistance to private entrepreneurs. Another imperative reason for reforming local government was the urgent need of dealing with pressing public health problems and of policing the motley population of the mushroom towns thrown up by the growth of industry.

Public education had previously been a craft adapted to the leisurely replenishment of the learned professions; it now had to be transformed into a factory capable of instructing, if not educating, the mass of the population and particularly the large corps of non-commissioned officers of the new industrial and commercial army—technicians, supervisors and clerks. A host of other problems with a direct bearing on economic progress, like the regulation of the currency, a rational and uniform system of weights and measures and an efficient postal system, also required determined action on a national scale. Only a rationalized and modernized State could cope with the new tasks thrust on it by the social and economic revolution due to the progress of modern industrialism. This force was embodied in the new middle class of business men and their allies amongst the professional classes who were clamouring for a share in political power.

The form of this struggle, and to some considerable extent even its outcome, depended on the different social and political heritage of each nation. This was much more than a matter of 'starting points', for political institutions are fundamentally machines for the conservation and transmission of power. Hence they do their utmost to suppress all tendencies dangerous to their survival and generally favour the social factors favourable to themselves. They may not always be very efficient judges of their best interests, but they are invariably strong enough to affect the pattern of development within their boundaries and are responsible for many differences in the lives of peoples which would otherwise be to all intents and purposes identical.

In most countries of continental Europe, 'the State' was in the first place identified with a ruling dynasty, whose position was generally founded on an uneasy balance of social forces. The ruling monarchy governed almost invariably in alliance with some social groups, usually the landowning gentry or aristocracy, but it jealously maintained sole control over the machinery of government, the armed forces as well as the civil service. This was the ideal soil for the growth of a professional public service which prided itself on its loyalty to 'King and Country'—or simply to the ruling dynasty—and on its independence of outside interests. In contrast to this development, it was the peculiar distinction of the British political system since the seventeenth century that the representatives of the landowners and the financial interests of the City of London had a large share in the exercise of power, although even in England the power of the Crown and its placemen remained a very real factor until the comparatively recent past.

The progress of modern industrialism was accompanied by a radical change in the social and economic balance from the landowners towards the representatives of business and particularly of industry. Corresponding political shifts were inevitable, but their form and extent depended not only on the relative strength of the social interests concerned but also on the strength of 'the State'. In a few cases this shift took place without any formal break in continuity, but many countries went through an era of political revolutions involving the violent overthrow of existing governments, though without radical changes in the structure of the State.

This was in particular the experience of the great continental monarchies—France, Germany, Austria-Hungary and Russia—where political catastrophes of the first order had relatively little effect on the administrative machine and even served to increase the political power of the bureaucracy. Under the *ancien régime*, the chiefs of the civil service wielded enormous influence, but their connection with the old ruling classes was relatively superficial and their more progressive elements were frequently on the side of the rising business classes. This enabled the bureaucracy to survive the change of rulers generally quite successfully, particularly because the victory of the business interests was in many cases far from complete, and their intrinsic social strength not nearly so overwhelming as that of their British counterpart. Instead of the virtually unchallenged predominance of a single class as in England, some continental countries developed a state of near-equilibrium between hostile forces which made the support of an old-established bureaucracy a very welcome accession of strength and thereby increased its independence still further.

In Great Britain, on the other hand, the civil service had been on the whole a reliable, if corrupt and inefficient, instrument of the aristocratic State. The replacement of the landowning aristocracy by the business classes as the predominant power was, therefore, accompanied by a radical re-fashioning of the civil service, which embraced its functions and methods as well as its sources of recruitment and social composition, until it became a 'representative bureaucracy'[1] of the new social order. The growth of bureaucratic tendencies in Great Britain and most other countries of the English-speaking world is, therefore, a more challenging problem than the survival of bureaucratic systems in France, Germany and Russia which had been ruled in this fashion for centuries.

The most obvious aspect of the growing bureaucratization of modern public life is, of course, the massive expansion of the State machine in response to the many new functions of national governments in all civilized countries. The modern State is operating over an ever wider area and entering more deeply into the lives of its citizens, especially in the economic field. This development corresponds to a change in the character of modern capitalism, the abandonment

[1] J. Donald Kingsley, *Representative Bureaucracy* (Yellow Springs, Ohio, 1944).

of the *laissez faire* principles of its early struggles in favour of the economy of 'imperfect competition', which forms the natural background for the rise of bureaucracy.

Bureaucracy and Social Tension

Threatened by wars between nations, split by the serious conflict of interests between capital and labour, agitated by less fundamental but still important divisions between town and country, expanding and decaying industries, free traders and protectionists, the present age lives in a state of permanent social tension.

The conflict between capital and labour is perhaps the most permanent feature of domestic politics in all countries outside the Communist sphere of influence. The tension created by this conflict cannot be measured in quantitative terms like that of an electric current, but its intensity clearly varies from country to country. In spite of outbreaks of great local violence, it is generally low in North America and Australasia, moderate in Great Britain and North-Western Europe as well as in some other countries of the Continent, but much higher elsewhere. With the inaccuracy inseparable from such generalizations it may be said that a low state of social tension prevails where the mass of the population, including the majority of the industrial workers, accepts the existing social order without reservations; where a large section of the population, generally including the majority of industrial workers, is persuaded of the unfairness of the ruling economic system but does not desire a break with social and political tradition, social tension is moderate; in countries where the clash of interests is so strong that the political framework and even the underlying social system is in danger, it is high. Within these general limits, internal social tension and its political expression waxes and wanes with the pressure of economic discontent. In periods of economic expansion, conflicts tend to lose their edge, while in times of depression they inevitably take on a more threatening form. The difference in temper between the crisis-haunted hungry 'thirties and the fat 'fifties in the advanced industrial countries of the Western world is obvious, and neither state provides a sound basis for an assessment of long-term trends.

Social tension is, of course, not confined to mature industrial nations nor to the capitalist social system. It is particularly acute in countries where racial oppression is combined with economic exploitation and social discrimination. In most, though not in all, communities of this kind, conditions are further complicated by sharp differences in the level of civilization between different racial groups, with the more advanced peoples abusing their superiority for the exploitation of the more backward races. But however important these problems are in some areas, these countries are at the periphery of modern society and not at its centre.

The degree of tension within the so-called 'people's democracies', from Czechoslovakia and Hungary to Poland and, perhaps, even Russia, may well be higher than in many capitalist countries, although their political system suppresses or modifies its symptoms. Its apologists either deny the existence of this tension until it comes into the open with devastating force, or they explain it away by the revolutionary character of these States which involves them at home in clashes with the remnants of the privileged classes of yesterday, and abroad in conflicts with the foreign backers of these groups. Though not entirely without foundation, this is at best a half truth which cannot disguise the stubborn persistence of social conflicts in these countries nor the part played by the ruling oligarchy itself in poisoning these conflicts and preventing their rational settlement.

Whatever the cause of social tension, it is directly linked with the growth of bureaucratic tendencies, because it weakens the control of the primary social force over the administrative machine of the State. Like every other form of organization, the State depends on the effective control of a primary force for the formulation of its policy and the supervision of its administrative system. If the power of the predominant group is permanently weakened by strong opposition, this affects both the political balance of the system and the position of the administrative machine of the government.

These preliminary considerations lead to the obvious conclusion that bureaucracy is generally weakest in political democracies and strongest in dictatorships, reflecting the inherent superiority of democracy as a method of controlling the executive, and thereby indirectly the administration of government. In a democracy, every social group has some opportunity of expressing its views, if not of influencing the policy of the Government. In practice, this may not amount to much, because the constitution may not be, in fact, as democratic as it claims to be in theory. Thus the chances of effective political action by the negroes in the southern States of America are almost as remote as the chance of the British Liberals to form an effective parliamentary party, because in both cases the electoral system precludes them from the share in political power which democratic principles would seem to reserve for them. Nevertheless, there is no doubt about the fact that it is easier for minorities to voice their grievances and to protect their interests in a political democracy than in countries where organized political expression of group interests is prohibited.

But parliamentary democracy, or democracy of any kind, is possible only in conditions where the dominant social forces within a State are sufficiently 'agreed about fundamentals' (A. J. Balfour) to abide by the constitutional rules of the game for the settlement of their differences; in other words, where social tension is relatively low. With the increase in tension the scope for majority rule after free discussion tends to contract, and finally to disappear, until a dictatorship takes the place of the democracy. Although inevitable in certain conditions, this change does nothing to reduce the level of social tension but simply drives it underground. This is bound to increase the power and independence of the administrative machine on which the safety of the dictatorship depends and thus provides the ideal breeding ground for bureaucratic degeneration.

Bureaucracy and the Police State

An absolutist government is of necessity bureaucratic and suffers from the classical weaknesses of bureaucracy—subordination of policy to administrative convenience, disregard of the interests of the governed and lack of foresight in critical situations. As it is based on the forcible suppression of opposition, it begins by strengthening the repressive organs of the State and ends by being dominated by them. The hypertrophy of the police and of the armed forces, whose services are needed not only against foreign enemies but also, at least potentially, against domestic opponents, is characteristic of absolutist governments and often leads to their ultimate breakdown through the degeneration of the army and the police.

The downfall of the old Prussian army, the embodiment of the traditions of Frederick the Great, in its clash with Napoleon I at Jena and Auerstaedt in 1806 was no less complete than the *débâcle* of the army of Napoleon III in its encounter with the re-organized Prussian army in 1870. In a different environment, the defeat of the Russians by the Japanese in 1904 was caused just as much by the corruption of a famous fighting machine through bureaucratic ossification and inability to adapt itself to changing circumstances as by the determination of their opponents.

Internal decay, though less spectacular than military collapse, is no less fatal to an absolutist regime. In this process the gradual degeneration of the police plays an important part, because of its key position in the supervision of the population and the prevention of subversion by the political opponents of the dictatorship. For this reason the description of such a system as a 'Police State' is basically justified, although the power of the police varies from country to country. It may, indeed, outlast the form of State under which it originated; thus the secret police of the French *ancien régime* achieved a splendid renaissance in Fouché's management of the police under Napoleon I and survived successive revolutions up to the democratic present. In the classical police States of history, Metternich's Austria between 1815 and 1848 or Tsarist Russia from 1825 to 1917, the political police was the very backbone of the government, and in the totalitarian states of the present or the recent past its power was no less deadly and its tendency to form a State within the State even more pronounced.

An almost normal but nonetheless pernicious form of degeneration of a political police is the use and abuse of its power in a way likely to strengthen opposition to the regime instead of suppressing it or, still better, preventing it from assuming dangerous forms. This excess of zeal is a characteristic bureaucratic defect which has more than once transformed a riot into a revolution. It was a prominent feature of police rule in the Soviet satellite regimes at critical moments, particularly in the Hungarian uprising of October 1956 and, on a smaller scale, in Poland during 1956 and 1957. On these occasions the brutal and inept behaviour of the forces of law and order was one of the most important factors responsible for making the crowds desperate.

The degeneration of the police is the most dangerous form of bureaucratic decay under an absolutist government. At the same time it is extremely difficult to prevent, because it is virtually impossible to maintain effective control over an all-powerful police, once circumstances have favoured its establishment. In the absence of such control, the police tends to show the extreme features of bureaucratic degeneration earlier and more completely than purely administrative government organs.

The secret police is in a particularly good position to make use of its functional authority for its own purposes and to acquire independent power, which may be abused either collectively or for the private purposes of its officers, because the calling of a secret police agent offers golden opportunities of corruption: 'It is vice itself which is precious, indispensable to the Secret Police, and not only do they not suppress it, but they actually encourage it. It is always in gambling dens and houses of ill-fame that detectives satisfy their professional curiosity. . . . The police have always allied themselves with those who profit from gambling and from prostitution, and the directors of every kind of vicious haunt invariably act as informers.'[1]

It is only a short step from this dubious partnership to the degeneration of the police agent into a corrupt beneficiary of the underworld or, still more important in the case of the political police, into an *agent provocateur*: 'The duty of the *mouchard* is to catch subversive conversations and denounce projected plots to the authorities. But the secret agent, in order to justify his salary, naturally tends to invite confidences by uttering with feigned violence his grievances against the regime, and the temptation is great to build up a complete conspiracy in order to gain later the merit of having discovered

[1] Galtier-Boissière, *Mysteries of the French Secret Police* (translated by R. Leslie-Melville), 1938, pp. 181 f.

it. In every informer who desires promotion and prizes there is a potential *agent provocateur*.'[1]

This system has been developed into a fine art in the prosecution of 'enemies of the people' and their state trials in Soviet Russia and the Communist regimes of Eastern Europe: 'First, upon the suggestion of party functionaries, the party police establish that someone is an "enemy" of existing conditions. . . . The next step is the preparation of the legal removal of the enemy. This is done either through a *provocateur*, who provokes the victim to make "embarrassing statements", to take part in illegal organizing, or to commit similar acts; or it is done through "stool pigeons" who simply bear witness against the victim according to the wishes of the police. Most of the illegal organizations in Communist regimes are created by the secret police in order to lure opponents into them and to put these opponents into a position where the police can settle accounts with them. The Communist government does not discourage "objectionable" citizens from committing law violations and crimes; in fact it prods them into such violations and crimes.'[2]

It is natural that the police should try to reap the greatest possible benefit from a real conspiracy, although this may involve the illustrious object of the proceedings in unexpected risks, as in Orsini's famous attempt on the life of Napoleon III. Alternatively, police agents may enter into close relations with genuine revolutionary terrorists and may have ostensibly to support a plot in order to be able to claim the credit of discovering it. It is possible that the assassination of the Austrian *Thronfolger* in 1914, which unleashed the first World War, belonged to this category. Finally, the police agents may themselves carry out a plot, as in the assassination of the Russian Prime Minister Stolypin in 1909 which may, however, have been to some extent a labour of love, because there was strong antagonism between Stolypin and the police authorities.

It is, therefore, only natural that in most really dangerous political crises reputedly omniscient and omnipotent police machines have abjectly failed to protect the governments which relied on their effi-

[1] Galtier-Boissière, *Mysteries of the French Sectret Police* (translated by R. Leslie-Melville), 1938, p. 183.　　[2] M. Diljas, *The New Class* (1957), p. 90.

ciency. In France, the political police of Louis XVI did little or nothing to anticipate the outbreak of the revolution, while the secret police of Napoleon III, which was probably better informed about the trends of thought amongst the enemies of the Empire, was unable or unwilling to prevent serious attempts on the life of its master. In Austria, Metternich's redoubtable police system during the *Vormaerz* collapsed completely at the outbreak of the revolution of 1848. In Ireland, the carelessness of the Royal Irish Constabulary was one of the main causes of the notorious Phoenix Park murders of 1882 which shocked late-Victorian England.

The climax of the degeneration of the police system was, however, reached in Russia and this state of affairs has persisted until the historical present. The Tsarist Okhrana, in spite of its brutality against its victims, was much more of a danger than a protection to the ruling system. The same must be said of its linear successor under the Soviets, the Cheka or GPU under its various names. The Secret police rule of terror from the assassination of Kirov in 1934 (which was almost certainly the act of a police agent) until the outbreak of the Russo-German war in 1941 all but fatally weakened the Soviet Union. The only compensation for these grave injuries to the Russian peoples was the steady growth in the occupational risks of the career of secret police chief which claimed a number of victims from Yagoda to Beria; more important, it seems to have caused a fairly determined reaction against the excesses of police rule amongst the Russian leaders, although it is too early to assume that the days of police terror in the Soviet Union are over for good.

Bureaucracy and the Welfare State
Until the rise of 'totalitarian' dictatorships after the first World War, the climate of official politics in the leading countries of the modern world indicated a gradual democratization of political life and a corresponding decline in internal social tension. This was illustrated in particular by the taming of the socialist Labour movement and its transformation from a revolutionary threat to the existing social order into the official opposition of today and the prospective government of tomorrow. Since then, the rise and fall of Fascism in Italy and

Germany, the establishment of Communist regimes in Russia, China and their satellites, and the failure of democracy to take root in Eastern Europe and the Moslem world have demanded a modification of this optimistic outlook. But at least in North-Western Europe and in the English-speaking countries political democracy has undoubtedly become more complete, and even its patchy progress in parts of Asia and in South America has been sufficiently encouraging to regard it as less of a luxury of a few wealthy nations and more of a—potential—world system.

The sovereignty of the people has, indeed, come to be the acknowledged political principle of most modern nations, although few of them have drawn all the practical conclusions from this radical proposition. Popular consent is regarded as an essential element of the process of government in all democratic countries, and the sham elections of totalitarian countries reflect their unwillingness to abandon the claim to 'true' democracy and are, therefore, the homage of political hypocrisy to democratic virtue. Failure to obtain the formal endorsement of the government by election or plebiscite has nowadays become a sure sign of backwardness for any political system.

However, in all modern democracies, the working of the political system has to take account of the fundamental paradox that the interests of a minority of property owners are in important respects opposed to those of the majority, most of whom earn their living by working in one form or another for the owners of property. The urgency of this dilemma varies according to the national standard of living, the social composition of the population and its political traditions; in addition, it may be affected by the state of the business cycle, for in times of acute depression social tension may reach a threatening intensity even in a rich country like the United States, while prosperity is everywhere the strongest argument in favour of the *status quo*.

This paradox has been the basis of the standard criticism of democracy as a political system by conservative political thinkers. In abstract terms, the inherent contradiction between 'democracy' and 'capitalism' is, indeed, formidable, and in the long run this may well prove to be the case even in practice, but it has been shown by experience that it is at least temporarily possible to make capitalism acceptable to the majority of the voting population through the device of the Welfare State.

The modern Welfare State may be defined as organized public interference with the functioning of the 'private enterprise system' and the rights of property and as systematic redistribution of the national income through taxation and social benefits for certain unprivileged groups. Although its main purpose is eminently conservative, shortsighted spokesmen of the business classes often make the mistake of denouncing the Welfare State as 'socialism', but this is no more justified than the parallel mistake of Labour politicians who want to persuade their followers that the establishment of the Welfare State is identical with the attainment of their original socialist objectives.

Historically, the growth of the Welfare State is closely connected with the rise of anti-capitalist popular movements. This connection is, perhaps, most obvious in the history of Imperial Germany, where Bismarck was responsible for the creation of a system of social insurance for the express purpose of taking the wind out of the sails of the Social Democrats whom he regarded as the mortal enemies of the established social order. In Britain, similar considerations were uppermost with Joseph Chamberlain who expressed the conviction, in his earlier radical days, that the possessing classes should pay a 'ransom' for the maintenance of their privileges; but the first great practical steps in the creation of the British Welfare State were sponsored by the radical wing of the Liberal Party in Asquith's government—though not without the spur of a growing independent Labour movement—and the virtual completion of its edifice was reserved for the Labour government of 1945.

With the exception of a small minority of *laissez faire* fanatics, most up-to-date supporters of the capitalist economic system are in favour of a certain amount of government interference in social and economic affairs, e.g. in the imposition of import duties and the management of the currency. In all modern countries, government regulation has, however, gone much further than this and includes a host of other measures. Some of these are less designed for the benefit of the general public than for ensuring fair play between different groups of business interests, while others attempt to protect the public against exploitation, such as Food and Drugs Acts, the regulation of transport charges and the limitation of monopolistic practices.

However, in the course of time further extensions of State activities have taken place in spheres where the interests of property owners have clashed with those of the population at large. Important industries may cease to conform to the changing demands of the market, and public assistance may be required in order to assist them temporarily or permanently. Where such measures are taken, even by governments which regard the protection of private enterprise as their sacred mission, they involve elaborate government regulation and control on a gigantic scale; perhaps the most striking contemporary example of such policies is the United States farm support programme.

More serious situations may call for more drastic remedies. It may prove impossible to run privately-owned branches of industry of public importance at a profit, except on terms unduly burdensome to the nation, e.g. a railway system in competition with road transport. Or an important national asset may be in danger of irremediable deterioration due to the neglect of its owners who find it unprofitable to make the necessary investments, as happened to British coal mining between the two World Wars. Finally, it may be unsafe to leave a key industry wholly or partly in private hands, such as the development of atomic energy. In cases of this kind, the nationalization of whole industries may be the only practicable solution even for governments hostile to a socialist policy.

Since the Great Depression of the 1930s and the Keynesian revolution in economic thought, the prevention of severe mass unemployment is generally regarded as a function of National Governments, since failure to act would endanger the very basis of political democracy by shaking the confidence of the democratic electorate in the existing social order. This new obligation may involve government interference at many points and particularly in the banking system and the flow of credit.

The interference of the Welfare State with the property rights of the individual is no less radical than its assumption of control over the mechanism of the economic system. Its most obvious symptom is the level of direct taxation which involves a more or less substantial redistribution of income in favour of the poorer sections of the population. The use of the 'weapon' of taxation for reducing inequalities of income is inseparable from the philosophy of the Welfare State which wishes to guarantee to all its citizens at least a 'decent minimum standard of life' or, more ambitiously, to each individual 'equal opportunity' in the obstacle race of living in modern society. These objectives frequently require the provision of 'benefits' financed out of taxes.

But taxes are not the only, and perhaps not even the most painful, tribute imposed by the Welfare State on the owners of property. In all modern countries, the progress of democracy has gone hand in hand with far-reaching limitations of the use which a man may make of what is legally his own, although it is generally not the personal use of property for consumption but its 'productive' use for the purpose of making profits in socially undesirable ways which has provoked opposition and consequently public regulation. This is obvious in the case of factory legislation, public health laws and food and drugs regulations, which are not confined to Welfare States in the proper sense, and to which only the most extreme disciples of Herbert Spencer would object. But the modern State also prescribes the type of buildings which must be removed (slum clearance) and the type of buildings which may be erected (town planning), and may interfere with the use of agricultural land. In times of emergency it may control the right of investing in certain types of undertakings or forbid the movement of funds from one country to another.

This process of regulating, controlling and hemming-in the consequences of the profit motive has been going on for more than half a century. It is not completely independent of party politics, for the conservative representatives of business interests view it with great distaste, while their 'progressive' opponents are wholeheartedly in its favour. It therefore tends to advance by more or less radical leaps when the latter are in power, while it may slow down, or even go temporarily in reverse, under conservative governments. The minimum acceptable to both tendencies was defined by the British *Report of the Committee on Administrative Tribunals and Enquiries* ('Franks Committee') which laid down 'the principle that the individual has the right to enjoy his property without interference from the administration, unless the interference is unmistakably justified in the public interest'.[1] 'Progressives' and 'Conservatives' may dispute the course of the dividing line between the categorical statement and its qualification, but whatever the complexion of the government of the day, in the old-established democracies of Western Europe and the New World a return to the unfettered rule of business interests has become a political impossibility; the only countries where this has proved even partially feasible are ex-Fascist Germany and Italy, whose political systems may not yet have reassumed their permanent shape. The outstanding political effect of this development has been a deepening distrust of State action on the part of the business classes. They are opposing this trend with great verbal vigour, although this does not prevent any section from invoking State aid for itself in suitable circumstances.

State regulation and control of large sections of the economic system is, of course, inseparable from bureaucracy in the popular sense, but it implies a movement towards bureaucratic rule only in so far as the control of the government machine by outside authorities is relaxed or becomes ineffective. Although opinions on this point are bound to vary, there is practically complete agreement on the fact that there has been a progressive decline in the efficacy of parliamentary control over the executive branch of the government and there is no doubt that the importance of the permanent officials has waxed as that of the legislative has waned. To this extent the conditions for the growth of bureaucracy in the strict sense have certainly become more favourable.

The heyday of parliamentary supremacy in Western Europe was the era of unchallenged middle-class rule towards the end of the nineteenth century, before the political consequences of the democratization of the suffrage were fully reflected in the parliamentary strength of anti-capitalist mass movements. This new force revolu-

[1] Cmnd. 218 (1957), p. 89, paragraph 405.

tionized the classical party system and introduced changes which have been blamed with good reason for the dwindling independence of parliamentary representatives and the corresponding decline in their influence on government policy. At the same time, parliament has been more and more compelled to abandon detailed legislation providing for all possible contingencies in favour of laws which are little more than a framework which has to be filled in by government regulations with statutory force.

This delegated legislation has become a focus for criticisms because it admits, and actually compels, a high degree of administrative discretion. Even in a comparatively simple and straightforward matter like taxation it is almost impossible to legislate in advance for the innumerable ways in which broad public purposes may be stultified by interested parties; in more complex matters affecting the economic well-being of powerful groups such an attempt would be foredoomed to failure. Legislation must, therefore, be confined to a broad statement of purposes and methods, including the provision of special machinery for carrying them out, while enabling the government to adopt the necessary detailed measures for ensuring that these purposes will be fulfilled.

Delegated legislation is thus a necessary instrument of government in the public interest in a situation where powerful private interests stubbornly contest every encroachment of public policy on their territory. The generally accepted explanation of the need for such legislation is the enormous expansion of parliamentary business; this is real enough, but detailed analysis would show that one of the main causes of this legislative congestion is the clash of interests between the demands of a more or less democratic mass society and the property rights of the minority.

The opposition of eminent lawyers to the principle of delegated legislation because it is repugnant to the 'rule of law' can be easily fitted into this view of the matter, for the English Common Law is not a timeless and absolute ideal; on the contrary, it is closely allied to specific social interests and conditions which are in important respects no longer those of contemporary society: 'Legislation means for the most part regulation of individual liberty in the old sense. Unlike the rules of judge-made common law the bulk of legislation is of application only to particular classes of subjects, e.g. to owners of certain types of property, to producers of a particular commodity, to those engaged in a particular industry. . . . But modern administrative methods seldom lead to unlawful interference with the person. They are, on the other hand, expressly designed for the regulation of private interests, particularly proprietary interests. In this respect they are the antithesis of the common law which seeks to protect the individual proprietor in the enjoyment of his land and goods.'[1]

However, not all measures of delegated legislation are well conceived nor is the discretion given to the civil service always well used. To furnish the executive government for certain purposes with the full powers of the legislature through the medium of delegated legislation has particularly drastic effects in a country like Great Britain, where the House of Commons, in the guise of the Queen in Parliament, is the absolute legal power in the land. In the United States, laws passed by the various legislatures are subject to review by the Courts, while in France a complex system of administrative law decides conflicts between the State and the citizen. In Great Britain, however, the immunity from legal review enjoyed by parliament extends as a rule to the minister acting under the powers delegated to him, and in many cases there is no appeal against his decision.

A further restriction on the power of the ordinary courts has resulted from the growth of administrative tribunals. Although this is not directly connected with the system of delegated legislation, it is rooted in the same basic situation: 'Disputes arise between, on the one hand, the individual whose rights are invaded and, on the other hand, the public authority bent on enforcing a policy or on maintaining or improving a standard: these were to be resolved by specially constituted tribunals outside the pattern of traditional courts or by the adjudication of the Minister himself.'[2] The advantages of this procedure are generally claimed to be cheapness, speed and the need for basing decisions on the public interest; from the point of view of

---

[1] E. C. S. Wade's editorial comment in the 1941 edition of Dicey's *Law of the Constitution*, pp. lxxxi and 522.

[2] *Rule of Law* (A Study of the Inns of Court Conservative and Unionist Society) (1955), p. 30.

the private interests affected these standards are, of course, irrelevant and increase the threat to their existence by making its operation more effective.

The haphazard growth of a host of administrative tribunals, like the corresponding growth of delegated legislation, has led to abuses and some safeguards—on the lines of those proposed by the Franks Committee—may well be required, particularly regarding the finality of the decisions reached. The defenders of the interests threatened by the trend of development of modern mass society naturally make the most of such defects and appeal to the traditional values of the freedom of the individual, and to the spirit of a legal system fashioned predominantly by their own spokesmen and their predecessors, in order to mobilize the maximum volume of public support for their stand.

In this battle they are inevitably on the defensive against power-ful, and in the long run irresistible, forces. The constant pressure by the democratic electorate for 'social progress', which cannot be ob-tained without substantial modifications of the capitalist economic system, is the ultimate cause of the complex system of checks on the operation of the profit motive which is characteristic of most modern countries. Even where the mass electorate is generally in favour of private enterprise and opposed to radical social change, this process may be seen at work, whenever the underlying conflict of interests takes the shape of specific burning issues. A large and growing mea-sure of governmental action is, therefore, more than a—regrettable or desirable—fashion; it is the form of political coexistence between capitalism and modern mass democracy in the Welfare State.

CHAPTER SEVEN

BUREAUCRACY AND THE PARTY SYSTEM

The State is the central repository of political power, and the right to determine the way in which it is run is the greatest political prize. The constitution or system of government provides the general framework for the activities of rival claimants to political power and, therefore, determines the outward forms of political life.

Parties and Factions
In despotic or absolute States, the typical form of political activity is of necessity that of cliques surrounding the ruler and trying to influence him in favour of the interests represented by their members. In such regimes hostile movements assume the character of conspiracies aimed either against the person of the ruler and the clique behind him or against the whole system of government; in the former case their purpose is a *coup d' état*, leading to the replacement of the existing incumbents by their opponents without any radical change in the character of the regime, in the latter a political revolution.

In oligarchic States, such as those of the Italian city republics, eighteenth-century Great Britain and a number of European countries during the nineteenth century, political currents crystallize in the form of factions, organized for carrying on the government in the interests of the dominant group, or trying to prevent the use of the resources of the State for purposes of which the opposition disapproves.

The growth of the modern State is matched by the growth of modern mass parties which are also a characteristic product of industrial society or, at least, of the process of industrialization. Just as the

H   113

modern State is not necessarily democratic but invariably plebeian, the mass party system is by no means confined to democratic countries, but its development is incompatible with a regime where the exercise of political power is restricted to a numerically small elite.

The fundamental aim of all political parties is the marshalling of mass support for the purpose of acquiring power over the State. The structure of the State is, therefore, the most important single factor determining the shape of the party system. This applies, above all, to its distribution of power and much less to its administrative arrangements. In broadest outline, the parallel between governmental and party structures is unmistakable even at a cursory glance. The disproportionate power of the party 'leader' in the British party system plainly reflects the corresponding position of the Prime Minister in the system of government. At the other pole of the political compass, the strict centralization of the Russian Bolshevist Party, and the corresponding atrophy in the independence of its local organs, was a faithful, if fateful, reflection of the distribution of power in the Tsarist State. In the Austro-Hungarian Empire with its medley of nationalities in different stages of development, the Socialist Labour movement assumed multi-national form, with the two most advanced nations, the Germans and Czechs, in uneasy alliance or open rivalry; across the border in Imperial Germany, the preponderance of Prussia was hardly less pronounced in the Social Democratic Party than in the government.

Even more pervasive, because less subject to national peculiarities or idiosyncrasies, are the social effects of industrial capitalism on the character of modern mass parties. The rise of the business classes was invariably connected with the creation or extension of representative parliamentary institutions. Unlike the aristocracies of precapitalist society they did not owe their influence to the predominant position of a few individuals but to their function as representatives of a new social power. This did not make the business classes democratic in the modern sense; on the contrary, in many countries they felt quite comfortable in conditions which gave them a growing measure of political influence, while excluding the masses entirely from active participation in the parliamentary game. But whereas the numerically insignificant aristocracy of landowners required very little formal organization, because it was a natural clique, the middle classes depended on political organization in order to make the most of the limited opportunities offered by the restrictive electoral systems of the time.

Before 1848, political democracy as understood at present was practically non-existent in the Old World of Western Europe. The transition to fully modern conditions was due to the interaction of three factors—the need of the business classes for political allies in their rivalry with the aristocratic or bureaucratic guardians of political power, the attempts by the most intelligent conservatives to exploit the latent conflict of interests between the middle classes and the unprivileged masses, and the independent protest movements of the masses against their social and political serfdom.

British democracy owed its comparatively smooth advance mainly to the first factor, represented broadly by the classical Liberal Party, though not without some assistance from the more far-sighted leaders of the Conservatives, notably Disraeli. The outstanding representatives of plebiscitarian conservatism were the Third Empire of Napoleon III and the German Empire which adopted manhood suffrage partly as a result of Bismarck's observations as Prussian ambassador to the Court of Napoleon III. A number of other continental countries were pushed along the road towards democracy largely by the strength of the independent Labour movement.

The progress of democracy was, however, so slow that at the beginning of the twentieth century electoral systems approaching manhood suffrage were, amongst European countries, limited to Great Britain, France, Germany (where the franchise in the most important States was, however, severely restrictive), Switzerland and Denmark. A number of other countries followed suit during the period before 1914, mainly under the spur of the first Russian Revolution of 1905, whose impact was particularly strong in Austria-Hungary, Sweden and Finland, but there and in such a highly-developed country as Belgium the end of the long struggle for political democracy was delayed until after the first World War, while Switzerland excludes women from voting even now.

Despite the natural optimism of the supporters of the extension of the franchise to the unprivileged masses, the practical result of 'democracy' in this technical sense was nowhere a system of 'government of the people, by the people, for the people'. The effect of universal franchise was essentially a change in the rules for access to the machinery of the State in favour of one of the contestants, and not a fundamental change in the character of the State. Its political effects are subject to the rules of the electoral system, which invariably safeguards the interests of the dominant social groups or classes by dry technicalities like the choice of single or double ballot, large or small constituencies or simple majority voting versus proportional representation, And even after a radical political party has cleared the electoral hurdles protecting the established social order, the *status quo* can rely on the constitutional rules for the distribution of power between different institutions and on the vested interests of the government machine itself.

Parties and 'Machines'

Although triggered-off by rivalries between powerful minority interests, the extension of political rights to the bulk of the industrial workers and small farmers (or agricultural labourers) invariably assumed a momentum which transformed at least the surface of politics. The advent of 'democracy' in this limited sense created new opportunities for changing the political balance of power, and thereby compelled even the defenders of the old order to adopt the new techniques for preventing encroachments on their strongholds. The result of these hostile but complementary forces is the modern party system.

This system is best understood as the political reflection of the great dilemma of modern democratic society, the contrast between the equality of all men as citizens and their social and economic inequality. This fact confronts the possessing classes with a difficult task which is, nevertheless, often solved with a great deal of success: to persuade the masses to join them in upholding the interests and defending the privileges of the minority. It also creates opportunities for the opponents of the business interests to translate their ideas from theoretical speculation or underground conspiracy into practical politics and to gain control of the government in order to curb, or even to destroy, the power of capital; in the advanced nations of Europe and the Western world the achievement of this aim has so far proved elusive.

All modern parties, however strongly they differ in their political aims, are therefore at one in their acceptance of the importance of mass organization, and this distinguishes them from the cliques and factions of earlier days which exerted their influence by more personal and less formal means. The need for such organizations is in the first place technical, for large-scale action requires some form of permanent institutions. As a good many party activities are carried out by voluntary workers, party organizations are less formal and professional than the government service or big business but they constitute administrative systems of a comparable kind.

Like all administrative systems, party organizations were originally designed as instruments for the achievement of the purposes of their primary social forces. But while it is relatively easy to discern the nature of these forces in broad outline, it is much more difficult to understand how they control the activities of their administrative 'servants'. This control is, in fact, remarkably defective, particularly as many parties do not directly represent clear-cut social groups but are amalgamations or coalitions invariably suffering from friction between their partners. In such conditions the party organization becomes the strongest link between disparate elements, and control of the organization is normally the key to party leadership.

The less complete the fusion of the social interests behind a party, the more important the role of the organization in rallying lukewarm supporters and marshalling them behind the official leadership. Thus it is much more than a passive piece of social machinery, serving the sole purpose of providing a primary social force with the most efficient leverage on the government. In coalition parties it serves, above all, as an indispensable means of safeguarding the interests of the dominant group within the party. As such it tends to acquire a growing measure of independent power which may transform it into a 'machine'.

An administrative system becomes a machine when its organization functions independently of the opinions, and ultimately of the interests, of its membership. The inherent paradox of machine rule in political parties, trade unions and such like organizations is the fact that this process takes place within formally democratic and voluntary bodies.

The first step towards the establishment of machine rule is the occupation of the key positions of the organization by a group of people intent on using them in their own interests and manipulating the constitution of the party for this purpose—the 'bosses' and their henchmen. Once the machine has gained power, it employs its position for the purpose of eliminating its opponents and preventing all attempts at a palace revolution. Thus the earliest symptom of machine rule is the substitution of orders given by the bosses for the more or less democratic decisions of the members or their representatives. As soon as the machine is safely in the saddle, it begins to make use of its ascendancy for its own purposes. At first these may be pursued side by side with the primary aims of the organization, though with the unspoken proviso that in case of a conflict of interests those of the machine take precedence. The full implications of this bureaucratic degeneration of the organization are felt only at a later stage, when the machine uses its—by then—absolute power entirely for its own ends, even at the cost of neglecting or perverting the original interests of the organization.

Machine rule as such has few, if any, apologists; on the other hand, it has been plausibly contended that a certain measure of administrative absolutism in large bodies such as trade unions (or, of course, political parties) is relatively harmless, because their voluntary character compels the leadership to act in the best interests of their members: 'If, however, members of voluntary societies are dissatisfied, then they can leave. This right of members to "contract out" is of greater potency than any other single factor in determining that the activities of a society shall respond to the wishes of its members. It must always retain the interest of its members.'[1]

This argument confuses legal with social categories. An organiza-

[1] V. L. Allen, *Power in Trade Unions* (1954), p. 10.

tion may be legally voluntary in the sense that non-membership does not violate any law, but it may have achieved a position of such importance that it is in practice essential for the pursuit of certain social purposes to belong to it. A trade union commanding the allegiance of the great majority of workers in an industry may, indeed, make membership a condition of employment for all persons in certain occupations. Apart from that, the power of a modern mass trade union may be so great in other respects that it is in practice impossible for individuals or minorities to affect its policy or leadership either by democratic means or by founding splinter groups or 'break-away' unions.

The same is true of established political parties in countries ruled by the two-party system. The effort of establishing a third party is not necessarily doomed in advance, as illustrated by the success of the British Labour Party, but it is truly gigantic and requires the sustained endeavours of a great social interest. However widespread public dissatisfaction with the operation of an established party, its expression will be seriously limited, and may be stifled, if the party organization has taken on the character of a machine. Once this has happened, the machine will resist all attempts at reform, because it is by definition ruled only by its own interests and not open to intellectual conviction or moral persuasion.

To regard the silent protest of resignation from a party or trade union in this stage of its degeneration as an effective means of influencing its policy is an optimistic illusion. Its result will usually simply be a further consolidation of the power of the machine through the withdrawal of its critics. The machine may actually take the initiative and expel awkward members, often with grave consequences for their livelihood. Neither in economics nor in politics is there any reliance on the operation of a hidden hand as assumed in the argument that 'dissatisfaction would be reflected in a declining membership, and in the interests of self-preservation union leadership would be compelled to stem the tide. They would have to get a correct impression of the needs of the workers. The democratic mechanism would be operated from the top.'[1] The democratic mechanism can

[1] Allen, op. cit., p. 28.

not be reversed at will; it either operates from the bottom or not at all. In practice, a powerful ruling machine accepts external defeat rather than internal reform which would result in loss of power for itself.

The shifts in the facts of political life have been accompanied by corresponding changes in the prevailing ideas concerning the nature of political parties. The eighteenth-century view was perfectly expressed in Burke's famous definition of party as 'a body of men united, for promoting by their joint endeavours the national interest, upon some particular principle in which they are all agreed'.[1] Since then, the growth of the modern party system has attracted the attention of a number of brilliant, though predominantly hostile, observers such as de Tocqueville, Ostrogorski and Michels, followed by the more objective approach of Max Weber and his school of sociologists. At present it is less fashionable to distinguish parties 'by their programme or the class of their members' than 'by the nature of their organization', and it is regarded as more realistic to define a party as 'a group of citizens united in acceptance of one discipline'.[2]

Like most definitions, this statement illuminates, perhaps, more the attitude of its author than the nature of its subject, but it is striking evidence of the radical reorientation of political thought brought about by a century of modern party politics. Although more down-to-earth than Burke's ideological approach, its formalism is just as one-sided.

Coalition Parties

The original hostility of conservative thinkers and politicians to political democracy was based on their fear of the clash of interests between the property-owning minority and the property-hungry majority. They assumed that the natural and inevitable consequence of granting political rights to the masses would be an overwhelming attack on private property and the outbreak of a social revolution. In practice, events in the political democracies of today have taken a

---

[1] E. Burke, *Thoughts on the Cause of the Present Discontents, Works* (1854 edn.), I, 375.
[2] Duverger, op. cit., pp. xv and 175.

very different course, for their dominant interests have managed to combine a high degree of social stability on the basis of the capitalist system with a substantial measure of public participation in political life. By offering timely concessions they have either prevented the adherence of the mass of the population to movements of radical social change or gradually transformed the aims and the character of such movements, where they had taken root.

In this process political parties are playing a vital part. They are the main device by which the business classes, which on a counting of heads are a small minority in every advanced industrial society, have solved at least temporarily the delicate task of rallying mass support for themselves, or at least of neutralizing the political expression of mass dissatisfaction with the established social order.

Conservative parties with a broad mass basis are not governed by the material interests of the mass of their members or supporters who must, nevertheless, be induced to accept willingly their discipline or, at least, their policy. Though on good authority it is possible to fool some of the people all the time, and politicians of all ages have made ample use of this possibility, it would be a crude mistake to regard deception as the main cause of the lasting hold which conservative parties manage to retain in most advanced industrial countries on a large section of democratic electorates.

Conservative parties have other and better means of tackling their permanent dilemma of maintaining mass support for a policy which benefits in the first place the propertied minority. Their real mass basis is provided by the numerically large and growing lower middle classes. Though the number of farmers, shopkeepers and independent small business men is on the decline, that of 'black-coated' workers—clerks, supervisors and technicians—is rising with the mechanization of manufacture and the growth of service industries. These classes are, on the whole, critical of the advance of the manual workers resulting from political democracy and full employment, and their insistence on their own superior status is reflected in their willingness to follow the lead of their betters in the defence of their common values against the claims of the lower orders.

The necessary condition of their docility—and therefore of conservative rule in a democracy—is economic prosperity. The expansion of State interference in the economic field since the war and the responsibility for preventing a catastrophic depression which is accepted by all governments, while in many ways irksome and unwelcome to the business classes, has created the condition for the revival of conservatism characteristic of the democracies during the 1950s. The close ties between it and the business community, so far from being a handicap, have become a definite asset, because they may be represented as a guarantee of further economic well being—and the disappointment of this expectation could have cataclysmic political results.

Conservative parties are thus by their very nature political amalgamations. They consist of a 'dominant' group and one or more 'captive' groups whose members genuinely share some interests with those of the dominant group and who give it their support on other political issues as well, either from traditional loyalty or from party discipline. The latter fact explains the vital part of the party organization in the life of such parties.

There is little room for genuine party democracy in conservative coalition parties, because they are not dominated by the numerical majority of their members but serve primarily the interests of powerful minorities. On the other hand, this distribution of power is an effective brake on the party organization and prevents its degeneration into a party machine: The dominant group is far too vitally interested in maintaining its control of the party organization. In such parties the primary social force is therefore usually able to retain its hold on the administrative system, and thereby prevents any serious bureaucratic degeneration.

Sometimes the dominant interests are not sufficiently strong to create an effective party organization or to prevent the captive groups from obtaining an uncomfortably large share in running it. In this case, they have to rely on coalitions with non-political organizations capable of exerting independent pressure on the mass of the party's supporters. Such additional ties are commonly found in religious beliefs or denominational connections. A classical case in point is the party with religious orientation, such as the German Centre Party before Hitler, the Austrian People's Party and the Dutch Catholics, or the post-war Christian Democrats in France, Germany and Italy. The hold of the Church on the people provides the social minority interests in control of the party organizations with a mass basis which they might otherwise find beyond their reach.

Religious affiliations have played a particularly important part in nationalist movements, from the Irish struggle for independence to the Muslim League in Pakistan and the Greek Cypriot Church. Such movements represent the most dynamic type of coalition parties. They owe their success to the universal appeal of their professed aim, the liberation of the country from foreign rule, through a common struggle against the national enemy.

The leadership of nationalist movements is in the early stages almost invariably in the hands of the 'moderates' who are by and large identified with the wealthier classes with a stake in the country. Their rank and file consists of the unprivileged or underprivileged masses whose material conditions are usually deplorable and whose social radicalism tends to take the form of a determined, and indeed exaggerated, nationalism; hence the frequently observed eclipse of the middle classes during the climax of the nationalist struggle.

It is relatively easy to maintain unity in the nationalist camp, while internal conflicts are repressed by common hostility towards the national enemy, but once this bond has been removed by victory, the comrades-in-arms of yesterday may confront each other with undisguised hostility. From the point of view of the moderates, the most critical task of a broad-based nationalist movement is, therefore, the continuation of the coalition in the new era. The prestige of the old leaders may suffice to make this possible, but it will be put to a formidable test.

In this critical situation the solid support of a disciplined party organization may prove decisive. The prestige of success will make its representatives the real rulers of the moment, while its ranks will be swelled by the accession of people who did not join the fighting movement from fear of personal or economic danger, but who now jump with enthusiasm on to the band waggon of the successful party which they support financially and whose established leaders they idolize with all the fervour of the neophyte. The party organization thus occupies the central point of the social balance; it becomes indispensable to the new regime and virtually independent of outside control. Thus the seeds of its bureaucratic degeneration begin to sprout in the hour of its public triumph.

An exceedingly complex form of coalition party is the Fascist Party which had its short but devastating vogue during the 1930s and which may reappear again, should similar conditions favour it. The Fascist parties were genuine mass movements exploiting the dissatisfaction of the lower middle classes with the sharp deterioration in their position brought about by the catastrophic upheavals of the first World War and the Great Depression. Their political aims were just as undemocratic as their organization, and this made them ideal allies for the more adventurous sections of the business classes eager to destroy the mass organizations of the workers who had benefited from the same events which had radicalized the lower middle classes. This alliance was immensely lucrative for the leaders of the Fascist gangs and it was perhaps the main reason for the sharp distinction between the leadership and its supporters.

The Fascist parties were a special type of coalition and showed the familiar sharp distinction between dominant group and captive public. But the dominant group was the product of an era of social disintegration; the greater the success of the party leaders, the less docile they were in their relations with their former backers and paymasters, until final victory transformed them into the absolute rulers of their countries. Their party machines thus became not only independent from outside control but were at the same time the supreme masters of the government machine. Their ambiguous position provoked the growth of bureaucratic symptoms from a very early stage, long before their conquest of power; victorious Fascism was, therefore, a hotbed of bureaucratic degeneration and a huge parasite on the body of society, a bureaucracy intensified by gangsterism.

Democratic Mass Parties

With the progress of political democracy the more articulate elements of the unprivileged majority of the population were enabled to throw the weight of numbers into the political scales against the wealth and position of the traditional rulers of the State.

The first great nation to evolve a broadly democratic political system was the United States, and it was there that the implications of democracy for the party system were worked out in practice in the party machines with their conventions and caucuses. The 'convention' originated as a device for ensuring the genuine expression of popular will in opposition to the manipulations of small cliques which had established themselves in the legislative assemblies. The 'caucus' was the democratically elected steering committee of the convention.

The ultimate political destiny of these broadly conceived democratic bodies is an ironic commentary on the practical weakness of abstract principles or formulae in a society dominated by conflicting social interests, but they retain a lasting importance as valid patterns of democratic political action in a mass society. The political movements of farmers and urban lower middle classes in other parts of the world provide a number of parallels to this American model.

These radical mass movements were in form aggressive, but in content almost invariably defensive, alliances against the social and economic effects of modern capitalism on the living conditions of the 'old' lower middle classes in town and country. For this reason, their social aims were frequently unrealistic in terms of practical politics but quite tangible and specific, because they were a direct reflection of the material interests of their supporters—nowhere more clearly than in the radical agrarian movements of nineteenth-century America with their clamour for legal measures directly benefiting the farmers in their capacities of commodity producers and debtors.

Democratic protest movements are by definition movements of the unprivileged or underprivileged in a society ruled by a privileged minority. Their primary social purpose is the alteration of the existing social balance by political means. As they gather force, their leaders acquire considerable power, and in a society split into groups and classes with conflicting interests, but organized on democratic political lines, the disposal of such power is worth a good deal to the ruling minority which wants to retain its privileged position.

The normal and healthy method of achieving this purpose is through compromise with the dissatisfied elements, where this is possible at a 'reasonable' cost, i.e. without injury to vital interests. If the compromise is successful, the edge of discontent is blunted, the social radicalism of the movement is softened and its dynamism weakened. The movement slows down, while its administrative system expands in response to the growing power and prestige of the organization. Its leaders change from dangerous demagogues into respectable administrators.

This process creates the conditions of a different and by no means healthy form of compromise. In a reform movement which has outlived its original purpose but still retains all the formal instruments of action on a mass scale, the administrators of yesterday may become the bosses of today's party machine, able to deliver power irrespective of the purpose for which it is used, and which is therefore worth buying by the vested interests who were originally the declared enemy of the democratic mass movement.

This situation is, of course, familiar to the student of American politics, but it may be observed just as well in other countries where conditions favour development on the same lines. It is, however, dependent on such conditions and these are by no means always available. They exist only in countries where the social system is stable and where social tension is therefore low. In an expanding economy there may be room for a rise in mass living standards parallel with increased incomes for the owners of property; in a mature capitalist society there may be room for a redistribution of the national income in favour of the masses, which can be accepted as a lesser evil by the ruling classes as a whole and as a positive boon by their enlightened minority. Movements of social reform are unlikely to arise in such circumstances or, if they have originated in times of sharper social tension, to retain their missionary zeal for long; they will either become one of the vested interests haggling for a greater share in the good things of life or degenerate into political machines exploited by their owners in their own selfish interests.

In conditions where there is less room for compromise without radical changes in the fundamental balance of power, the course of events will not be so smooth and predictable, and a good deal will depend on the character of the democratic mass parties, their aims and their organization.

The Labour Movement

The protest movements of the industrial workers against poor living conditions and unbridled exploitation began early and often assumed violent forms. From arson, riots and Luddite machine-smashing they developed into more permanent 'combinations', first with the make-believe ritual of secret societies, but afterwards in the clear, cold light of workaday trade unionism. Painful experience taught the pioneers of the movement to refrain from over-ambitious schemes and to concentrate on the humdrum but more rewarding task of organizing the workers of individual crafts or industries.

In the countries of the English-speaking world, the trade unions were from the outset the backbone of the Labour movement, and political Labour parties were comparatively dependent off-shoots of the unions. In Great Britain the conversion of the union leaders to the idea of an Independent Labour Party was slow and frequently half-hearted, and the British Labour Party remains to this day in important respects an auxiliary of the unions. In the United States of America the political Labour movement has so far failed to take root, because the unions are by and large satisfied with their ability to look after their specific interests through one or the other of the traditional parties.

Labour parties of the British type owe their position to a combination of two factors: the backing of the trade unions and the mass appeal of a socialist, or at least anti-capitalist, platform to broad sections of a democratic electorate. Their policy is influenced at least as much by the interests of the union leaders as by the wishes of their democratically organized party members. To this extent they bear some resemblance to the coalition parties on the right of the political spectrum, though the community of interests between dominant and captive groups is generally much closer.

In most countries of Europe, however, the creation of an organized political working-class party was inspired by and based on definitely socialist theories. 'Socialism', if it was more than a party label or a collection of magic incantations, implied a re-orientation of political action in line with purposes which transcended the bread-and-butter interests pursued by other organizations, including the modern trade unions and their political auxiliaries. This is particularly true of Marxism which soon became the most influential socialist theory, because it forged a link between socialist ideals and working-class aims. Thus it was a dominant force in the Labour movement of those countries, where rigid class barriers and narrow political restrictions forced the workers and their organizations into unyielding opposition to the existing social system. In Marxist terms, it was a suitable 'ideology' for such parties, i.e. an adequate reflection of their practical purposes and interests in the sphere of thought. In fact, the possibility of applying Marxist categories successfully to practical politics depends on the existence of a state of acute social tension between opponents whose interests are too irreconcilable to allow of a compromise settlement.

The difficulties of a working-class movement with specific socialist aims are formidable. Its purpose is the reorganization of the whole pattern of social relations in a way which is directly opposed to the interests of the most powerful groups and classes, and not even directly related to the day-to-day interests of the workers on whose support it relies. Its motive force is, therefore, idealistic to an extent quite unusual in party politics and in all other forms of organization with the exception of religious bodies in their evangelistic phase, and its primary social force is correspondingly nebulous: it consists in theory of the underprivileged classes to whom it appeals and whose long-term interests it claims to represent.

These interests undoubtedly exert a strong pressure on the course of events and on the attitude of the more articulate sections of society but they are quite unfitted for the task of controlling the operation of the mass organizations developed by the growing Labour movement. Within its framework, the masses are represented by the party members whose function is that of controlling their organization through the ordinary processes of voluntary democratic bodies. In practice, this is patently impossible, not only due to the increase in the power of the administration characteristic of all large-scale organizations but also for more specific reasons.

A movement of the underprivileged sections of society with a strongly idealistic appeal will inevitably consist of an *élite* comprising mainly the more articulate and politically active members of the working classes with a sprinkling of recruits from the professional classes. The more intelligent and energetic members of the movement are inevitably absorbed by the varied tasks of running the movement in its different branches. Apart from its active administrative system, the party is a mere skeleton, and its leaders are, therefore, virtually uncontrolled by any organized independent power.

In countries such as Great Britain, where the Labour movement grew out of the radical fringe of the existing political system, it is virtually limited to the framework of an electoral machine, in close alliance with the trade unions and loosely associated with the political minority of the consumers' co-operative movement. In countries where the Labour movement arose in bitter opposition to the established social order its organizations developed on much more ambitious lines. In Western and Central Europe it formed an all-embracing community catering for virtually all the social needs and aspirations of its members outside working hours. Its personnel comprised literally thousands of deputies and councillors, speakers and writers, publishers, printers and booksellers, as well as scores of separate organizations with full-time and part-time staffs assisted by armies of voluntary helpers. Membership contributions (collected by tens of thousands of voluntary party workers) and the success of the economic enterprises of the movement financed an impressive material accumulation of reserve funds, party centres, newspapers, printing presses, banks, insurances and other ancillary undertakings.

However genuine the idealism of the party workers and their leaders, however strong their conviction that they were assuring the final victory of socialism by strengthening their movement in all its forms, this luxurious growth took place entirely on the basis of the existing social system and was, in fact, a valuable pledge for the good behaviour of the Labour movement in its relations with the ruling powers. The material shell of the movement, the precious embodiment of decades of intense efforts by the devoted advocates of its socialist ideals, gradually assumed the character of a vested interest which regarded the maintenance and improvement of its position as its paramount purpose. In theory it remained the organized instrument of the democratic labour organizations and subject to the wishes of their members. In practice this relationship was transformed into its opposite: the hold of the 'machine' on the allegiance of the workers, and in particular the suppression of potential rival claimants for their support, became the most important task of the bureaucratic party organization in the relations with its members.

The policy of the party leadership towards outside forces was ultimately shaped by the same needs. It had always been the champion of working-class interests, at first more with an eye to the propaganda effects of its agitation than in the hope of effectively improving the material lot of the workers, but soon with considerable practical results. Representation in parliaments and local councils was no longer regarded primarily in the light of a tribune for effective mass agitation but as an opportunity for curbing the power of capital and obtaining benefits for the working classes. In most countries of Western and North-Western Europe, where social tension was high during the generation preceding the first World War, the growth of the Labour movement thus tended to reduce it. By giving the workers a modest stake in their countries, the socialist Labour movement made them increasingly less ready to risk everything in a life-and-death struggle for the overthrow of capitalism, just as the growth of the party machine induced their leaders to watch their steps and to eschew methods which might have endangered the basis of their position.

Where outside conditions favoured this policy, the party 'machine' found little difficulty in reconciling its independent interests with faithful service to the workers who obtained palpable benefits from its efficient work. In countries where the gradual change in the character of the Labour movement coincided with the progress of democracy and an improvement in mass living conditions, the socialist parties were content to shed their revolutionary traditions and to develop on the lines of the British Labour Party by concentrating on the progressive introduction of the Welfare State and the protection of working-class interests within the existing social framework. It was only in conditions where the progress of the masses depended on radical changes in the social and political environment that the transformation of the Labour movement into a bureaucratic machine became the source of irrepressible conflicts and catastrophic defeats. In such situations, the Labour movement was paralysed by the conflict between its radical past and its present reality as a vested interest, tied to the *status quo* by the bonds of self-preservation. Its main energies were concentrated on preventing its nominal supporters from acting in a way which might have endangered its existence, and it was easily destroyed by unscrupulous and determined enemies.

This was, by and large, the course of events in Germany, Austria and Italy after the first World War. These countries were deeply involved in the great power conflict culminating in the war of 1914-18 in which they underwent greater strains than their social fabric could accommodate. War preparations and the carnage of war intensified social tension to the point where the established system of government gave way, in Germany and Austria-Hungary under the impact of defeat, in Italy in spite of a hollow victory. The textbook case of a 'revolutionary situation' had arisen—but the socialist parties proved quite incapable of making use of it.

So far from exploiting the crisis for a 'conquest of power', the official Labour movement in Germany and Austria emerged as the strongest bulwark of the existing social order, while in Italy internal dissensions paralysed its energy and permitted the Fascist gangs of the ex-socialist Mussolini to establish their dictatorship and to crush their opponents at will. The victory of Fascist movements in Germany and Austria was delayed for more than a decade, but the highly organized socialist mass parties of these countries proved no less inadequate at the critical moment than their Italian comrades.

If these monumental failures demonstrated the unsuitability of the socialist Labour movement as the agent of the revolution which had been its professed aim for many decades, the later history of these countries provides striking proof of its deep roots. Hounded out of public life by the victory of Fascism and Nazism, persecuted and broken up as organized bodies, the socialist parties rose again at the end of the second World War—if not exactly like a phoenix from his ashes at least like grass growing over a battlefield. As a result of their descent into the hell of Fascism, they have been purged of all traces of their revolutionary past and desire nothing better than to function as the guardians of the material interests of the organized workers within the framework of the parliamentary democracies which were set up in all three countries after the defeat of their authoritarian rulers, though in Italy this change has not taken place without another split.

While the socialist movement thus developed through victories and defeats into a bureaucratic machine assuring the allegiance of broad sections of the workers through the hold of its organizations and the protection of their economic interests, an even more rigid bureaucratic machine has taken possession of the 'revolutionary' alternative to the 'reformists'—the Communist parties.

During the early years of the century, the internal balance of the Labour movement was seriously threatened by the growing friction between the radical minority, which regarded it primarily as a means to the end of reconstructing society on a socialist basis, and the moderates in control of the party machine who regarded it more and more as an end in itself. This growing conflict came to a climax during the first World War, and particularly after the Russian Revolution of 1917. Throughout Europe, left-wing opposition to the official policy of supporting the war and enthusiastic approval of the Soviets were two facets of one and the same attitude, and from this premise it was only a short step to the conclusion that the remedy for the defects of Social Democracy was the application of the theoretical and practical methods developed by the Bolsheviks: the 'radicals' of European socialism turned towards Russia and its Third International.

On the Russian side, the Communist leaders were just as convinced as their Western Allies that Communism was by no means a purely Russian affair and that its victory in Russia was merely the beginning of a new phase in its international development. At the same time, Lenin, Trotsky and most other Soviet leaders were certain that their new regime could only survive with the help of a socialist revolution in the West, or at least in Germany. Their attempt to rally the revolutionary forces of Europe to the support of Soviet Russia was thus based on thoroughly practical, if not necessarily realistic, considerations and therefore became one of the earliest preoccupations of Soviet foreign policy. The result of these efforts was the creation of a new international organization designed to unleash in the West the forces of social revolution which would prevent the capitalist governments from crushing the young Soviet State by military intervention.

The Communist International was modelled on the first International of 1864 in conscious opposition to the second International of 1889 which had been essentially a loose federation of autonomous national parties for the limited purpose of organizing Congresses and maintaining contact between the party leaders. It was to be a uniform organization with a uniform policy which had to be applied by its national sections according to local conditions but which was not subject to revision by these sections or their leaders. This meant that the primary force of each national Communist party was not even theoretically located within the party but elsewhere—in the Communist International, its Executive Committee and its leading group—while the party was simply the administrative machine for carrying out the policy dictated by its primary force. In view of the disproportionate power of the Russian Communist Party in an organization conceived on these lines, it was virtually inevitable that the policy and organization of the Communist International should have been dictated by the leaders of the Russian Communists and subordinated to their interests.

The slavish adoption of Russian concepts and the imitation of Russian forms in countries where these were alien and unsuitable was, perhaps, the least important aspect of this relationship. But with the consolidation of the Soviet regime, the direction of the Communist parties through the 'bureau' of the Communist International took less and less account of the differences in conditions in different parts of the world—with disastrous political results from China in 1927 to Germany in 1933. The maintenance of 'party discipline' degenerated into a veritable rule of terror against all 'deviationists', however justified their opposition to the party line of the moment which was determined by the ebb and flow of the struggle between different groups within the Russian Communist Party before Stalin's acquisition of complete power, and by the requirements of his dictatorship afterwards. In this process the Communist parties of most countries were purged of all elements capable of independent thought, and transformed into bureaucratic machines for the transmission and execution of orders from above.

The utter failure of this policy between the two world wars has been overshadowed by the enormous expansion of Communism after 1945, but it was far from accidental. Since the second World War, the weakness of Communism has been most clearly revealed in Western Europe where the Communist parties have failed to make any worthwhile political gains or to hold those made immediately after the end of the war. Even in France and Italy, where they have retained the allegiance of a large section or even of the majority of the industrial workers, they remained confined to the part of a frustrated and purely negative opposition. On the other hand, Communism has become a world system through its victory in China with its two bastions in Korea and Indochina, while in Eastern Europe it was installed as the governing system in the wake of the Soviet armies, except in Yugoslavia where Tito's Communist party acquired power mainly by its own efforts and has since developed on individual lines.

Where the victory of Communism has been due to military occupation by Soviet armies, satellite regimes in the true sense of the terms were set up which owe their existence in the last resort to the threat of Russian military intervention. This is itself a measure of the failure of Communism in the countries concerned; where the victory of Communism was, if not spontaneous, at least a victory of movements which had managed to make use of assistance from outside in order to oust the corrupt and degenerate governments of their own countries, it has taken place in economically and politically backward countries such as Yugoslavia and China, and by the use of a social technique superior to that of their opponents but worlds apart, in content even more than in geography, from the modern party system.

The Process of Political Bureaucratization

At this point it may be useful to survey the progress made so far and the path by which definite conclusions may be reached.

The discussion of the structure of modern large-scale organization in Chapter Two revealed the crucial position of the administrative system in the operation of mass organizations. The complexities of their tasks create inevitable difficulties which were called 'bureaucratic defects' in Chapter Three and which can be alleviated but not entirely removed by some of the measures outlined in Chapter Four.

Apart from these technical problems which are important in some respects but fairly parochial, the delegation of authority to the chiefs of the administrative system may create conditions in which the administrators may usurp uncontrolled power and establish their rule over the organization as a whole. This possibility was discussed in Chapter Five which also includes a sketch of the main features of a fully bureaucratic system.

This analysis does not provide an answer to the all-important question why some organizations degenerate into bureaucracies, while others remain the obedient tool of their primary social forces. Such an answer can only arise from an examination of the factual evidence. The simplified sketch of the development of the modern State and the party system in Chapters Six and Seven has set the scene for such an examination.

In its most exacting form, this task would involve a world survey, country by country, and extending back into history, because the present situation is in crucial respects incomprehensible without the study of its background. Such a task is far beyond the scope of one book and the powers of one man, though it might well find its place in a collective re-interpretation of modern history in the second half of the twentieth century. For the present purpose it may be attempted to summarize in bold outline the growth and structure of the machinery of government and the party system in a few contrasting countries of major importance, concentrating mainly on shifts in the balance of power between different groups and on the changes in the relative importance of government and parties as power centres.

The great continental States, where the bureaucracy of the central government has traditionally played a paramount part, are obvious choices for a study of the conditions of bureaucratic rule. They are represented in the following chapters by Russia and France, an Eastern autocracy and a Western democracy. The very different political structures and problems of the English-speaking world should be studied at least by reference to the United States and Great Britain, but for reasons of space Great Britain alone will be included. Russia, France and Great Britain provide not only striking illustrations of different forms of the machinery of government but contrasting party systems—totalitarian, multi-party and two-party.

However condensed and reduced to its barest essentials, this survey of the structure and functions of political administration in three important countries should provide basic factual material for an answer to the main problem of political bureaucracy—the identification of the forces responsible for the process of bureaucratic degeneration and the conditions of bureaucratic rule.

PART II

CHAPTER EIGHT

BUREAUCRATIC RULE IN RUSSIA

I. BEFORE THE REVOLUTION

The Soviet State as it exists today is the heir of the Tsarist State which was essentially an absolute bureaucracy of unusual strength and great staying power with an unbroken history going back at least to the period of Tartar rule over Russia from the thirteenth century onwards.

The Origin of Russian Absolutism

When the Tartars overran the vast expanse of territory west of the Ural mountains, it was an agglomeration of small principalities with a sprinkling of merchant republics such as Novgorod the Great and Pskov. The Tartar hordes did not transform this huge 'empire' into a cohesive State with themselves as a new ruling class on the lines of the Norman conquest of England: they were content with the collection of a tribute, first in furs but later on in precious metals, which became a genuine tax collected by Tartar officials not only from princes and republics but also from individuals. This system created the foundations of an administrative machine which embraced, in however primitive a fashion, the previously more or less independent local communities and thus introduced a potentially decisive new element into the political situation: the Tartars had created the basis of the future Russian State.

At first their own officials were used in order to run the new machine and thereby exercised political power unrestricted by the narrow local boundaries which primitive social conditions and difficult communications had imposed on the country after the decay of the loose agglomeration of principalities based on Kiev. It was, perhaps, an early sign of the decline of the Tartar regime that this crucial power was put into the hands of one of the native rulers and was finally acquired in 1328 by the Grand Princes of Moscow.

The position of chief tax collectors for the Khans of the Golden Horde, the key to Russia's political future, was obtained by the rulers of Moscow mainly in consequence of their ability to satisfy the rapacity of the Khans and their satraps. By insisting on a tribute in precious metals which could only be procured by foreign trade, the Tartars indirectly encouraged an alliance between the princes of Moscow and the main repositories of gold and silver in a backward peasant country—the merchants of the towns, who played a big part in the primitive fiscal system, and the Greek Orthodox Church and in particular its wealthy monasteries. The Church as the only other countrywide organization became the natural ally of the Grand Princes in their attempts to widen the radius of their power. This inevitably involved them in conflict with their erstwhile masters, the Khans of the Golden Horde, and with the local dignitaries, the Boyars.

From this long and bitter struggle the Grand Princes of Muscovy emerged as Tsars of Russia, as 'self-rulers' or autocrats in the double sense of independence from the Tartars abroad as well as from the traditional domestic limits on the power of the princes by representative organs. Although the Tartars remained formidable military opponents even during their period of decay, the Tsars found the struggle against this external enemy less difficult than the establishment of their absolutist rule in the face of the tenacious opposition of the Boyars. The old and time-honoured system of precedence acted as a brake on Tsarist administration, because it gave the aristocracy a share in the government which they were unwilling to abandon. Even their most determined enemy, Ivan the Terrible, who opposed them with a rule of ferocious terrorism, had to be satisfied with a rough-and-ready division of the country between areas subject to his personal rule and the rest of the country.

The Tsars fashioned their tools of military expansion and domestic rule partly in imitation of Tartar institutions; they relied mainly on an army of heavily armed knights, supplemented under Ivan the Terrible by the 'Streltsi' furnished with firearms, and on a civil service derived from the administration of their private estates which became the nucleus of a strictly bureaucratic State. In contrast to the feudal Boyars, the knights were the servants of their rulers who rewarded them mainly with service land (*pomestye*) which was at first strictly tied to the performance of their duties but in the course of time tended to become hereditary. The officials were rewarded either in the same way or by a share of the dues and fines collected by them, by taxes in kind paid by the local population for their keep, and by corrupt extortions which played a prominent part in Russian administration from the earliest times.

The whole system was imposed from above on a primitive subsistence economy, and therefore showed irresistible tendencies towards getting out of hand and degenerating by the transformation of functional officials into parasites living at the expense of the peasants in the same way as the landlords. The knights became a landowning gentry, and as such they played an important part in the struggles between Tsars and Boyars. The main victims of these developments were the peasants who were subject to multiple extortions by landlords of various descriptions and by hordes of tax gatherers who filled their own pockets in addition to collecting heavy taxes for the Tsarist exchequer. The pressure of taxation grew steadily with the wars for access to the Baltic waged by the Tsars against their Western and North-Western neighbours, the Poles and the Lithuanians, while the landlords, both knights and Boyars, tightened their hold on the peasants whose labour gave value to their landed properties.

In a vast country with a small population, the only power capable of inducing the peasants to put up with this situation was brute force. Their natural reaction was either to turn on their tormentors in order to tear them to pieces, or to escape into the masterless steppe or forest. The landlords as individuals were far too weak and too few to compel the peasants to obedience and were thus in the last resort dependent on the government of the Tsars for the maintenance of their position. Despite the friction between various groups of landowners and the government, all were agreed on the paramount necessity of keeping the peasants in subjection, and after a series of more and more stringent restrictions on their freedom of movement serfdom in the full sense of the word was finally introduced just before the social revolution during the Time of Troubles.

Any blow to the power of the State through confusion at the centre, such as the struggle for succession after the death of Boris Godunov, or any serious decline in its efficiency as an organ of repression through the periodical degeneration of the bureaucratic machine, was quickly reflected in peasant risings. If conditions were favourable, these assumed enormous dimensions as in the great rebellions of Stenka Razin and Pugachov, which put the great German Peasant War of 1525 in the shade and dwarfed the French *Jacquerie* or Wat Tyler's rising in England.

Withdrawal from the grip of the twin forces of government and landowners was the most prominent aim of the most energetic elements of the Russian people. Wherever possible, this urge took the form of flight into the Cossack communities in the no-man's-land between the Russian Empire and the Black Sea and Caucasus; elsewhere people simply took to the woods, particularly in the trackless North where they could easily hide from the police of the Tsars and form their own communities. Where all means of escape were closed, individuals, groups and whole villages took a desperate refuge from the power of the State in mass suicide: 'Since the end of the seventeenth century, self-immolation in the flames as an extreme form of protest against the power of the State had assumed a horrible and puzzling mass character. As early as 1691 the number of people who had thus killed themselves since 1675 was estimated at over twenty thousand.'[1]

The dependence of the main beneficiaries of the Russian social order on the Tsarist government was virtually complete. The bureaucracy owed its privileged position and its opportunities of illegally enriching itself entirely to its connection with the service of the State and was in its overwhelming majority blindly devoted to its superiors and opposed to any change. Even the landowners were in no position to pursue independent policies or to control in an effective manner

[1] V. Gitermann, *Geschichte Russlands* (Hamburg, 1949), II., 77.

the government and its servants. Not only were many landlords originally endowed with their lands as servants of the Tsars and were therefore the creatures of the State, but they relied entirely on the support of the government for the exploitation of their most valuable possession, their peasant serfs, who were straining at the leash to flee from their oppressors or even to turn on them with a ferocity bred from centuries of ruthless domination. On the other hand, although in an underpopulated country of continental size no resource was more valuable than its population, the unrestrained despotism of the Tsarist bureaucracy—coupled with habits inherited from centuries of Tartar rule—made the State tragically profligate in its treatment of the people, with mass exterminations as a means of internal repression and the callous sacrifice of its soldiers as its main strategic principle.

The only privileged group which from time to time turned the tables on the government was the officer corps whose power to dispose directly of physical force in its most effective form frequently gave Tsarism during the eighteenth century new rulers and a regime closely resembling that of other Eastern despotisms.

The Vicious Circle of Tsarism

The inevitable result of the distribution of power between the State and the social forces was stagnation in society and gigantic corruption in administration. At that time Western Europe went through the first stages of quick technical and economic advance through the gradual development of trade and industry on a modern basis and this different experience was felt in despotic Russia mainly in terms of an insulting contrast between the—theoretical—omnipotence of the Tsar at home and Russia's relative insignificance in international affairs. The most determined attempt to resolve this dilemma was Peter the Great's violent and heroic reform policy which aimed at driving Russia by administrative and military measures along the path pursued by the leading nations of Europe.

Peter freed the bureaucracy from the external traces of irrational and obsolete traditions, methods and institutions. He took the administration of indirect taxes into the hands of the central government and created a Board of Revenue on the Dutch model, he substituted a more rational poll tax for the primitive Tartar house tax, he abolished the council of Boyars and the *prikaz* (the traditional government bureau) and created the administrative Senate and five government departments or Colleges copied from his Swedish enemies. In State and Church he introduced the 'collegiate' or Board system of administration on the same lines as in Prussia, which was a fertile breeding ground for hordes of officials. He created special controlling organs within the bureaucracy, the Inspectors, who have been immortalized in Gogol's comedy. This system was amplified by the appointment of Fiscals and Imperial Upper Fiscals and the Procurator General, who at times became the real head of the government machine. The bureaucratic structure established by Peter the Great, though frequently revised in detail and particularly in the functions and composition of the central government boards and departments, remained essentially unchanged until after 1861 and, indeed, until the downfall of Tsarism.

Peter succeeded in putting Russia on the map as a military power by a similarly radical reorganization of the army which put crushing burdens on the Russian people and also on the nobility, but his concept of a *Dienststaat*, a society organized from top to bottom for the exclusive purpose of service to the State, was a complete failure, because it ignored the basic social relationships within the country.

In fact, the main beneficiaries of Peter's reform of the machinery of government were the noble landowners, because their position *vis-à-vis* the serfs was greatly strengthened by the increased efficiency of the administration. Secured in the rear, they managed to extract additional privileges from the State either through the personal influence of aristocratic cliques or through the bribery of its officials, while torpedoing all attempts by the Government to interfere with their power over the peasantry. The internal history of Russia in the eighteenth century consists largely of the successful stratagems of the aristocracy to free itself step by step from its obligations to serve the autocracy and, indeed, from any contributions to the State, while obtaining full government support for its privileges and interests and the unconditional use of the resources of the government for the repression of peasant discontent.

The clearest illustration of this process is the history of the *chin*, the system of fourteen dignities with parallel ranks for army and bureaucracy, which Peter introduced in 1722 for the purpose of subjecting the nobles thoroughly to the needs of his regime. In fact, he overawed the landowners without permanently changing their character and created or confirmed new privileged groups in addition to the existing upper classes with whom they gradually tended to coalesce. There is no more illuminating illustration of this process than the opening paragraph of Catherine II's great Charter of 1785 for the Aristocracy which defined nobility as 'a consequence of the qualities and virtues of those men who in earlier times distinguished themselves in the exercise of official functions and who thereby transformed their service into a privilege and bequeathed to their heirs the Estate of Nobility'.[1]

Catherine's reform of local government supplemented the inefficient and corrupt local administration after its complete breakdown in the face of Pugachov's rebellion by a modicum of local self-government for the aristocracy. This permission for the nobility to manage its own affairs was a considerable modification of the principles of the bureaucratic absolutism in the interests of the nobility. Nevertheless, Catherine's internal policy taken as a whole was a record of her gradual transformation from a reformer with 'western' ideals into a figure-head for the rule of the bureaucracy.

This may well have been inevitable, for the autocracy of the Tsars was in essence the legal form of bureaucratic rule, and the power of the Russian bureaucracy was more independent and less subject to outside control than anywhere else in Europe. Its absolutism was directly related to the destructive social tension between the mass of the peasants and their aristocratic owners, which made the nobles dependent on government support. Though firmly in the saddle, the bureaucracy, however, proved totally incapable of evolving any policy except the maintenance of the *status quo* at all costs. In its overwhelming majority it was a determined enemy of the reform policy advo-

[1] German version in Gitermann, II., 470 ff.

cated by the enlightened elements amongst the Russian upper classes
and by a tiny minority in its own ranks.

For this reason reform movements had a chance of success only
in situations where the bankruptcy of the ruling system assumed the
character of a public calamity. In the first internal crisis of the regime
during the nineteenth century, the murder of 'the first bureaucratic
Tsar'[1], Paul I, and his replacement by Alexander I, personal factors
played an important part, but the intrinsic sequence of events was
not very different from that under Alexander's grandmother
Catherine II.

The reign began with a period of reform proposals culminating in
the appointment of the reformer Michael Speranski as chief minister
for the purpose of preparing a new constitution and introducing order
into the chaos of the governing bureaucracy. Speranski aroused the
stubborn resistance and undying hatred of the bureaucracy by his
fiscal reforms and even more by establishing examinations as the
condition of higher office in the civil service. His fall was engineered
by bureaucratic intrigue at the time of the war against Napoleon in
1812, and the last years of Alexander's reign were a renaissance of the
most reactionary forces of the bureaucracy, personified by the pecu-
liarly repulsive Count Arakcheyev.

The pressure of this brutal and stupid regime was felt most strongly
by the younger generation of officers who may have harboured high
hopes of a better era after their experience of conditions in Western
Europe during the French wars. This was the direct cause of the
conspiracy of the Decabrists which came into the open after the
death of Alexander I and set a pattern which was to be repeated several times until the final fall of the Tsarist system.

The typical course of events was as follows: a phase of strictly
bureaucratic rule culminating in a discreditable breakdown; a reform era aiming at a more or less radical change in the structure of
the social, political and administrative system; a bureaucratic counter-
offensive resulting in the more or less complete frustration of the preceding reforms by administrative action or inaction; a corresponding
shift in the leadership of the reformers from moderates to radicals

[1] Sir Bernard Pares, *A History of Russia* (1926), p. 279.

favouring—and sometimes achieving—action by terrorist and revolutionary means; a period of violent persecution of the reformers leading to the complete restoration of a strictly bureaucratic system until the re-enactment of a discreditable breakdown on a bigger scale.

The reign of Alexander I ran through all phases of this cycle in a quarter of a century; that of his successor Nicholas I devoted thirty years to its final phase. Alexander II who took over the reins at a time of domestic and international crisis, acquired the title of 'The Liberator' through the series of reforms centred on the abolition of serfdom in 1861, and lost his life in the merciless struggle between the bureaucracy and the revolutionary wing of the progressive movement which was the direct outcome of the bureaucratic counter-offensive against the modest achievements of the reform era. His son Alexander III was again a figurehead *par excellence* for the bureaucracy and the period of its absolute rule lasted until the double crisis of the Japanese War and the first Revolution under his successor Nicholas II. The final cycle of reform, reaction and breakdown was compressed into a mere dozen years between 1905 and 1917.

This view of Russian history during the nineteenth and early twentieth century as a by-product of bureaucratic rule is reasonably consistent in its own terms, but it does not explain the increasing severity of the successive breakdowns of the system. Their main cause lies outside the purely bureaucratic sphere—in international relations and in social developments in Russia and elsewhere.

Until the end of the eighteenth century, Russia's social system was so static that these developments appeared mainly as a clash between the small minority of progressive 'Westerners' intent on importing European techniques into the country, and the bulk of the nobility, bureaucracy and officer class intent on maintaining the barbarian *status quo*. Yet for a country situated like Russia the maintenance of the existing state of affairs was an utter impossibility, in the international sphere even more than at home. The growing privileges of the nobility induced a strong demand for luxury goods from Europe which could only be satisfied by increased trade; hence Russian foreign policy was increasingly influenced by the search for ice-free ports. The pressure of the peasants against the borders of the Empire made it imperative to extend these borders more and more towards the South and East; hence Russia engaged in a series of expansionist wars against its neighbours, particularly the Ottoman Empire.

In this policy of predatory expansion, the combination of a certain amount of modern technical knowledge, imported from the West under Peter the Great and his successors, and a despotic use and abuse of first-class human raw material proved for a surprisingly long time very successful. During the eighteenth century Russia's external position improved almost miraculously. It started with a life-and-death struggle against Sweden and ended with the Tsar as the strongest counterweight to revolutionary France on the Continent of Europe. This dominant position was further strengthened by the failure of the invasion of 1812 and by the share of the Russian armies in the destruction of the Napoleonic Empire.

During the nineteenth century Russia maintained or even increased its superiority over its neighbours in the South and East, from Turkey to China, but the development of its relations with the West unleashed forces which ultimately were to prove fatal to the Tsarist regime. In terms of military events, the milestones of catastrophe were the Crimean War, the Russo-Japanese War and the first World War. These conflicts revealed the inefficiency and rottenness of the official civil and military machine and demonstrated by the merciless logic of armed struggle the need for a thorough change of system.

For a country at the stage of development reached by Russia about the middle of the nineteenth century, the Crimean War was not so much a military and political event as a social epoch. Even more painful was Russia's defeat at the hands of the Japanese after almost half a century of reorganizing and re-equiping the army and navy at prohibitive cost. This war demonstrated with unmistakable emphasis how far Russia under its bureaucratic rulers had fallen behind in the assimilation of Western techniques by comparison not only with its originators but with a despised oriental imitator of the West such as Japan. The final proof of the backwardness of the Tsarist system rendered by the first World War could no longer be accommodated within its framework.

The Tsarist State as a Ruling Bureaucracy

By the vicious circle of its swings from reform to catastrophe, Tsarism exhibited in extreme form the ultimate consequences of bureaucratic degeneration in the sphere of policy. It is, therefore, not surprising that its structure and methods exhibited with unusual completeness the characteristics of a ruling bureaucracy.

Autocracy in the sense of uncontrolled exercise of supreme power by the government—in modern parlance, dictatorship—was the legal foundation of the Tsarist State up to the Manifesto of October 30, 1905, which promised a constitutional regime, and its factual condition up to the Revolution of 1917. In practice, the omnipotence of the Tsar was, of course, simply a cloak for the uncontrolled rule of the bureaucracy. The Tsar chose his ministers according to his whims or wishes, and he was also supposed personally to appoint all officials of the four highest rank classes, but his effective influence on the administration, though always capricious and sometimes profound, inevitably waned with the expansion of the Empire and the growth of a huge bureaucratic sytem. Each individual bureaucrat was exposed to arbitrary action on the part of his superiors, from the Tsar downwards, but the system as a whole functioned as a sovereign power unchecked by any effective outside control, though subject to unending internal checks.

The outstanding feature of such an organization was inevitably its boundless inertia and consequently its failure to adapt itself by small adjustments to changes in conditions. Hence the succession of sweeping administrative reforms—especially under Peter I, Catherine II and Alexander II—designed to reorganize whole branches of the administration on a new basis in accordance with contemporary needs. In fact, none of these reforms managed to achieve their purpose, because the tenacity of the old institutions was equal to their inefficiency as instruments of policy. Their typical result was, therefore, the construction of superficially new institutions on old foundations which were only imperfectly remodelled in the process. With every reform the system as a whole became less and less rational, with unreformed elements tending to reassert themselves in the course of time, until in the end the complexity of the administration defied any attempt at rational direction from the top.

In its penultimate stage, before the emergency changes introduced in the course of the first World War, the central administration consisted of three main bodies—the Imperial Council, the Senate and the Council of Ministers—in association with a variety of other organizations with partly overlapping functions. The formal conduct of business at the top was, therefore, a matter of labyrinthine complexity. In times of emergency, there was a strong but invariably ineffective urge to cut through the chronic complications of the system by setting up special Boards with over-riding authority, charged with the duty of getting things done somehow at whatever cost. In the first World War four special Councils were placed above all other government institutions, with the Defence Council ranking higher than the others.

The organization of business within each government department reflected the organized chaos at the top of the administration and contributed not a little to it. Apart from the usual subdivision into branches, sections, subsections, etc., where the 'bureaucratic principle' of personal authority and responsibility applied, there was a host of other bodies varying in composition from ministry to ministry. These included standing committees for different purposes and, in a number of departments, administrative Boards under the chairmanship of the minister himself. In addition there was a complex system of inter-ministerial standing committees to deal with matters affecting the interests of a number of government departments, with provision for resolving differences of opinion, if necessary by reference to the Council of Ministers.

While the main structural weakness of the central administration was thus the proliferation of overlapping organizations with ill-defined areas of competence, the system of provincial administration suffered from the undue centralization of power in the hands of the provincial Governor. He was at the same time the head of the provincial department of the Ministry of the Interior and the representative of the central government in his province—a concentration of functions copied from the French prefects which created another serious bottle-neck at one of the strategic centres of the administrative machine. One of the main causes of this congestion was the deliberate policy of the bureaucracy which kept the *Zemstva* and municipal councils under control to the extent of duplicating their functions by its own officials who formed part of the Governor's establishment.

The patent defects of the bureaucratic administration called for remedies. In the absence of effective outside control over its activities, the bureaucracy created its own organs for supervising the execution of their duties by the bureaucrats. This bureaucratic method suffers from the incurable defect that it cannot provide a satisfactory answer to the question *quis custodiet custodes ipsos?*

The most impressive organ of general supervision of the administration was the Senate, created by Peter the Great as a controlling and co-ordinating body on the largest scale. The Senate first lost its administrative powers and later on its effective supervisory functions, though in theory it remained the supreme supervising office. In addition to the Senate, a special department was set up under a Procurator General whose duties consisted in the exercise of control functions over all parts of the bureaucracy from the Senate downward, with procurators' offices virtually duplicating the whole structure of the administration—not excluding the Church—in order to keep all its branches under permanent review. In the course of time, this institution became largely merged in the administration of justice, and a separate system of State control was created for the primary purpose of supervising receipts and expenditure and acting as an audit department for the greater part of the public service, but excluding the Privy Purse. Like the original procurators' offices, the department of State Control was organized as an independent ministry, duplicating by and large the whole organization of the bureaucracy, and subject to the same defects as the rest.

In addition, the government employed special inspectors at central and regional level, whose task was to observe on the spot how the bureaucracy carried out its duties, and how closely its practice corresponded to the endless reports which all officials had to make on their activities. This distrust of the reliability of official documents was only too well justified, but the same applied to the reports of the inspectors themselves who were just as much affected by the general drift towards inefficiency and corruption as their fellow officials.

The abuse of official power for private gain was endemic in a State whose original function had largely been the extortion of tribute for a foreign conqueror. More important, the material position of the office holders in a primitive and grossly overtaxed society depended mainly on their ability to squeeze the subjects as much as possible in order to satisfy the exchequer, with a surplus for themselves. It was, therefore, accepted as a matter of course that the performance of public functions had to be purchased by the public at a usurious price and that justice was a marketable commodity. At the Sobor of 1642 it was said that the bureaucrats, 'getting salaries, estates and patrimonies, growing rich off bribes, have bought up large estates and have made themselves brick houses such as even well born used not to have before'[1]—obviously to the great disgust of the aristocracy. Catherine II complained that 'the taking of gifts, bribery and blackmail are a radical defect of the Empire. There is hardly a judge who is not affected by this disease in the dispensation of justice. . . . If one wants to be protected from slander, one has to pay for it in cash; if one wishes to slander somebody else, bribes will be used in support of it. The judges transform the holy place where justice should be administered into a market place.'[2]

The prevention of corruption, at least so far as it affected the interests of the State, was a frequently proclaimed but never achieved objective of policy. Peter the Great created the Fiscals as professional watchdogs against corruption charged with the secret denunciation of dishonest officials, but this desperate remedy was open to all the temptations which caused the original evil and failed to achieve its aim. When Peter demanded that everybody defrauding the State even by the value of a rope ought to be hanged, one of his highest officials asked him whether he wished to be a Tsar without subjects: 'For we all steal—only some more, and more blatantly than others.'[3]

---

[1] Sir Bernard Pares, *A History of Russia* (1926), p. 160.
[2] Gitermann, op. cit., II, 204, quoting Ukase of July 18, 1762.
[3] *Ibid.*, II, 133.

The thorough corruption of public life had two main facets—the serious, and at times catastrophic, decline in the efficiency of the machine of government, and the additional oppression of the over-taxed subject. Corruption on this truly monumental scale kept the Treasury empty and enormously added to the cost of administration everywhere, but more especially in the army and navy, through collusion between suppliers and officials, thus making a substantial contribution to the successive breakdowns of the regime.

The main social effect of the corrupt bureaucracy was the imposition of an almost unbearable burden on the people. This intensified the pressure of the top-heavy State on all classes and thereby increased the social tension within Russian society. 'All sections of the people were getting restive', wrote a Decabrist leader to Tsar Nicholas I, 'only the government dozed unconcerned on top of the volcano; only the judges were delighted, because for them alone Russia was the land of promise. Their corruption reached an unheard-of level of shamelessness. Clerks could afford their own horses, and their superiors bought whole villages. . . . In short: the same picture in tax offices, Courts and supply agencies, before Governors and Governors General, wherever a private interest could enter. Those who had a chance robbed, those who did not dare, stole. Everywhere honest people suffered, while slanderers and crooks had a good time.'[1]

For the suppression of dissatisfaction the government relied more and more on its police forces. The whole system of local administration centred on the police, although during the period of serfdom police powers over the peasants were in the hands of their landlords. The secret police of the central government was used, and dreaded, as early as the time of Peter I and his immediate successors. Its main purpose was the discovery of oppositional tendencies and conspiracies and it was so unpopular that its abolition was promised whenever a new Tsar felt it necessary to keep the Capital in good humour.

The extension of the political police network to the whole country was carried out under Nicholas I after the suppression of the Decabrist rising. It took the form of the notorious 'Third Division', and the liberation of the serfs and the growth of a mutinous and semi-

[1] Gitermann, op. cit., II, 515.

nomadic industrial working class widened the field of the security police (*Okhrana*). The activities of the Narodniks of the 1870s took the form of a veritable duel between the revolutionary terrorists and the Secret Police in which the latter finally triumphed at the expense of the life of Alexander II. The intensification of the police terror under his two successors did not prevent occasional terrorist attempts on the life of prominent officials of the highest rank, but the real and invincible enemy of the police became more and more the growing Labour movement.

In its struggle against socialist tendencies amongst the workers the police went far beyond the sphere of police operations in the normal, or even in the Tsarist, sense of the term and used means of truly revolutionary consequences. The employment of *agents provocateurs* for the purpose of penetrating the secret circles of the opposition was a time-honoured and, on the whole, successful police weapon, even though it sometimes involved the murder of some prominent nobleman or high official whom the police was supposed to protect. However, the extension of this practice into the sphere of mass organization by the 'police socialism' of the chief of the secret Police of St Petersburg, Subatov, though officially disowned, led straight to the Bloody Sunday, January 22, 1905, and the first Russian revolution.

Tsarism and Modern Society

In the early part of the nineteenth century, Russian society consisted of a privileged class of noble landowners, closely allied with the ruling bureaucracy and the army officers, a mere sprinkling of urban tradesmen and 'intelligentsia' and a submerged peasantry.

This social structure made it inevitable that opposition to the dictatorship of the bureaucracy should start with the 'enlightened' minority of the upper classes which maintained at least some contact with Western ideas. The experience of the Napoleonic Wars extended the area of contact and made comparisons between conditions in Europe and Russia more and more frequent. The rising tide of dissatisfaction with the state of Russia was one of the main reasons for the tightening of the absolutist regime towards the end of Alexander I's reign, and dissatisfaction crystallized into conspiracy. Amongst the 121 men tried after the failure of the Decabrist *coup* in 1826 high aristocrats and army officers played a prominent part: there were no fewer than 7 princes, 2 counts, 3 barons, 2 generals and 23 colonels.

Although individual aristocrats continued to occupy high places in the administration of the country, the government of Nicholas I was highly suspicious of the aristocracy as a class and hostile towards any independent political manifestations on its part. Nicholas went so far as to give preference to foreigners who had to rely entirely on their official position and had no social backing in the country where they were, indeed, regarded with barely concealed hostility by Russians of all classes. The share of Germans from the Baltic provinces in the officer corps and the higher branches of the civil bureaucracy was outstanding, partly due no doubt to their higher educational level and technical efficiency, but mainly because the authorities regarded them as absolutely reliable tools of the government. The prevalence of foreigners was particularly marked in the diplomatic corps.

During the thirty years of Nicholas I's reign the pressure of the bureaucracy and its police continued unabated on all sections of the population, but the growth of trade and industry and of a professional middle class in the towns produced a change in the attitude of the nobility towards the government. The fundamental obstacle to progress on the lines of the West was the maintenance of serfdom, and the continued existence of this 'peculiar institution' depended entirely on the attitude of the government towards the growing pressure for its abolition. Hence the aristocracy lost its oppositional tendencies, which had been confined in any case to a small minority, and rallied round the Tsar and his government as the ultimate defenders of its privileges—a policy which proved fully justified by the terms on which the liberation of the peasants was ultimately brought about.

There would have been no night of August 4, 1789, in France without the background of burning chateaux and murdered noblemen, and such a background on the necessary scale was lacking in Russia on February 19, 1861. Russia had suffered a military defeat in the Crimean War, but the power of the bureaucracy at home had remained almost unimpaired and the repressive organs of the government were strong enough to maintain law and order, or at least to revenge its breaches with the customary ferocity. For this reason the reforms introduced by Alexander II went only as far as the rulers' realization of their necessity, and their insight was limited by their interests and by the close alliance between the bureaucracy and the nobility. Although carried out mainly by the more liberal officials, the reforms, and particularly ıthe abolition of serfdom, were very tender of vested interests. Thus it was enthusiastically welcomed in the towns but received with discontent, and sometimes even with riots, in the countryside. The abolition of serfdom did not create a broad class of well-contented peasant farmers owning their own homesteads and attached to the government which protected them in the enjoyment of their property, and its failure to do so was one of the main causes of the instability of the Tsarist regime and of its ultimate downfall.

Although liberal aristocrats continued to play some part in the opposition to Tsarism until its destruction, and some of its most illustrious critics such as Count Leo Tolstoy and Prince Kropotkin belonged to this class, the leadership of the reform movement from the middle of the nineteenth century onwards passed into the hands of the middle classes, and especially of the so-called intelligentsia.

Despite the quick growth of industry during the second half of the nineteenth century, the authentic middle classes remained numerically weak, socially unimportant and far too engrossed in making the most of their considerable economic opportunities to engage actively in political propaganda which was unpromising in terms of practical results and exceedingly dangerous for its participants. Only very rarely did their ambitions stray beyond their local interests and the 'reformed' municipalities and the *zemstva* which had taken over most of the functions previously carried out by the assemblies of the nobility.

These organs of provincial self-government had been created in the liberal opening phase of the reign of Alexander II and became the main theatre of the endeavours of the moderate reformers, although they were elected on extremely narrow and undemocratic franchises, closely supervised by a hostile bureaucracy, surrounded by petty restrictions and severely confined to their own localities, because the authorities feared with some justification that they might otherwise become a nucleus for nation-wide representative assemblies hostile to the autocracy. Their leaders and supporters were liberals in the Western European sense, critical of the corrupt, old-fashioned and hopelessly inefficient Tsarist government which was the very opposite of the kind of State they wanted, but at the same time opposed to violent action against the autocracy which might endanger the foundations of the social system within which they were trying to establish themselves as equal, if junior, partners with the traditional upper classes.

Their hopes of quick results along these comfortable lines were thwarted by the determined resistance of the entrenched bureaucracy, and the resulting political vacuum was filled by the revolutionary movement of a handful of students and intellectuals who regarded the overthrow of the Tsarist dictatorship as the basic condition of progress and who expected the regeneration of the country from the Russian peasantry and its ancient communistic organization, the *Mir* (village community), and not from the adoption of Western capitalism. The attempts of these *Navoduiks* to 'go amongst the people' were a dismal failure, and their revolutionary wing turned more and more to terrorism against high government officials. This policy culminated in the assassination of Alexander II in 1881 after a systematic hunt lasting for several years. The price paid for this achievement was the destruction of their organization, the death of their leaders on the scaffold, in prison or in exile, the intensification of the reactionary regime for a quarter of a century—and a widening gulf between revolutionaries and moderate reformers.

This turn of events was not entirely, or even mainly, due to lack of energy and political conviction on the part of the moderates but to the fact that their attitude towards Tsarism was considerably modified by the arrival of a new force on the social scene. With industry developing quickly on a fairly high technical level, large concentrations of industrial workers appeared in the towns. Their living conditions were atrocious and they eagerly absorbed the revolutionary propaganda of the radical intelligentsia. With this emergence of a new social class the camp of the revolutionaries split into two groups. One of them continued to follow the traditional propaganda amongst the peasants, coupled with the renewal of terrorist attempts against prominent individuals (Social Revolutionaries); the other went over to the 'Western' theory of Marxist socialism and regarded the industrial working class as the spearhead of the coming revolution (Social Democrats), though it split within a few years on questions of organization and policy into the hostile factions of Bolsheviks and Mensheviks.

The revolution of 1905 was the most important political watershed in Russian history since the reforms of the 1860s. Like them it followed military defeat, but while the changes after the Crimean War were entirely administrative, popular reaction to the Japanese War took the form of mass risings by the peasants and mass strikes by the workers in the towns who formed the nucleus of a revolutionary government in the 'Soviets'. Against the background of revolutionary events in town and country, and under the combined pressure of the middle classes organized in the *zemstva* and the more far-sighted amongst his own officials, led by Count Witte, Tsar Nicholas II granted a Constitution which appeared to limit the powers of the autocracy by the creation of a parliament with a popular House based on a fairly wide franchise. This Constitution was virtually abolished by the *coup d'etat* of June 1907, when the second Duma was dissolved and the franchise radically changed; though less progressive than the first Duma, it had likewise refused to support the dictatorship of Prime Minister Stolypin, who had meanwhile crushed the revolutionary forces by an effective reign of terror.

However critical the more influential leaders of the growing middle classes were of the policy pursued by the government of the Tsar, the revelation of the strength of the subversive forces during the revolution curbed their oppositional tendencies. Despite its patent defects, the Tsarist State with its bureaucracy and police changed in their eyes from a negation of progress and civilization into the champion of law and order against the enemies of society. The revolution of 1905, which had been hailed by the business interests as the dawn of a new era, thus was in fact the grave of their political hopes.

This disappointment and the well-founded fear of the only practicable alternative to the Tsarist regime thus tied the middle classes much more closely than in the past to the established political order. Without the repressive forces of the State they would not have been able to guide the course of the revolutionary masses and the ensuing catastrophe would have engulfed them no less surely than the government. Thus they found their Bismarck eventually not in the liberal bureaucrat Witte but in the business-minded conservative Stolypin who boldly tackled the reorganization of the Russian village on lines compatible with the needs of modern capitalism. However, the point of no return had been passed for all of them: Stolypin was murdered by a cross between a revolutionary and an *agent provocateur* of a type familiar in the political underworld of Tsarist Russia, and the great war which Stolypin had tried to avoid, because he had no illusions about the effect of another violent shock on the tottering system, broke out less than three years after his death.

Its consequences were disastrous for Russia, for the Tsarist regime and for the Russian business classes which had been its only wholehearted supporters. The only alternative to the Tsarist State was not, as the middle classes hoped, a democratic reform regime on parliamentary lines but a radical revolution which proved incompatible with the prosecution of the war and with the existence of the established social order as a whole. For this reason, far-sighted reactionaries like the French Ambassador Paléologue were convinced that Tsarism had to be kept in power at all costs, if Russia was not to drop out of the war.

The February revolution of 1917 confirmed the correctness of this judgment. Every endeavour of the Provisional Government, in which the middle classes played the leading part at first openly and until the end behind the scenes, to direct the energies of the Russian people towards the war ended in failure. The only result was a further radicalization of the masses and the fall of the Provisional Government by the action of Lenin and his Bolsheviks. Democracy, in Western Europe the classical form of the political rule of the middle classes, was in Russia incompatible with the very existence of private capitalism—but not less with the rule of its determined enemies.

Political Parties before the Revolution

Political parties in the Western sense could not grow and flourish in Tsarist Russia. Before 1905 the central government was completely autocratic, without even a semblance of national popular representation, and constitutional parties on a national scale were, therefore, out of the question. In local affairs the *zemstva* and the municipal councils offered some form of representative institutions. Their great political aim was the creation of a central body which might finally develop into a national parliament, but the hopes of their respectable leaders were disappointed by Nicholas II on his accession, and the growing pressure of police and bureaucracy actually goaded these highly respectable persons into the formation of an illegal 'Liberation Society' shortly before the outbreak of the Russo-Japanese War.

The revolution of 1905 gave unexpected emphasis to their demands for a Constitution, and when the Manifesto of October 30, 1905, seemed to meet them on this point, the Society quickly split into two sections. The right wing, which represented mainly the wealthier industrial and financial interests, expressed itself as satisfied with the position created by the October Manifesto and formed its own party under the name of *Octobrists*; the left wing in which the professional classes played a more important part, demanded something better than a sham constitution and looked to Western Europe for their political models. Hence the name of 'Constitutional Democrats' (or *Kadets*) adopted by them and their policy of constructive opposition in the Duma.

Neither Octobrists nor Kadets represented more than the very narrow social groups from which their leaders were recruited. In a democracy this would obviously have condemned them to political insignificance, but in Tsarist Russia this was by no means the case. The Duma was divided into classes which corresponded broadly to the main social groups—landowners, urban middle classes, peasants and industrial workers—and the wealthy minority was thereby spared the effort of obtaining the allegiance of the unprivileged majority in order to be sure of parliamentary representation. As long as the real power was safely in the hands of the bureaucracy, this did not make much difference, although it prevented the middle-class parties from creating effective party machines. However, the hollowness of the claims of the respectable parties to independent po litical leadership was exposed after the Revolution of February 1917, when they proved quite incapable of persuading the authentic Ru ssian people—the nation of land-starved peasants and poverty-striken workers—that they were fit to speak and act for them in a crisis of unprecedented gravity.

It is, therefore, problematical how far Octobrists and Kadets really deserved to be called political parties in the true sense of the term; they resembled rather the cliques and factions of earlier times which were also able to dispense with the mass organization which is the distinguishing feature of modern parties. However, they certainly had a better claim to this description than the groups of the Right whose influence depended entirely on their connection with the autocracy and on the support of the Black Hundreds which they received as a result of careful police management and which did not reflect any true political allegiance to their leaders but rather to the police which paid and controlled them.

Amongst all the political organizations of Tsarist Russia only those of the revolutionary Left could be described as parties, though of a different type than those of parliamentary regimes. They consisted mainly of three sections: the *Narodniks*, who called themselves from 1902 onwards Social Revolutionaries like their precursors in the days of Alexander II, the *Mensheviks* and the *Bolsheviks*. Like the political parties of other countries they sponsored certain social interests as a means of influencing the distribution of political power in their own favour, but for a considerable time this link between the parties and their primary social interests was more imagined than real, and it never completely lost this somewhat theoretical quality. In fact, their membership was largely confined to tiny groups of (mainly young) intellectuals, with not more than a sprinkling of industrial workers, and the oppressive dictatorship of Tsarism prevented them from establishing really firm relations with the classes which they claimed to represent.

The Social Revolutionaries followed the Narodnik tradition in looking to the peasants as the main force of Russia's social regeneration and combined a programme of the revolutionary redivision of the land with rather vague semi-socialist ideas. Their influence extended to those sections of the middle classes which regarded the peasants as the big batallions most likely to help them to win their own battles and whose sympathy with the sufferings of the *Muzhik* was therefore mainly a by-product of their own political requirements. As the peasants constituted the overwhelming majority of the population, a political movement specializing in gaining their support was naturally sure of finding a mass audience as soon as conditions favoured the wider dissemination of its propaganda.

Mensheviks and Bolsheviks, the warring factions of the numerically tiny Russian Social Democratic Party, accepted the Marxist approach to history and with it the expectation that socialism was bound to follow the progress of capitalism. The latter was plain for all to see since the 1880s or 1890s, and with it developed a sturdy and rebellious working class which was hailed by all Marxists as the instrument for social revolution. But whereas the Mensheviks thought that after the overthrow of Tsarism the business classes would grasp the reins in a more or less democratic republic, the Bolsheviks derided the Menshevik assumption that the workers' party would from a parliamentary opposition until the outbreak of the socialist revolution; instead of this they tried to prepare for a quick transition from Tsarism to a republic dominated by a 'democratic dictatorship' of the workers in close alliance with the revolutionary peasants.

From these conceptions flowed different strategic principles and different organizational structures. All three parties were necessarily composed of small 'cells', but while with the Social Revolutionaries these were by and large autonomous and connected only by loose ties, the Social Democrats formed fairly cohesive parties, for both factions regarded it as their main task to create organizations capable of serving as a genuine working-class party after the overthrow of Tsarism. The Mensheviks conceived it in terms of a democratic mass movement on Western lines, while the Bolsheviks under Lenin's tireless and single-minded leadership built up a cadre composed of 'professional revolutionaries'. This Leninist party was subject to a system of strict central control which was in principle democratic but in fact very tight, and not at all unlike the bureaucratic dictatorship of the autocracy which stood between the revolutionary parties and the achievement of their aims. The Bolshevik leaders insisted on a measure of political conformity amongst their followers which was unheard of in contemporary politics, and they were willing to adopt ways and means which to most other revolutionaries were beyond the pale of the political struggle.

The distinctive feature of all three revolutionary parties was their acceptance of the need for a violent overthrow of the Tsarist regime as a condition of the realization of their programmes, but they differed radically in their views as to the best means of getting rid of Tsarism. The Social Revolutionaries, like their Narodnik ancestors, relied mainly on political assassination—a running fight between the conspiratorial circles and the State aiming at unnerving the autocracy and thereby forcing it into granting a constitutional regime. Both fractions of the 'Marxist' labour movement, on the other hand, regarded the movement of the main social forces as the ultimate agent of the overthrow of the regime, but while the Mensheviks were inclined to regard this essentially as a spontaneous process, the Bolsheviks organized their small party consciously as the general staff and officer corps of the revolutionary forces.

Of the main political groupings of Tsarist Russia, the parliamentary moderates (Octobrists and Kadets) and the Mensheviks were essentially offshoots of West European movements and ill adapted to the political realities of the Russian situation—above all to its outstanding fact, the Tsarist State. Social Revolutionaries and Bolsheviks were both effective in their ways, because they represented revolutionary responses to the social and political conditions of Tsarist Russia. However, the former were essentially a symptom of the popular reaction against the intolerable pressure of the regime on the mass of the people, while the latter represented in their closely knit and ruthlessly led secret organization the nucleus of an anti-State. This was, indeed, potentially far superior to the all-powerful machine of Tsarism, partly as a result of the unquestioning and heroic devotion of the 'professional revolutionaries' to their ideals but mainly due to their leaders' insight into the motive forces of history and their ability to transform their conclusions into political energy by a remarkable feat of social engineering on the largest historical scale.

2. THE SOVIET PARTY STATE

The Tsarist system was a dictatorship of the civil and military bureaucracy in league with, but not controlled by, the privileged classes of Russian society—landowning nobles and a thin layer of big business and financial interests. The Revolution submerged the existing bureaucratic structure, killed or expelled virtually all its leaders and destroyed the power of private landlords and capitalists for ever. Its immediate effect was the creation of a political vacuum which was filled in Communist theory by the 'democratic dictatorship' of workers and peasants but in practice more and more by the Communist Party, the name adopted by the Bolsheviks after their forcible victory over all competitors.

The Supremacy of the Party Bureaucracy

Although the Communists were much better prepared than any other group or party to ride out the hurricane of anarchy, violence and war which swept with destructive force over the vast country, their survival was by no means a foregone conclusion either to themselves or to the outside world. In order to maintain their bare existence as an organized government, the Communists resorted to methods of single-minded brutality which accentuated all the dangerous features of their organization and policy which had provoked the criticism of their more far-sighted fellow socialists almost from the moment of their separate existence as a party.

The absence of a firm social and political basis for a democratic regime in Russia was reflected in the stark choice between bureaucratic rule and anarchy; the absence of an organizational basis for internal party democracy implied that it depended mainly on the intentions of the party leaders whether they would accept the rules of a democratic system, and with the increasing stress and strain of War Communism the democratic possibilities of the Soviet system remained completely unrealized and the dictatorial features of the Bolshevik tradition triumphed: military discipline was exacted from party members even more strictly than from ordinary citizens, and the 'dictatorship of the proletariat' proved in fact a dictatorship of the Communist Party over the people. The effect of this basic balance of power on the ruling party had been forecast with uncanny accuracy by Trotsky at the very time of the split between Mensheviks and Bolsheviks: 'The organization of the party will take the place of the party itself; the Central Committee will take the place of the organization; and, finally, the Dictator will take the place of the Central Committee.'[1]

At the end of the Civil War, the interventionist powers withdrew, all internal opposition to the Soviet regime was crushed and the Communists remained in undisputed control of the administrative machine, such as it was. The Tsarist bureaucratic autocracy had been replaced by another despotism. Under Tsarism, absolute power was in the hands of unscrupulous, corrupt and inefficient careerists, bent on perpetuating the rule of privilege and injustice and persecuting their enemies with all the determination which their inefficiency and corruption permitted; under the new regime power was in the hands of just as unscrupulous, much more honest and efficient and at first completely selfless revolutionaries—but it remained absolute and uncontrolled. From being a revolutionary party, held together almost as much by its common aims as by its organization, the ruling clique became the effective government of the country.

Even if the tradition of the Communists had encouraged internal democracy instead of tight central control, circumstances would have forced this effective government to adopt methods and policies in keeping with the almost unchanged bureaucratic structure of the Soviet State. In fact, not the least important amongst the features responsible for the practical success of the Communists in the struggle for power was Lenin's conception of a revolutionary anti-State constructed in the negative image of the system he wanted to overturn. Thus it was fatefully easy for the victorious Communists to step into the shoes of their defeated enemies.

[1] Quoted by Bertram D. Wolfe, *Khrushchev and Stalin's Ghost* (New York, 1957), p. 99.

If the seeds of a bureaucratic dictatorship were sown long before the victory of the Communists, the state of Russia during the Civil War period provided an ideal climate for its growth. Left in exclusive control of affairs by outlawing all other political parties, the Communist Party was at that stage by no means 'monolithic', but reflected vividly, if not faithfully, the growing dissatisfaction and disillusionment amongst workers and peasants with the policy of the Soviet government. In the absence of other forms of political expression, these tendencies appeared as 'oppositions' within the Communist Party which were met by the party leadership under Lenin by a succession of measures including the banning of organized party 'factions', purge of party members, removal of opposition leaders from Moscow by assignments to distant provinces, all of which had the effect of strengthening the administrative control of the party machine. The most fateful of Lenin's false steps was the appointment of Joseph Stalin as General Secretary of the Communist Party in the summer of 1922. Lenin tried in vain to undo the harm, when his removal from practical leadership through illness a few months later gave him an opportunity for contemplating at leisure the disastrous effects of his own policy, while evidence of Stalin's ruthlessness in the use of his power as head of the party machine accumulated almost day by day.

The withdrawal of the dictatorship in the face of the physical impossibility of making the peasants accept the ill-conceived economy of War Communism led to a temporary reversal of economic policy. This New Economic Policy provided the regime with an indispensable breathing space, but after a few years it created a very real threat to its very existence: hostile forces had succeeded in gaining a stranglehold over its basic resource—the food required to feed the towns and to obtain funds for financing the import from abroad of capital goods for the reconstruction of Russian industry. Hence the apparent paradox that the era of the New Economic Policy was a time of violent clashes within the ruling party which ended only with the establishment of Stalin's personal dictatorship at the outset of the 'Plan Period' of forcible industrialization.

The struggle against the million-headed hydra of the individual

peasantry needed the strength of a whole army of tough and fana-
tical fighters who could starve whole villages into surrender to the
'General Line' of the Kremlin. The hurried building of huge fact-
ories, the speeding up of work in industry and the disastrous fall in
mass living standards required another vast army of representatives
of the State power in order to apply the pressure for the final turn of
the screw which made the difference between failure and success at
critical moments. At the same time, the ambitious new planning
schemes and their considerable success enormously extended the
range of the economic bureaucracy, and for the most responsible positions in every field the dictatorship inevitably turned to the members
of the ruling Communist party which thus underwent its final transformation into a gigantic bureaucracy, super-imposed on all other
bureaucratic organs of State rule and management.

These changes enormously complicated the balance of power within the party. It was by now a strictly 'monolithic' pyramid, with
power emanating exclusively from the top; but at the same time its
members occupied the leading positions in organizations with conflicting and competing interests—State bureaucracy, police and defence, industrial investment and farming, even labour and consumer
interests in general. While the party expected its members to further
the interests of the party in whatever positions they occupied, this
frequently involved inconsistent methods and policies, and their
dual capacity made them inexorably, and generally against their own
will, the representatives of the conflicting interests. In a period of
quick but uneven growth, directed from above with bureaucratic
ruthlessness and lack of subtlety, without regard for social consequences or even for technical necessities, tension became sufficiently
acute to endanger the existence of the regime and to destroy the last
remnants of internal cohesion within the party: nothing remained
but a bureaucratic structure ruled despotically by its General Secretary and the party machine.

The most sinister reflection of this destruction of the ruling party
as a voluntary organization reflecting different trends and subordinating them to common political ends, was the rise of the secret
police to its dominant position which was the most spectacular fea-

ture of Stalin's fully-fledged bureaucratic dictatorship from the 1930s onward.

The use of the secret police as an instrument of government went back to the earliest days of the Soviet system, when large-scale 'Red Terror' was employed against the opponents of the government. Like many other repellent Soviet institutions it was of Tsarist origin and could trace its descent through the *Okhrana*, the security police of the *ancien régime*, to the days of Peter the Great. The *Okhrana* was one of the first casualties of the Revolution, only to be revived under the abbreviated title of Cheka which employed not a few of the servants of the old regime, particularly in its lower strata.

At the end of the Civil War the secret police had become far too powerful simply to disappear from the scene, and during the next few years it settled down to a routine which was in many ways similar to that of its Tsarist predecessor; its main purpose was the suppression of political opposition, at first against the new regime as a whole, but in due course opposition against the ruling clique within the regime. The part played by police terror and by the degeneration of the police into a virtually masterless and unmanageable bureaucracy of extinction and annihilation in the purges of the 1930s may never be fully known. From Khrushchev's revelations at the 20th Congress of the Communist Party (February 1956) and from the stories of some of its victims, mainly foreigners who lived to tell the tale, it was obviously enormous. When the fever had run its course with its nightmares of State trials, secret executions and mass deportations, the personnel of the Communist Party had changed just as thoroughly as its character and its functions.

The uncontrolled use of the powers of compulsion wielded by the secret police transformed it into a parallel and at times competing body largely independent of the Communist Party[1] which had itself become a bureaucracy in control of the other bureaucracies. In competing with the party machine, the secret police had the advantage of being endowed with particularly effective means of getting its way, but it was subject to exactly the same secret rule of terror within its own organization as all other parts of the government machine.

[1] Merle Fainsod, *Smolensk under Soviet Rule* (1959), pp. 165 ff.

The mass basis of the power wielded by the secret police under a multitude of names was the prodigious expansion of physical compulsion against the peasants during the early years of the Five-year Plan period. Collectivization involved the deportation of millions of persons and was not forced on the peasantry without acts of war on both sides, with the State authorities ultimately always successful, though at a terrible price. The disposal of the deported 'kulaks' was in the hands of the OGPU, which was the incarnation of the Cheka at that time. The numbers of prisoners in the hands of the secret police exceeded the population, first of some of the smaller but soon afterwards of some of the more important sovereign nations of the world, and the absolutism of its power was of a different order of intensity from that to which the 'free' population of Russia was subjected. The secret police founded gigantic forced labour camps whose inmates were freely expendable for the toughest and most dangerous tasks arising from the grandiose construction works of the reconstruction period, such as the famous White Sea Canal. The quickly consumed population of these camps had to be replenished in the interests of the gigantic machine of the secret police which was a moloch crying out for more and more victims. This 'racing' of the bureaucratic police system may well have been one of the contributory factors of the insensate mass purges of the later 1930s which kept the GPU camps brimful, until huge armies of further victims were found in the course of the war and its aftermath.

The State police thus tended to form a second independent system of administration, a State within the State which was a Police State in a uniquely literal sense and which showed all the characteristics of the Soviet dictatorship in grotesque exaggeration. Its members were a feared and privileged group even amongst party members, and their creature comforts were well cared for in the darkest days of the regime, just as their prisoners were even more wretched and degraded than the lowest and most depressed sections of the common people. During the last few years of Stalin's rule a kind of uneasy truce seems to have been established between the chiefs of the party bureaucracy (under Malenkov and Khrushchev) and the police (mainly under Beria), but this balance was disturbed by the removal of the keystone of the complex structure through Stalin's death in March 1953. This was soon followed by a short and sharp clash, in which the supremacy of the party was asserted by the time-honoured practice of killing off the bosses of the rival body, which seems to have lost since then a good deal of its former influence.

Only time can tell whether this change is comparable with the temporary quiescence of the Cheka during the earlier NEP or whether it is a more permanent feature. The trial and execution of Beria and his associates by his partners was not a revulsion against the illegality of the secret police system but an indication that the good intentions of Stalin's successors were not strong enough to withstand the powerful forces which had once before led the Soviet system into a dangerous impasse. Despite many glittering external successes, it had become inflexible to the point of almost complete ossification, and the prostration of even the highest 'leaders' before Stalin's personal whims made them powerless to influence policy, even on questions where the vital interests of the Soviet Union were at stake. After Stalin's death they were, therefore, determined not to make the same mistakes as their old boss, and there is no reason to doubt their good faith in forswearing the 'cult of personality' and extolling the virtues of 'collective leadership'.

The celebrated exposure of Stalin's character in Khrushchev's secret report to the 20th Congress,[1] though invaluable as an authentic description of Stalin during the final phase of his career, was on an infinitely lower level as a political document than Trotsky's merciless dissections of his victorious rival. It was lacking, above all, in any understanding of the forces within Soviet society which made a Stalin possible, and almost necessary. The main burden of Khrushchev's accusations was the plaintive claim that there was no real need for Stalin's departure from the principle of 'collective leadership', and the implicit assertion that the degeneration of the Soviet Communist Party was merely the result of the mistakes of a single individual. The absence of any reasoned analysis of the process as a whole was, indeed, the outstanding feature of this sensational speech

---

[1] Reprinted in Bertram D. Wolfe, *Khrushchev and Stalin's Ghost* (New York, 1957).

which got no nearer to the realities of the situation than a few remarks against 'careerists without conscience' in the secret police (p.
138), and which tried in vain to answer its own questions why
Stalin's excesses had not been prevented by the 'majority of the
Political Bureau' (p. 194).

It is, therefore, not surprising that the internal stresses of a system
where political decisions depend on the ability to dispose of the
levers of power in a bureaucratic party machine have continued to
make themselves felt after Stalin's death in exactly the same way as
before. On the personal plane this has meant that the leaders of the
party bureaucracy clashed first with the heads of the Secret Police
and then with each other. In the past, Stalin had opposed Trotsky
with the help of Zinoviev and Kamenev, only to oppose Zinoviev and
Kamenev with the help of Bukharin and Rykov, until he remained in
exclusive and disastrous control of the party machine and the government as absolute dictator. After Stalin's death, Khrushchev opposed
and killed Beria with the help of Malenkov, Molotov and Kaganovich, only to demote first Malenkov through Bulganin and then
Molotov and Kaganovich through Zhukov, until five short years
after Stalin's death the last remnants of 'collective leadership' had
disappeared and a new personal regime been established. Although
the person of the new ruler strikingly reflects the resourcefulness and
originality of Russian society and his policy makes him one of the
great reformers in Russian history, the persistence of the framework
of bureaucratic rule may well triumph in the end over good intentions.

The Machine of Soviet Government

Lenin's judgment of the Communist Party as the faithful guardian of
working-class interests was clearly warped by the bias of the practical politician in favour of the system which gave him power, but he
had no illusions about the character of the machine of government
operated by his party. In his own words, it was the old Tsarist 'ap-
paratus' only thinly anointed with Soviet holy oil, which the Communists had inherited from the old regime and which they had been
unable to reorganize during the first five years of Soviet rule. Hence

Lenin's repeated (and quite unsuccessful) attempts to cure this radical evil by tinkering with it, through the formation of a special People's Commissariat of Workers' and Peasants' Inspection—a method which ominously resembled earlier attempts at bureaucratic self-control during the Tsarist regime from the days of Peter the Great. The inevitable failure of the new device simply added one more bureaucratic institution to those plaguing the regime and the Russian people by their inefficiency and arrogance.

Amongst Lenin's other attempts to overcome the menace of bureaucratic rule perhaps the most significant was the campaign for individual authority and against the practice of 'collegiate' or 'Board' management in public administration. Such boards played an important part in the running of the unwieldy Tsarist government departments, and under the new dispensation they performed the task, at least to some extent, of putting a brake on the government machine in its relations with the workers. Hence Lenin's advocacy of 'bureaucratic' management was much more than a technical matter, and its beneficiaries were the very bureaucrats whose existence he later on came to regard as one of the most serious blemishes of the Soviet regime. Nevertheless, the inertia of administrative tradition was so strong, and the similarity of methods between Tsarist and Soviet bureaucracy so enduring, that the Boards castigated by Lenin outlived him as well as later attempts to destroy them.

The consolidation of the Communist dictatorship and its change into a bureaucratic dictatorship of the party machine frustrated all hope that the inherited system of public administration might be reorganized on democratic lines. Thus it retained its extreme bureaucratic character, particularly in its day-to-day relations with the common people, and the expansion of its functions in the economic field was reflected in a corresponding proliferation of administrative agencies. The detailed history of the methods and devices used by the Communists in their attempts to cope with this problem would have to distinguish between formal administrative measures and the informal, and often illegal, ways in which these measures were made to work by managers entrusted with the direction of the unwieldy machine. The formal system was characterized by the sequence of inefficient operation and sweeping changes, usually in diametrically opposite directions, which is a feature of bureaucratic rule; its working was further complicated by the intimate connection between semi-technical administrative problems and the exigencies of the factional struggle for power which was driven underground but not finally terminated by the political victory of Stalin and his associates. The glimpses available of the informal working of the system, though tantalizingly incomplete, are even more fascinating.

The machinery of government was in danger of getting completely out of hand with the creation of a host of new ministries for individual branches of the national economy, with special emphasis on armaments. Immediately after the second World War, in 1946, the Council of Ministers had sixty-four voting members compared with thirteen in 1917. The central system of government comprised 'fifty-five ministries, less than a dozen committees and councils, and about half a dozen chief administrations, as well as a number of other organs attached to it';[1] apart from the much larger numbers of separate ministries, this chaotic system resembled in many ways that of pre-1914, except for the existence of a separate centre of power in the Communist Party organization.

However, even for purely administrative functions a body of the size of the full Council of Ministers was worse than useless, and the effective leadership of the administration rested with a small inner cabinet of non-departmental ministers, the 'praesidium', whose changing size and composition reflected the shifts in the balance of forces within the party and between the party and the government bureaucracy.

Perhaps the most spectacular of these shifts was the reform of May 1957, which reduced the number of All-Union and Union-Republican ministries to less than half and established about one hundred managing 'economic councils', similar to the regional councils of the national economy at the start of the First Five Year Plan. These appointed bodies were made responsible for managing the bulk of the industries within their area under the control of their 'Union-Republican' governments, subject to the exercise of broad central

[1] Towster, *Political Power in the USSR* (New York, 1948), p. 280.

planning powers by the State Planning Committe of the central government.

In proposing the new system, Khrushchev collected a formidable body of evidence highly damaging to the previous system of industrial management by centralized government departments.[1] He showed that these had been guilty of all the bureaucratic defects in the calendar such as lack of co-operation between related and neighbouring enterprises under different ministries (p. 15), duplication or, indeed, multiplication of identical activities, e.g. in building (pp. 17 f.), delays and inter-departmental friction (pp. 28 ff.), etc. Above all, the system involved a misuse of scarce manpower on a gigantic scale, for staffs remained grossly excessive, despite the fact that during the previous three years the 'managerial, procurement and other staffs as a whole' had been cut by more than 900,000 (p. 34).

On the basis of more than forty years experience it may be doubted that these reforms will succeed in their professed purpose, and that the creation of scores of independent managing authorities without a convincing system of co-ordination is sound in principle and workable in practice. The scheme may be more important and successful as a move in the game of bureaucratic power politics; the dispersion of the centralized ministerial bureaucracies over the face of the Soviet Union—so far as it has actually been carried out—may create two new obstacles to the efficient running of the Russian economy for every one which it removes, but it should greatly enhance the power of the entrenched party bureaucracy at the centre and that of its local exponents in the provinces.

The outstanding feature of bureaucratic rule in the Soviet Union is, indeed, the prominence which administrative problems assume, because they frequently are political problems in disguise. This is the inevitable result of a system which has not managed to abolish conflicts of interests between the main social groups and the ruling bureaucracy but which does not tolerate independent organizations outside the bureaucratized system. The resulting internal strains and stresses thus appear as 'mistakes' which are diagnosed in true bureau-

[1] N. S. Khrushchev, *Improvement of Industrial Management in the USSR*, Report at the Seventh Session of the Supreme Soviet, May 1957 (1957).

cratic fashion as administrative defects. These mistakes are rectified by organizational changes which are in turn discarded in favour of new administrative patent medicines, when it becomes clear that the earlier cure had only suppressed one symptom of a radical disease by giving rise to another.

3. THE SOCIAL ROOTS OF BUREAUCRATIC RULE IN RUSSIA

After tracing the forces responsible for moulding the Tsarist State in its rigid bureaucratic frame and those responsible for the resurrection of a bureaucracy of vastly greater power and complexity under the Soviets, it remains to consider their general character and the bearing of the Russian experience on the problem of political bureaucracy in State and parties.

The Tartar conquest of Russia played a crucial part in the origin of the Muscovite absolutism and the forms taken by the Tsarist State. It was a clash of interests of the most elemental kind—the extraction of tribute from a conquered people by its conquerors—which created the administrative system from which the State of the Tsars was descended. The persistence of the conflict with the Tartars for more than two centuries favoured the growth of Tsarism; the leadership of the Russian forces in the struggle against the Horde was a great national cause from which the private interests of the Grand Princes of Muscovy benefited even more than from their function as chief tax collectors for the Khans. Their State became the decisive power factor in the life of the vast country, and they succeeded, though not without occasional setbacks, in freeing themselves from the organized political interference of the aristocracy and in establishing Tsarist autocracy. The destructive internal tension between landowners and serfs resulted in complete independence for the State, which was the only reliable defence of the established social order against the spontaneous attempts of the peasants to escape from their deplorable position by flight or by the extermination of their masters.

This brutal and backward system might well have settled down to an indefinite existence of stagnation or decay, had it not been for its contacts and conflicts with the vigorously expanding mercantile and military societies of Western and Central Europe. Their result was a series of radical changes in the economic and social structure of Russian society and, from the middle of the nineteenth century onwards, of military defeats. In the end these defeats destroyed the power of the Tsarist State and thereby removed the only obstacle which had prevented the explosion of irreconcilable social interests within the country.

The outstanding difference between the organization of the Tsarist regime and the Soviet regime of today is the Communist Party whose position is the key to some of the most puzzling features of Soviet history. The political rulers of pre-war Russia, the Tsars and their military and political bureaucrats, formed part of a static pre-industrial society which could be held in subjection from outside, by the superior physical force of the organs of the State. This system was ill-adapted to the dynamic forces of modern capitalism which undermined the old Russian village and created new antagonistic classes in the towns: the conflict between *entrepreneurs* and industrial workers could not be permanently contained within the framework of the old-fashioned bureaucratic absolutism of the Tsarist regime.

After the revolution of 1917 and the years of civil war and military intervention the old bureaucratic State emerged in many ways remarkably unchanged from apparently total destruction, but it was no longer the true repository of political power. The new political power centre had moved outside the old bureaucracy, into a body specializing in the manipulation of the social forces of post-revolutionary society. This body was the Communist Party.

Having achieved its primary object of obtaining 'power' in the sense of exclusive disposal of the machinery of government, the Communist Party changed its character to an extent which distinguishes it radically from other parties outside the Communist world. It is the prototype of the 'totalitarian' party which is a different species from the political parties of more or less democratic countries. Its transformation from a political group with socialist aims into the bureaucratic dictatorship of today took the form of a succession of steps in which changes in the balance of power within the organization played a conspicuous part. However predisposed towards such a development by its early history, the root cause of this process was the pressure of internal and external social tension which can be traced as the decisive influence at every important step of Soviet history about which adequate information is available.

The process of bureaucratization advanced by a succession of organizational devices for the suppression of opposition within the Communist Party. Thus congresses and party conferences 'withered away' as policy controlling bodies, until in the end the party bureaucracy under its General Secretary established itself as the ruling power by eliminating all effective opposition.

The Soviet Communist Party as the totalitarian party *par excellence* does not serve the purpose of influencing the government in the interests of its primary social group, like the parties of democratic countries; its main function consists in influencing the social classes in the interests of the government. It does not rely on mass support in order to obtain control of the government, but supervises the way in which the government controls the people. Its leaders are not subject to the dictation of primary social interests, but dictate their policy to all sections of the people by virtue of their control over the party machine.

In non-totalitarian parties, membership is usually open to all who wish to join, and the attraction of the largest possible number of members is an important element of strength; in the Soviet Communist Party membership is a valuable privilege and the necessary condition of prominence in most walks of life. Expulsion from the party, though for the time being decreed much less freely than during the Stalin era, is a dreaded form of punishment, generally followed by loss of influence, status and income.

A bureaucratic State machine such as that of Tsarist Russia, acting in isolation, is unlikely to maintain its rule for long in a society subject to the forces of modern industrialism. In the Soviet State the positions of real power are no longer in the hands of the government and its bureaucracy but in those of an organization specializing in the manipulation of the more important social groups, partly by ideological means (persuasion, propaganda, etc.) but mainly by the operations of its own machine.

M

The Ruling Servants

The Russian experience thus illustrates with extreme clarity and in extreme form the intimate connection between the process of bureaucratization and the operation of primary social forces: the rise to power of a bureaucracy as a result of irreconcilable conflicts between opposed groups none of which can dominate the other without the help of an outside agent, the maintenance of a bureaucratic system for a long time, while the basic social equation remains unchanged, its final collapse under the impact of new social forces which cannot be accommodated within the old system—and its replacement by a more sophisticated regime thrown up by an acute social emergency and combining the use of the traditional resources of a bureaucratic government with the ability to control society by a new bureaucratic machine *sui generis*.

CHAPTER NINE

BUREAUCRACY AND DEMOCRACY IN FRANCE

I. THE MACHINERY OF GOVERNMENT

The French State can trace its descent from the time of Hugh Capet and his successors who built their feudal kingdom on the firm basis of their personal dominions in the heart of France. The expansion of their possessions was carried through against the bitter resistance of the feudal magnates who were no less strongly entrenched in their own possessions than the king in his, and whose allegiance to the Crown was often little more than nominal. At times the royal rulers took the offensive; at other times they were forced into a desperate defence against superior enemies, while on other occasions they managed to expand their territory through successful marriages. The process was by and large completed by the end of the seventeenth century, although rounded off by later territorial gains.

Perhaps the most critical stage in the history of the French monarchy was the Hundred Years' War against England and Burgundy in the early fifteenth century which undermined the feudal system and prepared the way for the rise of the absolutism of Louis XI, who leaned heavily on the bourgeoisie of the towns in order to balance, and finally to defeat, the political aspirations of the nobility. The clash of interests between the privileged classes and the 'Third Estate' was also the main cause of the decay of the States General, the traditional representative bodies of the feudal Middle Ages which did not meet once between 1614 and 1789, though provincial Estates continued in some provinces, notably in Brittany and Languedoc.

The Ancien Régime

The final victory of the royal power after the collapse of the Fronde in the middle of the seventeenth century marks the end of the pre-history of the French State. Its modern history in the sense of a chain of events effectively linked with present-day realities dates back to the era of Louis XIV.

In a populous nation inhabiting a large country, the absolute rule of the king was in practice inevitably that of the royal administration. Throughout the transition from feudalism to absolute monarchy, functions originally carried out by feudal dignitaries or officers of the States General were taken over by the servants of the Crown. The political power of the old feudal nobility, the aristocracy of 'race' or of the 'sword', declined steadily, but at the same time the royal servants became increasingly independent of their royal masters and developed into a new caste—the aristocracy of the 'robe'. The main characteristics of this new social group were the virtual heredity of originally functional administrative and judicial offices and the establishment of private property rights in them.

Although this process was in some respects similar to bureaucratic degeneration, its real basis was the practice of purchasing public offices which was forced on the king by his chronic lack of funds. The penury of the French treasury was as much a social and political as a strictly financial problem; it was, in the last resort, another facet of the practical limitations of the theoretically unlimited royal power. The political victory over the nobility had to be paid for in hard cash, partly by the enormous expense of keeping a large part of the higher nobility at Court at the expense of the exchequer and partly by the loss of revenue from tax exemptions for the privileged estates, the clergy and the nobility. The position was alleviated at the cost of the future by creating large numbers of public 'offices', which could be purchased and bequeathed like any other property and which generally also included valuable immunities from taxation. The result was the creation of a powerful class of 'officers' in possession of important public functions who owed their position to their wealth and who were virtually independent of the king and his government. As the direct income from such posts was extremely modest, only very rich men could afford such careers.

Although less important in the administration than in the judicial field, this system was a serious brake on the efficiency of the government, particularly in view of the Court's vigorous interference in the process of administration. In Tocqueville's classic phrase, the greed of the royal power 'had created a balance for its ambition. Thus it was constantly reduced to employing in its service tools which it had not fashioned and which it could not discard. Frequently it had to watch its most absolute decisions losing their force in the execution. This bizarre and vicious constitution of the public offices became a sort of political guarantee against the omnipotence of the central power.'[1]

Had the administration of the State remained entirely in the hands of the 'officers', the royal absolutism would inevitably have become a mere façade for the rule of an oligarchy consisting of the aristocracy of the robe in alliance with the old nobility of feudal landowners with whom it tended to amalgamate completely by land purchase and inter-marriage. Such a system might sooner or later have grown into an aristocratic State determined to defend the social *status quo* at all costs.

It was, therefore, vitally important for the royal power to oppose this threat, and in this matter its interests were the same as those of the rising urban middle class. After the defeat of the Fronde, Louis XIV distrusted the *Parlements* just as much as the feudal aristocracy. In his new machine of government under Mazarin and Colbert commoners played a prominent part, and the economic policy of the monarchy was strongly influenced by the interests of the business community.

Although the government could not entirely by-pass the 'officers' in their purchased and hereditary positions, it tried to neutralize their powers of obstruction by setting up a strictly centralized administration not subject to the veto of the aristocracy of the robe. The new officials owed their place entirely to the royal commission appointing them, had no proprietary interest in their positions and could be dismissed at any time. They were functional administrators in the modern sense, known as 'commissars' from the commission

[1] Alexis de Tocqueville, *L'Ancien Régime et la Revolution*, Oeuvres Complètes, Vol. iv, p. 162.

under which they acted and, in contrast to the 'officers' with their aristocratic associations, they were mainly of bourgeois origin and inclined to an interpretation of the royal power which stressed the impersonal character of the State.

The effective government and its most important organs were largely in the hands of commissars and represented a formidable instrument of power as well as a reasonably efficient administrative machine. The central organ of government was the Royal Council operating through a number of committees and co-ordinating the activities of the Ministers who were mainly experts in charge of departments, though since Louis XIV the Controller General of Finances tended to play the part of Prime Minister. The functions of the committees partly overlapped, the number of officials was excessive and they were frequently far too willing to oblige the powers that be, and the rigidly centralized machine worked slowly and clumsily, with ample opportunities for backstairs intrigues. Its most characteristic organs were the secret police and the intendants in charge of the administration of the country.

France was a police State of a vicious kind whose 'Bastille' and *lettres de cachet* were notorious beyond the French frontiers. The special task of the police was the suppression of opposition and the maintenance of order by what have since been called police methods. However, the police soon developed independent interests, and its usefulness to the government was correspondingly reduced. On balance it probably was a liability to the regime and its chiefs presently abused their power to hoodwink the king, particularly through the underhand censorship of the *cabinet noir* which supplied the king in case of need with false letters for the purpose of influencing official policy in accordance with the interests of the police and its financial backers.

Although the influence of the police in French political life has proved remarkably tenacious, its political importance was incomparably less prominent than that of the intendants. Before the Revolution, France was essentially an agglomeration of provinces whose laws and customs differed as much as their history. This would have in any case presented great administrative difficulties which were multiplied by the tendency of the representatives of the government to become feudal dignitaries, as in the case of the provincial governors during the sixteenth and seventeenth centuries. The coalition between these governors and the provincial *Parlements* created a serious crisis during the period of the Fronde, and the government tried to break their power by sending its own agents into the provinces; after the defeat of the Fronde Mazarin extended this practice to the whole country.

It was a reflection of the prominence of finance that the financial areas (*généralités*) became the main administrative divisions, under thirty-two intendants who were the virtual rulers of their regions. They were generally taken from the *maîtres des requêtes* and were, therefore, 'officers' but as intendants they acted as 'commissars' under the direct control of the central government and particularly of the Controller General of Finances. They appointed sub-delegates for smaller areas for supervising the local government in towns and villages and ruled with virtually plenipotentiary powers. The system ensured the unity of the administration against the entrenched local *Parlements* by stifling all opposition and excluding the nobles from political influence in their own strongholds.

Though a strictly bureaucratic and authoritarian system, the *ancien régime* was protected from complete bureaucratic degeneration by the co-existence of two kinds of officials with a different background and different interests which generally acted as a check on both; where such a check was missing, as in the police, the result was, indeed, disastrous. Although the abuses of the 'officers' in their own sphere, and particularly in the judiciary, were a public scandal, their independence made them a powerful and effective enemy of the central administration which otherwise would have ruled unchecked. The main weakness of the system was the intimate connection between the aristocracy of the robe and the privileged classes. It was an excellent watchdog for all vested interests but unconcerned about the interests of the common people at whose expense it and its allies maintained their comfortable existence.

The state of tension between the government and the nobility was not primarily a matter of administration but a serious political issue.

Throughout the eighteenth century, the aristocracy systematically opposed the government, particularly through the *Parlements*, and 'enforced the dismantling rather than the consolidation of the centralized absolutism of the administrative bureaucracy'.[1] The result was a near-stalemate, broken by short-lived bursts of energy by one or the other of the contending parties. The ensuing political and administrative chaos was bound to lead to the breakdown of the system in the long run, but the immediate cause of the Revolution was the threatening bankruptcy of the Treasury.

Wars, extravagant court expenditure and the tax exemptions of nobility, clergy and bureaucracy resulted in crushing taxes for the masses of the people, and especially the peasants, without enabling the government to pay its way. A tax reform was inevitable, but it affected the opposing interests of different social groups so intimately that it could not be undertaken without calling the whole regime into question; every step towards a solution of the financial crisis was, therefore, a step towards the dissolution of the monarchy.

This was true in particular of the reform measures undertaken by the bureaucracy during the twenty years before 1789. The great intellectual upsurge which makes the eighteenth century unparalleled in French history was increasingly dominated by ideas reflecting the growth of the urban middle class—nowhere more than in the theories of the physiocrats which were one of the main French contributions to the nascent science of economics.

The physiocrats supported the royal government, and a number of their most prominent spokesmen held important positions at Court or in the bureaucracy. In politics they were convinced defenders of the absolute monarchy as the most suitable instrument for the realization of their ideas against opposition by vested interests. These ideas reflected the broad aims of the bourgeoisie in a form which at first sight was more than a little paradoxical. By extolling agriculture as the only form of economic activity producing a genuine surplus or net product, they tried to prove that all taxes ought to come out of the net revenue of the landlords—a revolutionary

---

[1] Hans Rosenberg, *Bureaucracy, Aristocracy and Autocracy—the Prussian Experience 1660-1815* (Cambridge, Mass., 1958), p. 154.

break with French fiscal traditions which contributed to the convulsions of the last period of the *ancien régime*.

The economic theories of the physiocrats prepared the outbreak of the revolution in other unforeseen ways. They were free traders in the eighteenth-century sense of wanting to sweep away the many obstacles to the internal circulation of goods and to permit imports from abroad, though not without the payment of import duties. They were also in favour of the 'Eden Treaty' of 1786 which opened the French market to the superior competition of English products, with the result of making the textile districts implacably hostile to the government. The social and political consequences of their agricultural reforms were no less far-reaching. They wanted to remodel French agriculture on the English pattern and encouraged the enclosure of commons at the expense of the livelihood of the poorest sections of the peasants, and every step on this road brought the country nearer to the social revolution which flared up with devastating force in the summer of 1789.

Centralization and the Bureaucracy

Centralization under the *ancien régime* was one of the chief weapons of the monarchy in its struggle against the feudal power of the nobility in their territorial strongholds, and the intendants watched for any tendency on the part of the aristocracy to spend too much time on their estates instead of living at Court. Centralization was also the government's main defence against the unceasing attempts of the 'officers' to frustrate official policy whenever it clashed with their own interests or those of the nobility.

The nobles and even the clergy were, therefore, in favour of local self-government by more or less representative bodies, and sometimes their *cahiers* for the States General of 1789 demanded at the same time the abolition of the intendants. In the reorganization of the government by the Constituent Assembly—in which privileges of wealth, if not of birth, were strongly represented—its centralized character was modified fairly radically in relation to the wealthier classes. Although the delicate balance of the new system of local self-government tempered by central supervision did not survive long in the face of sharpening internal struggles and growing external dangers, it left a permanent legacy in the abolition of the *généralités* of the old regime and of the intendants, and in the division of the country into some eighty departments.

The pace of the Revolution was set by the temper of the common people of Paris, where the wealthy bourgeoisie quickly lost most of its political influence to the lower middle class of shopkeepers and artisans, frequently under pressure from the workmen who formed a large part of the population. The clash between the Radicals of the Montagne and the moderates of the Gironde was decided in favour of the former by the intervention of the people of Paris, and the new leaders of the Convention had to make good their disputed authority by armed force against a federation of local interests from many parts of the provinces, especially the South and West.

The Convention as a whole as well as its Committee of Public Safety despatched 'special commissars' into the provinces. These were taken from amongst their own members as plenipotentiaries for the restoration of order by means of revolutionary terror. For this purpose the existing departmental and communal administrations were 'purged' of the opponents of the Montagne, and the powers of the departments were reduced in favour of the districts and the municipalities which were at the same time put under the control of 'national agents' appointed by the government. *Mutatis mutandis* this was similar to the method by which the monarchy had broken the power of the feudal nobility through the intendants. In its revolutionary version centralization was the necessary administrative result of the growing tension between the Radicals in power in Paris (and a few other towns) and the peasants who were compelled by superior force to subordinate their immediate interests to the prosecution of a revolutionary war.

This emergency regime could not last indefinitely, and the combination of military triumph and internecine conflict amongst the Montagnards brought it to a violent end in July 1794. After the fall of Robespierre and his associates, tension slackened, the moderates gained the upper hand and centralization was relinquished; not, however, in favour of the orderly rule of the beneficiaries of the revolution in town and country, but in favour of near-anarchy because these beneficiaries were not strong enough to control their enemies on the right and left. This situation put a premium on organized power, and in Napoleon Bonaparte the victorious army produced a leader of transcendent ability and commensurate personal ambition. The bourgeoisie which wanted to reap the fruits of the revolution without being able to organize French society on its own threw itself into the hands of the generals. The result was the Napoleonic dictatorship which created the classical forms of the centralized modern French State.

In the hands of Napoleon, centralization was partly a method of extracting from the nation the necessary human and material resources for the army, and partly a system enabling him to balance the politically passive countryside against the restless towns with their continuing revolutionary traditions. In this system Paris was far from omnipotent; on the contrary, it was subject to close supervision and policed by methods resembling those of the *ancien régime*. The proud capital of the revolution was from the point of view of the government simply a department like any other, with the invidious distinction of having a separate prefect in charge of its police.

In the social and political sense, the centralization of government during this crucial period of French history was the chosen tool for the direction of the country by dominant minority interests, from the Montagne to Napoleon and his marshals. From an administrative point of view, centralization under the new system was much more complete and thorough than under the absolute monarchy. The most important reason for this change was the disappearance of its counterweight under the *ancien régime*, the corps of 'officers' in full possession of their freehold positions in the administration and the courts.

The first and heaviest blow to the 'officer' class was the abolition of office purchase in the famous night of August 4, 1789, at the time when the feudal burdens of the peasantry were swept away. This liquidation of the 'officers' as a class was followed by the dissolution of the *Parlements*, their judicial and political strongholds, which were too hostile to the Revolution to be allowed to survive and were sent on indefinite vacation in November 1789.

With the removal of the 'officers', the 'commissars' of the *ancien régime* remained in undisputed control of the administration, and the hostility of the revolutionary leaders towards the pretensions of the *Parlements* strengthened the powers of the bureaucracy in an unexpected way. In these circumstances, the law of August 1790, which applied the theory of the separation of powers to the relations between the administration and the judiciary, became a veritable charter of bureaucratic privilege: 'The judicial functions are distinct and remain for always separate from the administrative functions. The judges must not, on pain of forfeiture, interfere in any way whatever with the operations of the administrative bodies nor must they summon administrators before the courts for actions taken in the exercise of their duties.'[1]

Though the times were too unsettled to permit the bureaucracy to make full use of its newly-gained freedom, this was an important principle which would by itself justify the assertion that 'the confiscation of power by the officials of the State is no less characteristic of the Revolution of 1789 than the confiscation of the land by the peasants'.[2] In addition, however, the weakness of the political executive during the early years of the Revolution strengthened the relative position of the permanent officials both at the centre and in the provinces. With the creation of a new form of local government in the departments the intendants of the *ancien régime* were swept away, but their archives and their officials remained, and by and large they continued to operate in the same way as before.

During the revolutionary period of the Convention, the new masters asserted themselves with ferocious energy in the administrative field as well as in purely political matters. Unreliable officials were purged, though there was a dearth of efficient 'patriots' to replace them. However, under the Directorate the power of the political executive decayed progressively and the bureaucracy correspondingly strengthened its political position, though it suffered financially from the progress of inflation. Finally, its independence was fully recog-

---

[1] G. Lepointe, *Histoire des Institutions et des Faits Sociaux* (987-1875), (Paris, 1956), p. 746.
[2] Herbert Lüthy, *A L'Heure de Son Clocher* (Paris, 1955), p. 27.

nized in Napoleon Bonaparte's first constitution and in his reorganization of the machinery of government. Bureaucratic rule was, indeed, the administrative side of the coalition between army and bourgeoisie in Napoleon's authoritarian State.

The Napoleonic State

The revolutionary decade 1789-99 swept away most of the obstacles to quick social, economic and political advance and enacted a whole host of measures expressing the rationalism of their authors and their keen urge for a thorough reconstruction of society. However, the efforts of these years, and above all the almost superhuman strain of foreign and civil wars, quickly exhausted the forces which had borne the brunt of the forward movement, while the beneficiaries of the Revolution in towns and country wished for nothing more than the peaceful consolidation of their gains.

This situation was the ideal environment for the *coup d' état* of the 18th Brumaire by which Bonaparte and his associates set up a military dictatorship destined to last until the downfall of the first Empire. The urban bourgeoisie which had lost the reins at the height of the Revolution managed to resume them under the Directorate, but its rule was so unstable that it was punctuated by a whole series of dangerous risings. It was, therefore, on the look out for a strong ally and Bonaparte appeared the ideal man for the part. In the villages, the peasants had got rid of the feudal burdens and the more substantial among them managed to enrich themselves by cheap land purchases for depreciated *assignats*; their main aspiration was to be left in peace, and this aversion to further political exertions was exactly what the military dictator needed in order to get into the saddle—and to stay there.

However, the army soon proved more of a master than a servant of the satisfied middle class in town and country, and its leader more masterful than any absolute king. The series of successful wars which spread French power to the borders of Russia and kept British goods out of Europe created a hot-house atmosphere for the growth of trade and industry and made the fortune of countless speculators, but the growing claims of the army on French manpower and material resources became more and more unbearable, and the reckless pursuit of *gloire* reflected the disproportionate weight of the army in French life and the exploitation of society for the personal and dynastic purposes of the new ruler.

These purposes were not only irrational from a national point of view but involved Napoleon in policies which were sure sooner or later to lead to defeat. In the early stages of his career, Napoleon pursued a clever and reasonably successful balancing policy between the right and the left. But with the establishment of the Empire, Napoleon not only reverted more and more to the forms of the old monarchy, e.g. in the creation of a hereditary nobility, but increasingly favoured old victims and enemies of the Revolution in appointments to such key positions as those of departmental prefects whose loyalty did not outlast his good fortune.

In many other respects, however, the Napoleonic era fulfilled the expectations of Napoleon's civilian backers. It was a time of consolidation of the revolutionary achievements for the bourgeoisie, and the stupendous energy of the new ruler and his able associates was embodied in a number of striking achievements. A great effort of codification gave France a legal system in many respects superior to anything known elsewhere, which became the model for similar legislation abroad. At the same time, the administrative system received the shape which it was to retain for well over a century.

The prominence of administrative matters in the minds of the new rulers was reflected in the immediate action programme after the *coup d'état*—'to organize order in all parts of the administration, to restore tranquillity at home and to obtain an honourable and lasting peace'.[1] This priority of administration reappears in the personnel of the Consulate itself. Bonaparte as first Consul and ruler of the country was assisted by Cambacérès and Lebrun, the former an important ex-member of the Convention whose interests had been mainly legal and administrative, the latter a man of sixty and an ex-bureaucrat of the *ancien régime* who had played a part in its most radical reform attempt, the abolition of the *Parlements* in 1770. The balan-

[1] J. Godechot, *Les Institutions de la France sous la Révolution et l'Empire* (Paris, 1951), p. 473.

cing policy of the new regime was thus embodied in the composition of the supreme executive, and its administrative personnel was a skilful blend of the old and the new.

The outstanding representative of the old order amongst Napoleon's ministers was the Minister of Finance, Gaudin, who was a *protégé* of Lebrun's and the only man to retain his original position throughout the Napoleonic era; and he was only the most prominent amongst 'hundreds of prefects, sub-prefects, engineers, district managers, tax collectors, treasurers, who, across the gulf of the Reign of Terror, had gathered up the threads of the old Regime and its administrative traditions'.[1]

Even more important than the personal identity of many individual officials was the similarity of structure and functions between the Napoleonic State and the pre-revolutionary monarchy. What had changed radically was the social environment which was no longer a motley collection of provinces with different laws, customs and 'privileges', hampered by internal excise lines and other obstacles to the circulation of resources, with industry shackled by guild restrictions and an administration checked and thwarted by the aristocracy of the robe. By removing these obstacles to industrial, commercial and administrative progress the Revolution had made France safe for bureaucracy, and the weakness of the bourgeoisie removed all hope of strong and independent outside control of the executive and its servants.

For these reasons the Napoleonic State was a streamlined version of the *ancien régime*, differing from its predecessor mainly in the consistency and efficiency of its arrangements. The personal character of Napoleon's rule did not remove the need for a powerful central government machine and, as under the Bourbons, this was not a single co-ordinating body but a complex organization. Near its apex was a small Privy Council and a Council of State closely modelled on the old Royal Council. The ministers in charge of individual departments played a subordinate part in policy making, though some of them were men of great ability and personal influence, such as Talleyrand or Fouché. Above all, they had no corporate existence as a

[1] P. Gaxotte (trans. J. Lewis May), *Louis the Fifteenth and his Times* (1934), p. 299.

Cabinet and were in some respects subordinate to the Council of State. There was a fair amount of duplication and overlapping, primarily as a check on individual ambition.

The administration of local affairs also followed in important respects the institutions of the absolute monarchy. During the Revolution, the general trend had been towards representative local government bodies, though agents of the central government continued to play an important part. Napoleon did not abolish such bodies but replaced election by nomination and limited them to purely consultative functions. Executive powers were, on the model of the army, reserved to appointed officials on the principle 'Administration is a function of the individual'.

The most important of these officials were the prefects in charge of individual departments. They were the direct descendants of the commissioners of the Directorate and the remote descendants of the intendants of the old monarchy. The prefects were 'small-scale emperors' in sole charge of departmental administration, chosen as a rule from amongst men without ties in the department and under close control by the central government acting through the Minister of the Interior.

The new intermediate unit, the *arrondissement*, was in the charge of sub-prefects corresponding to the sub-delegates of the pre-revolutionary intendants, while nominated mayors were in sole charge of municipal administration. A single chain of responsibility, no less clear-cut and effective than in the army, led from the local mayor through sub-prefect, prefect and minister to the Emperor. The corresponding representative institutions at all levels were of little practical account.

Like the *ancien régime*, the Napoleonic State was in the hands of a predominant executive but without any check on the power of the administration comparable to that exercised by the *Parlements*. The twin results of this position were the confirmation of the privileges of the bureaucracy over the private citizen and the complete ascendancy of the central authorities over the individual official, both classical features of bureaucratic rule.

The first Napoleonic Constitution of 1799 confirmed the prohibition of judicial inquiry into administrative acts and made the Council of State the supreme judge of administrative legality, for 'agents of the government other than Ministers could not be called to account before the courts except by a special decision of the Council of State'.[1] Original jurisdiction in administrative disputes was in the hands of the *conseils de préfecture* or in those of the minister concerned, with the Council of State as the supreme administrative court.

While the official as an agent of the government was thus well protected against society, as an individual he was closely controlled and strictly disciplined from above. All important office holders were appointed and removed by the Emperor, from ministers, members of the Council of State and prefects down to the mayors of all but the smaller municipalities. In addition, the Emperor had to approve the way in which the Council of State exercised its wide disciplinary powers over the bureaucracy. These powers gave the Council of State the power to reprimand, censure, suspend or depose every official.

Although changes in general conditions in France have been less radical since the early nineteenth century than in most other countries, they have been many and frequent, but the administrative system created under Napoleon has remained relatively intact until the present century. This astonishing longevity must have been partly due to the practical merits of the system as an administrative machine, but it cannot be entirely, or even predominantly, explained by technical considerations.

The French system of government is in the first place an instrument of rule in the double sense of a political weapon in the hands of certain social groups and in that of a factor influencing the social distribution of power more or less independently. Under Napoleon I, support of the rulers against hostile forces was virtually the exclusive province of the bureaucracy, though administrative control had to be supplemented by strict police supervision of the population, particularly during the later years of the Empire and in the great towns. With the fitful and incomplete, but in the long-run irresistible, progress of democracy since the days of Napoleon, the political tasks of

[1] Godechot, op. cit.

the centralized administration have become less direct and more subtle but no less important. The inter-relations of the powers of bureaucracy and democracy form, indeed, the warp and woof of French politics from the time of the Revolution until the present day.

The Survival of the Bureaucratic State

The connection between the instability of French government and the strength of the permanent bureaucracy is one of the common-places of French political literature. During the first seventy years of the nineteenth century France was governed by five different poli-tical systems none of which lasted for as much as twenty years, while under the Third Republic—which lasted as long as the previous five forms of government taken together—well over a hundred ministries followed one another with bewildering speed. It is, however, far from clear that this was either the cause or the effect of the survival of the Napoleonic State which underwent only secondary changes until the first World War and which is essentially intact today.

The effectiveness of the Napoleonic system made it a first-rate political factor for any government and the potentially decisive force in case of serious dispute between approximately equal powers. When the balance was clearly in favour of one social group, its superiority was confirmed by its command over the bureaucracy; the masters of the moment invariably proceeded to change the leading personnel of the administration, to fill the key positions with their own agents and to use and abuse the machinery of government for the suppression of oppositional tendencies.

The political system under the Restoration was dominated by the aristocracy of landed proprietors. The bureaucracy was by and large an inheritance from the Napoleonic Empire; most of its members were ready to accept the Bourbons, provided they were acceptable to them. Louis XVIII on his part was quite willing to let bygones be bygones and replaced only eight gravely compromised members of the crucial prefectoral corps. On Napoleon's return from Elba, all officials who had served the king were dismissed, but Louis XVIII re-established the *status quo* on the very day of his re-entry into Paris. However, on every subsequent political change in direction the higher bureaucracy, and particularly the prefects, were purged of opponents of the new rulers.

The substitution of the financial aristocracy for the landowners as the dominant class under the July monarchy involved the wholesale replacement of Restoration prefects, mayors, etc., by adherents of the new order. The regime of Louis Philippe 'was nothing but a limited company for the exploitation of French national resources whose dividends were distributed amongst ministers, members of parliament, 240,000 electors and their dependants, with Louis Philippe as company director'.[1] Like the Restoration, it was ruled by a small privileged minority exercising political influence through representative bodies elected on an extremely narrow franchise. However, it was opposed from both flanks—the 'Legitimists' on the Right, and the majority of the middle class as well as the unprivileged people on the Left.

This balance of forces resulted in a considerable increase in the power of the bureaucracy, except in local government where the July monarchy was rather less centralized and bureaucratic than under Napoleon or Charles X. In the strictly political sphere, however, the part played by the bureaucracy in ensuring the election of government nominees and the defeat of opposition candidates was, if anything, greater than before. Although it was by no means invariably successful, the general impression was one of almost mechanical political perfection. Right up to the moment of Louis Philippe's overthrow, 'everything there seemed combined to produce with the machinery of liberty a preponderance of Royal power which verged upon despotism; and, in fact, this result was produced almost without effort by the regular and tranquil movement of the machine'.[2]

The political power of the bureaucracy was a doubtful blessing for the regime in whose favour it was exercised. By loading the dice consistently against the opposition, the bureaucratic falsification of the political struggle was a permanent incitement to unconstitutional action, while the threat of revolution was a further reason for its chiefs to demand the strengthening of police powers. The combination of

[1] Karl Marx, *Die Klassenkaempfe in Frankreich* (Berlin, 1951 edn.), p. 32.
[2] A. de Tocqueville, *Recollections* (edited by J. P. Mayer) (1948), p. 9.

political rule by a hated minority and administrative rule by an over-bearing bureaucracy could only be overcome by a revolutionary combination of all opposition forces which was achieved for a short period during the revolutions of 1830 and 1848. In the former, the dissatisfaction of the bourgeoisie with the rule of the landowners transformed bankers, financiers and other pillars of society into revolutionaries for the duration; in 1848, the acute discontent of the middle classes as a whole with the narrow rule of the financial oligarchy in a period of severe economic and financial crisis overthrew the July monarchy by the energetic action of the workers of Paris.

The proletariat of the capital acted both in 1830 and 1848 as the temporary ally of the oppositional sections of the middle classes, because it lived in a state of permanent discontent which could easily break out into revolutionary fervour when the power of the repressive state machine was weakened. However, the regimes established mainly through the sacrifices of the workers showed little interest in their grievances. Their neglect of their awkward allies after the hour of victory was the main cause of the serious revolts in the early years of the July Monarchy and of the much more important June Days of 1848. On these occasions the workers were made painfully aware that they had been used as the catspaw of astute vested interests.

The most that can be said about the importance of the bureaucracy in French politics during the first half of the nineteenth century is that it was to some extent responsible if events took the form of revolutionary changes in the system of government instead of gradual changes in the personnel and policy of the ruling group. The content of French politics was largely determined by the dynamic classes of French society, the business classes and the workers, concentrated in the towns—and above all in Paris.

In the February revolution of 1848, another important social factor was brought back into politics—the peasants. This was a by-product of the fact that the growing influence of the workers and the lower middle classes, led by more or less socialist groups and personalities ranging from Louis Blanc to Auguste Blanqui, compelled the opponents of Louis Philippe to commit themselves to the principle of manhood suffrage. Apart from giving the urban masses a chance of organized political expression which they had lacked since the heyday of the Great Revolution, this measure made the peasants the potential arbiter of the new regime—and though disgruntled with their growing indebtedness to the financial aristocracy, the peasants were by no means revolutionary.

The resulting change in the balance of forces gave added weight to the bureaucracy. The new Minister of the Interior, Ledru-Rollin, immediately tried to exploit it in the interests of the new regime. Royalist magistrates and officials were dismissed, and the prefects were replaced by commissars instructed to deliver the provincial vote in the interests of the new Republican government at the forthcoming elections. This attempt however, was a failure, partly because one of the first measures of the government had been a swingeing increase in the Land Tax which infuriated the peasant proprietors, but perhaps also because the task of rigging elections under a system of universal suffrage needed a new technique which could not be improvised in a moment.

The Constituent Assembly of 1848 thus had an anti-revolutionary majority which rallied round General Cavaignac, the victor over the workers of Paris. The new authorities immediately replaced Ledru-Rollin's commissars by prefects of their own choosing and took over the key positions of the administration. But in their eagerness to restore the *status quo* in everything but name, they confirmed the independent power of the Executive as an indispensable guarantee against the danger of further outbreaks from the Left. Coolheaded observers such as Tocqueville clearly saw the dangers of this policy: 'To allow the President the same power that the King had enjoyed and to have him elected by the people would make the Republic impossible.'[1] In these circumstances, the very measure enacted in order to ensure the ultimate supremacy of parliament, the limitation of the President to one single term, was bound to overthrow the regime.

This became a certainty with the choice of the heir to the Napoleonic tradition as first President of the Republic: instead of making the Republic safe for the middle classes by voting for their hero,

[1] *Recollections*, p. 207.

General Cavaignac, the peasant voters put Louis Napoleon into the saddle. Against a parliament weakened by rifts between Legitimists and Orleanists amongst the privileged minority and by the gulf between the middle classes as a whole and the workers, the President claimed to speak for the whole nation, and particularly for its rural majority. The duel between President and Parliament lasted until the *coup d'état* of December 1851 which was soon followed by Louis Napoleon's establishment of the Second Empire with its Napoleonic trappings.

Like its predecessors, the Second Empire employed the bureaucracy as the chief guardian of its power. Louis Napoleon purged the moderate Republicans from the key positions in army and administration and replaced them by his own creatures. Immediately after the dissolution of parliament, he systematically strengthened the power of the bureaucracy: cuts in civil service salaries were restored, the prefects were again furnished with secretaries general who had been abolished by Louis Philippe and their authority was considerably increased. On the other hand, Napoleon III relied on his prefects to whip up the anti-Red hysteria which was the background to the establishment of the Second Empire, and to deal with all opposition to his regime. Under the rule of the Emperor, the prefects reached the peak of their political power.

Although not an exclusively bureaucratic regime, the Second Empire leaned very heavily on the bureaucracy for its survival. After the 1848 Revolution had brought the masses back into politics, force alone could not guarantee this result for any length of time, and Napoleon III made repeated use of the plebiscite which had been employed by his greater model as a formal sanction for the exercise of dictatorial power. This appeal to the people as a whole enabled the machine of government to exert to full advantage the greatest possible pressure on the electorate through prefects, sub-prefects, mayors and officials, and eliminated the local influence of the 'notables'. However, the growing weight of the middle classes gradually changed the character of the Second Empire. During its last few years it tended to take on the features of a constitutional monarchy but this process was cut short by the collapse of the regime in the Franco-German war of 1870 which involved all parts of the dictatorship—political leadership, army and bureaucracy.

With the third Republic begins the modern era of French politics. In 1870, as in 1848, the decisive part in the overthrow of a discredited regime was played by the workers of Paris who were again defeated by the new authorities in a violent clash. On both occasions, the new regimes expressed the hostility of the middle classes and the peasant-farmers towards the revolutionary capital but with very different political results: in 1848, this cleavage of interests enabled Louis Napoleon to establish his own dictatorship, but in 1871 the collapse of the Paris Commune left the middle classes in complete control. The outstanding difference between the Second and the Third Republics was, therefore, the changed attitude of the bourgeoisie towards the Executive. It had been taught by the experience of the second Empire that the complete separation of powers with an independent Executive as bulwark against the revolutionary workers was a dangerous expedient, and the ruthless suppression of the Commune made it sufficiently confident of its own position to keep the reins in the hands of a legislative assembly in which it was the undisputed master.

An anti-revolutionary republic was contrary to French political tradition, and the Third Republic was at first regarded as a simple stop-gap. However, it was kept alive during the first critical years by the friction between the monarchist parties and the proverbial inability of the Bourbons to learn and to forget. Karl Marx had noted more than twenty years earlier that 'the nameless rule of the republic was the only one where both factions could maintain their common class interests in uniform rule without dropping their mutual rivalry',[1] and the man who now acted on this insight was Adolphe Thiers who laid the foundations of the Third Republic and became its first President.

After the royalist majority had regretfully buried its hopes of a restoration of the monarchy, the Assembly adopted the compromise Constitution of 1875 which was not so much republican in the revolutionary French sense as monarchist without a king. It involved the

---

[1] *Klassenkaempfe*, etc., p. 90.

de facto acceptance of the republic by some of the monarchists, and the acceptance by the republicans of institutions admirably fitted for a constitutional monarchy. Effective power was divided between the Chamber of Deputies and the Senate, with the government reduced to almost complete dependence on parliament. The President was deprived of executive power and became a ceremonial figurehead in the actual operation of the constitution, a position confirmed by the premature resignation of a large number of Presidents.

The France of the Third Republic was thus a parliamentary democracy of a very thorough type in a country, where the modern business classes and the industrial workers were confined mainly to the capital and a few large centres, with a majority of the people consisting of peasant-farmers and of the old middle class—shopkeepers, artisans and professional men of the many country towns living mainly on the farmers. Both houses of parliament, and particularly the Senate, tended to reflect local interests, and this feature was strengthened by the introduction of single-member constituencies through the conservative majority of the first Chamber. The partial democratization of local government—everywhere except in the suspect capital—had a similar effect, and the typical deputy and senator were representative of the dominant local interests and their position depended largely on the services he rendered them as a condition of continued re-election.

Though the Constitution was strongly biased against the towns with their radical political tendencies, it did not favour the countryside from any special sympathy with the small farmers. The Conservatives had more than a sprinkling of local notables and they expected to control the village vote partly through the clergy and, above all, through the bureaucracy. In particular, the influence of the prefects and their staff on elections in rural areas continued to be almost as important in the early years of the Republic as it had been under the second Empire.

The existence of a centralized bureaucracy thus remained the central fact of French politics, but its control became localized to an unusual extent. Each senator and deputy regarded it as his foremost task to obtain a say in the exercise of administration within his constituency, either by ensuring the appointment of his own candidates as prefects, sub-prefects or other key officials, or at least by obtaining the removal of obnoxious members of the bureaucracy. In view of the enormous size of the French bureaucracy and its importance for the life of the country this was a matter which only the most prominent politicians could afford to neglect and it was one of the conditions for their support of the government of the day. The governments themselves were, above all, the central lever of control over the composition and operation of the bureaucracy as a whole, and the crucial battles for political supremacy were as much administrative as parliamentary.

The consolidation of the Republic after the unsuccessful attempt of the conservatives to stage a legal *coup d'état* in May 1877 was therefore followed by sweeping removals of royalist officials and their replacement by reliable adherents of the republican regime, a policy which was later on extended from the upper strata of the bureaucracy to the magistracy. These measures were in the tradition followed by every new regime since the establishment of the Napoleonic State, but the Third Republic differed from its predecessors in combining bureaucratic government with democratic political institutions. In a parliamentary system such institutions cannot be worked for any length of time without the intervention of political parties.

2. THE PARTY SYSTEM AND THE SOCIAL FORCES

The defects of the French party system are not the result of a peculiar political mentality of the French people but of the facts of French history and politics.

Highly organized voluntary political associations date back at least to the time of the revolution, when political 'clubs' played an outstanding part—none more so than the club of the Paris Jacobins with its close relations with corresponding and affiliated bodies in many provincial towns. The clubs acted as co-ordinators and supervisors of the machine of government which they supplemented by methods appropriate to a time of revolutionary crisis. For this reason they were incompatible with the Napoleonic dictatorship and the restored monarchy.

The small privileged minorities which ruled France until 1848 to the exclusion of the majority of the population, were little more than cliques reflecting the various short-lived systems of government between the First and the Second Republic. The narrow franchises and the fairly tight police rule of the government in power, whatever its complexion, prevented the formation of genuine opposition parties. Even the respectable opposition to Louis Philippe went no further than the organization of reform banquets, while the radicals either took refuge from the overwhelming strength of the State machine in utopias, like Saint Simon and the other utopian socialists, or concentrated on the preparation of conspiracies by secret societies according to the doctrine of Auguste Blanqui.

With the introduction of manhood suffrage after the February revolution of 1848, political groups representing almost every section of French society appeared on the scene, only to be swept away within a few years and without forming political parties in the modern sense of the word. When the fall of the Second Empire and the suppression of the revolutionary pretensions of Paris through Galliffet and Thiers cleared the stage for their re-apearance under more favourable conditions, many were recognizably the same as more than twenty years earlier. On the Right there were various shades of monarchists whose right wing opposed the existing regime root and branch and advocated its speedy overthrow. The centre was formed by moderate Republicans known as 'opportunists' who cared less for the form of government than for the maintenance of law and order against attempts by the revolutionary Left which remained outside the pale for upwards of twenty years after the fall of the Paris Commune. The respectable Left was formed by the Radicals.

The party system of the Third Republic was an essential element, and a faithful reflection, of the French system of government. It was based on the elimination of the danger of revolution from the Left through the political emasculation of Paris by an extremely narrow system of local government and on the thorough control of the whole country by a strictly centralized administration. In these conditions, parliamentary government was limited to the question of who was to determine the way in which the bureaucracy carried out its functions, and this subtle game was further complicated by the frequency with which the parliamentary majority of the day changed its rules in order to perpetuate its ascendancy.

The comparative weakness of the business classes in French society was reflected in politics in an exaggerated form by the division of their representatives into monarchists and republicans. The split between the anti-republican Right (which was itself far from united) and the republican Moderates weakened the political effectiveness of the privileged classes as a whole, prevented their political leaders from running the country with the approval of the majority of voters and forced them to form complicated combinations with other groups. In these combinations the extreme Right had usually to be excluded and the republican Moderates had to rely on support from other republican groups.

The National Assembly, and later on the Chamber of Deputies and the Senate, therefore consisted of a number of loosely knit groups, held together mainly by the backing of similar interests with hardly more than a veneer of common ideas or principles. They were supported in their constituencies by small coteries of notables without formal contacts with the mass of sympathizers and voters. Their technique of political rule was the use of their parliamentary position for the purpose of running the bureaucracy through the government; just as in Paris cliques and coteries established and overthrew governments according to minor shifts in the parliamentary balance of power, the main issue in the constituencies was not the mobilization of popular forces but the conquest of political influence over the local administration, and a share in the spoils of running the national administration, through the person of the local Deputy. Where the local balance of power was settled more or less permanently, as in many parts of rural France, the development of political parties remained arrested right until the end of the third Republic; where different interests were in some kind of equilibrium parties with rather more clearly recognizable traits opposed each other or formed alliances according to marginal shifts in the balance of popular discontent.

Before the first World War, the old middle classes, including the peasant-farmers, formed the predominant group in French society, although with the progress of industrialism their situation tended to deteriorate. They were, therefore, critical of the privileged groups and their political spokesmen, and they soon found their most characteristic political expression in the Radical party, the Left opposition in the early years of the Third Republic. The strength of the Radicals lay in their local roots. Their political organization was much less rudimentary than that of the parties of the Right and that of the republican Moderates and included local 'cadres' as well as national congresses whose influence was, however, much smaller than that of the parliamentary leaders. In addition, they made effective use of their close connection with the para-political organization of the freemasons and made a strong and effective attack on the most important para-political ally of the Right, the Catholic Church, by opposing the parish priest with the schoolmaster. At the same time, they did not despise the assistance of the bureaucracy in cementing their electoral position, and the key Ministry of the Interior, which controlled the prefects throughout France, was for many years almost their private preserve. Perhaps the most important limitation of their political power was their failure to purge the officer corps after the Dreyfus affair; their attempt to carry out such a purge produced a serious crisis which in the long run strengthened the reactionary sympathies of the army leaders.

The rise of the Radicals to the political leadership of the Third Republic towards the end of the nineteenth century was paralleled, and to some extent caused, by the vigorous growth of the socialist movement at the periphery of the French party system. The absence of a radical Left wing in the first period of the Third Republic was, indeed, the necessary condition of the comfortable rule of political cliques which differed in their opinions as to the most suitable form of government but were of one mind about the need to maintain the existing social order against the extreme Left. The gradual revival of socialism after the disastrous end of the Paris Commune was assisted by the long economic depression of the 1880s and by the radicalization of the small vinegrowers of the south whose economic existence was threatened by the ravages of phylloxera.

The socialist movement bore from its inception as a political force under the Third Republic a coalition character which weakened its ideological and tactical unity. The party contained the successors of the old Communards who represented the workers and many shopkeepers of Paris, modern Marxists with their base amongst the miners and steel workers of the north and east, as well as a large contingent of fervent idealists, often with a strongly anarchist flavour, from the south with its mainly rural population whose backward economy contrasted with their lively intelligence and ancient civilization. At a relatively early stage, the socialist movement also became the political home of substantial numbers of teachers, postmen, railway workers and the lower grades of the civil service who benefited materially from the spread of trade unionism amongst the huge army of public servants whose parliamentary spokesmen were the socialist members of the Chamber of Deputies. For a party of this type a stable organization was vitally important and this marked the socialists as a national party in a different sense from the loose groups of the Right and even from the Radicals.

From their first appearance in the Chamber of 1893, the Socialists steadily increased their votes and seats until the first World War, when they accounted for over one-sixth of the Chamber of Deputies. At that time they were a much more important parliamentary force than the British Labour Party, and although the German Socialists had a numerically stronger parliamentary group in the *Reichstag*, the effective political power of the German parliament was incomparably weaker than that of the French Chamber which made and unmade governments in embarrassing profusion. The existence of a large, growing and relatively disciplined block of seats made the French socialists an important factor in the political game almost from their entry into the Chamber.

The structure of French society set fairly rigid limits to the growth of socialism, but the political system offered their parliamentary representatives tempting opportunities of obtaining political influence. This tantalizing dilemma was a more invidious test than the open persecution of earlier times, and subjected the cohesion of the party to strains which were at times unbearable. The first occasion when this problem arose in the concrete form of participation of a socialist leader in a bourgeois government became a test case not only for the French socialists but for the Socialist International. In 1899, Alexandre Millerand, at that time Jaurès' right-hand man and one of the most prominent socialists, entered the Waldeck-Rousseau government and initiated a pattern which was to become characteristic of many leading politicians of the Third Republic; they started at the extreme Left and ended either at the extreme Right, like Millerand himself, Laval, Doriot, etc., or as elder statesmen, like Briand and, in a sense, even Léon Blum.

The attraction of the 'bourgeois' Republic for the socialist leaders was the cause of frequent splits within the socialist ranks which could not accommodate both supporters and opponents of the policy of cooperation. But the temporary withdrawal of Vaillant and his 'revolutionary' supporters on the occasion of Millerand's entry into a middle-class government was little more than symbolical compared with the cleavage caused by the great dilemma of the socialist attitude towards the first World War. In a country where national sentiments and revolutionary politics had never been regarded as incompatible, the great majority of socialist leaders and their supporters enthusiastically endorsed the war and the national government formed soon after its outbreak. However, the realities of the struggle in due course created a growing opposition to the war and to the subordination of working-class interests to its prosecution by Clemenceau's methods. The conflict between 'radicals' and 'reformists' within the socialist party gathered strength, until shortly after the end of the war the party split permanently at the Congress of Tours (1920) into Socialists and Communists.

Although the opponents of affiliation to the Communist International were in a minority at that Congress, they rallied the greater part of the 'militants' and the voters to their side, and at most elections during the inter-war years the Socialists polled about twice the number of supporters of the Communists. This relative failure of the Communists was mainly due to the disastrous effects of their subjection to the Soviet power acting through the Communist International. Their adherence to a rigid party line dictated from abroad accorded so little with the real interests of the French workers that it had to be forced on the supporters of the Communist party through a bureaucratic dictatorship of the party machine which dominated the organization and policy of the French Communist Party. At the same time, the refusal of the Communists to take part in electoral combinations with other parties excluded them, as much from necessity as from choice, from the corrupting influence of the political horse-trading of the final era of the third Republic; this reduced their parliamentary strength almost to insignificance, for their representation in the Chamber fell from a modest twenty-six in 1924 to twelve in 1932 compared with well over one hundred Socialists for about double their voting strength, but it made them almost automatically the beneficiaries of the growing opposition amongst the workers to the policy of the Socialists.

The position of the latter was in many respects the exact opposite of the Communist attitude. They had lost a good deal of electoral support through the split, but their parliamentary position benefited greatly from the practice of electoral alliances with Radicals of varying shades which paid handsome dividends in the shape of generous parliamentary representation for both parties. However, the political consequences of this attitude were much more favourable for the Radicals than for their Socialist partners. The system enabled the Radicals to elect Deputies with the help of socialist voters in the name of 'Republican discipline', while supporting socially conservative governments in the Chamber. So they got the best, or at least the second best, of both political worlds. The Socialists, on the other hand, had to give grudging support to policies which could not be reconciled with their professed aims even by the most lavish use of political rhetoric and imagination. This caused a permanent loss of militant supporters to the Communists and a steadily increasing internal tension within the Socialist Party whose party machine asserted itself by disciplinary measures, culminating in splits and expulsions, against opponents from Right and Left.

The period between the wars was thus marked by a steady increase in the power of the party machines in both working-class parties, the Communists as well as the Socialists, for broadly similar reasons—the pursuit of policies which did not represent the fundamental interests of their members and supporters but those of unrepresentative cliques; on the one side the Soviet-installed and Soviet-directed party bureaucracy, on the other side the parliamentary leaders. The political bankruptcy of both parties was fully revealed in public shortly after their greatest ostensible triumph, the victory of the Popular Front in 1936 which brought the smouldering crisis of French democracy into the open.

3. THE CRISIS OF FRENCH DEMOCRACY

It is a relatively harmless form of nostalgia amongst French political commentators with their roots in earlier generations to distinguish between the heroic era of the Third Republic before 1914 and its decay in the inter-war years; in fact the roots of the dramatic and tragic course of French politics during the last generation lie in the deeper soil of social and economic conditions. They may be described as the relative backwardness of the French economy compared with that of most other industrial nations, particularly Germany, and the effects of the unspectacular but nevertheless continuous process of capitalist industrialization on French society.

The Polarization of Politics

France's pretensions as a world power were put to a searching test in the acute international rivalries preceding the first World War, and the narrow economic base of French overseas expansion and rearmament was insufficient to support them. The conquest of a large overseas empire, the unprofitable investment of large sums in Tsarist Russia for purely political reasons and, above all, the huge losses of the first World War caused a chronic financial crisis which dealt the death-blow to the most characteristic class of French pre-war society, the small *rentier*. Although the franc was stabilised by Poincaré—at one-fifth of its pre-war value—the effort of maintaining a dominant military position in Europe, of bolstering the rickety alliance of the

'Little Entente' and supporting the drain of an ever more restive empire, exposed the inadequacy of French resources more clearly with every passing year.

The political effects of the decline in French currency and finance were felt most strongly by a section of the lower middle classes which were the backbone of the most representative party of the Third Republic, the Radicals. Their traditional policy was a strong attachment to the slogans of the Revolution of 1789 combined with an even stronger sense of the sanctity of private property. The emergence of a conflict between these allegiances was one of the main causes of the crisis of French democracy which developed during the 1920s, matured during the Depression, erupted with full force with the French defeat in 1940 and has continued ever since.

The main feature of this crisis is the progressive polarization of French politics, with the politically liberal but socially conservative Radicals steadily losing influence compared with the extreme Right and the extreme Left, and forced to move now in one direction and then in the other. During the inter-war period their leftward movement was mainly noticeable at election times, while for the serious business of governing between elections they followed increasingly the leadership of the Right. The spokesmen of the respectable Right, for their part, differed considerably from the lunatic fringe, the *Action Francaise*, but the growing strength of the dissatisfied sections of the lower middle class encouraged less respectable rival leaders to exploit the mounting tension for their own ends.

While the Right benefited mainly from the decomposition of the old lower middle class, the declared enemies of the capitalist system, the Socialists and the Communists, used the opportunities provided by the slow but sure progress of industry and the growth in urban population for a steady increase in their voting strength. The leftward trend of the electorate had been one of the outstanding characteristics of the party system, and still more of the political phraseology, of the Third Republic almost from its inception; during the inter-war period it gathered speed at the same time as the extreme Right gained supporters at the expense of the Radical centre. It only needed a serious worsening of economic conditions to transform the political scene, and this was provided with a vengeance by the Great Depression of the 1930s.

At first the course of French politics seemed to follow the traditional pattern of earlier crises with a moderate swing to the Left at the elections of 1932, followed by the equally time-honoured erosion of the 'progressive' forces in parliament. But the measured swing of the pendulum towards the respectable Right was disturbed by distinctly fascist tendencies feeding on the patent inadequacy of the Radical government, which was backed and kept in office by the Socialists. These tendencies assumed almost irresistible force with the Stavisky scandal and its political aftermath, when the attempt by a Paris mob to coerce the parliamentary government marked the end of the long era of unchallenged rule by the solid middle class of the provinces. The riots of February 6, 1934, overthrew the Radical government without answering the question whether democracy could survive the polarization of internal politics at a time of growing dangers from fascist regimes in Germany and Italy.

The violent shock of this combination of domestic and foreign threats of an unfamiliar kind forced the Radicals out of the strategic position from which they had managed so long to run with the hares of the Left and to hunt with the hounds of the Right. Instead of using the Left for their own parliamentary interests in the name of 'Republican discipline', they found themselves in the unusual position of helping to elect Communist deputies in the cause of anti-fascism under the banner of the Popular Front. In the elections of 1936, the combined forces of the Right maintained their strength virtually undiminished and still accounted for 42 per cent of the electorate, while the share of the Radicals fell to 22 per cent. The real victors were the Communists with over 15 per cent of the votes, and for the first time with a parliamentary representation broadly in line with their popular strength.

The Socialist leadership of the short-lived Popular Front government took the polarization of French politics a big step further. The quick disillusionment of the industrial workers with 'their' government discredited the Socialist leaders in favour of the Communists whose 'independent support' of the government enabled them to evade responsibility for unpopular measures and soon degenerated into an unscrupulous poker game for the allegiance of the workers. At the elections of 1936 the Communist vote, though almost twice as high as in 1932, had been substantially lower than that of the Socialists; two years later they were well on the way towards wresting the leadership of the Left from their Socialist rivals, only to tarnish their reputation by their approval of the Hitler-Stalin pact and their open subservience to Russian politics during the early part of the second World War. The expulsion of the Communists from parliament in 1939 altered the parliamentary balance of power radically in favour of the reactionary enemies of the Republic whose hour of triumph was fast approaching.

The subordination of national to sectional interests was no less complete on the extreme Right. The government of Léon Blum hoped to pacify the workers by long overdue social reforms and to allay their revolutionary mood. The success of the reform measures was complete in this respect, but at the same time they acted as the catalyst which changed the bourgeoisie and a substantial part of the lower middle class from conservative republicans into reactionaries at any price: the slogan 'rather Hitler than Blum' assumed terrifying reality with every intensification of the threat from abroad—the loss of Spain to Franco, the Austrian *Anschluss*, the rape of Czechoslovakia and finally the outbreak of the second World War.

Political polarization limited the scope of the traditional process of parliamentary combinations, and the Chamber became more adept at overthrowing governments but less capable of forming new ones. With parliamentary government becoming progressively more difficult, methods of by-passing the parliamentary labyrinth and the formally omnipotent Chamber and Senate assumed growing importance, above all the practice of government by decree (*décret-loi*) which closely resembled the situation of the Weimar Republic before the advent of Hitler.

Bureaucratic Rule and the Great Crash

The main beneficiaries of this process of governing formally with parliamentary approval but actually without reference to parliament were not the fleeting Cabinets of the moment but the permanent bureaucrats whose power and independence increased by leaps and bounds during the years between the wars.

The political importance of this change was at first disguised by the far-reaching identity of views between the heads of the bureaucracy and their titular masters, but the crisis of the regime during the depression brought it into the open. The clash between the Radical Prime Minister, Edouard Daladier, and the Right extremist head of the Paris police, M. Chiappe, was a spectacular illustration of this conflict, and the Popular Front government was compelled in the main to entrust the execution of its policies to officials whose lack of sympathy with its aims was faithfully reflected in their actions: the most it could do to outspoken enemies of its policies was to transfer them to less influential posts. The privileges of the chiefs of the bureaucracy had become enshrined by law and custom and were under the powerful protection of the Council of State which had obtained the right to quash government decisions affecting the career of the officials on whom the government had to rely for the execution of its policy.

At the same time, the mass of the lower ranks of the bureaucracy managed to consolidate their positions by the same means as other pressure groups—economic and political action. During the nineteenth century, junior officials of the Third Republic were treated by their superiors almost as arbitrarily as the employees of private firms. Recruitment, promotion and disciplinary measures frequently depended on the discretion of the minister and the chiefs of the hierarchy. The appeal of the growing trade union movement to the lower grades of the civil service was, therefore, very strong, and after a protracted struggle with the governments of the day—which were mainly Radical in political complexion—trade unionism amongst public employees was recognized and made rapid progress, particularly amongst teachers, railwaymen, postmen, etc. The unions frequently obtained not only improvements in living conditions but also a say in promotion and disciplinary procedures, subjects of special interest to public officials.

The claims of the struggling civil service unions were championed from the beginning by the Socialists, and it was only natural that the lower ranks of the bureaucracy repaid this service by their allegiance to the Socialist Party. This alliance became even closer after the split within the Labour movement which weakened the working-class element within the Socialist Party and made it increasingly dependent on the support of the white collar workers and particularly the organized civil servants; the bureaucracy thus obtained an influential representation in parliament, thereby closing the vicious circle: the individual deputy demanded, and frequently obtained, a direct say in the appointment of the prefect and other leading officials in his constituency in order to be sure of official backing at all times and especially during elections; the organized bureaucracy, on the other hand, was sure of important political friends in the Chamber for the protection of its specific interests.

The growing independence of the bureaucracy was not confined to the level of group interests and assumed steadily growing proportions with the extension of government activities which was almost as considerable in France as in other modern States with a less centralized administrative system. Although under the Third Republic local self government made considerable progress, it remained under the 'tutelage' of the central government in all except purely local matters. This power of supervision was exercised by the prefects who were more than ever in a crucial position and used their wide powers more and more independently.

The Prefect was and remains the sole 'government delegate', charged with the duty of ensuring 'the co-ordination of the activity of civil servants, the representation of the national interests, and the administrative supervision of the territorial collectivities', as the 1946 Constitution said.[1] The ministerial control of the Ministry of the Interior over his eighty or ninety prefects is an illusion from the administrative point of view and the accumulation of functions in the hands of the Prefect makes him a serious bottleneck—and in times of crisis a menace to the spirit of local initiative.

The almost complete independence of the bureaucratic machine from the political government which was its nominal master was one

[1] Article 88.

of the main causes of administrative decay during the closing years of the Third Republic. The Stavisky scandal revealed serious defects in the police and the judicial system. With the approach of the final crisis, other branches of the bureaucracy were tried and found wanting. In the Ministry of Foreign Affairs, power was concentrated in the hands of the permanent head, Alexis Léger, who shared the bureaucratic dislike of awkward reports by forward subordinates to the extent of discouraging diplomatic representatives from warning their government of the danger of a Soviet-Nazi agreement in the summer of 1939.

The outbreak of war found the bureaucracy unable to adjust itself to the emergency which had been imminent for over a year. The Prime Minister asked in vain for an end to bureaucratic methods, 'especially in war time', but the disease was too deep-seated to give way to rhetoric: 'From top to bottom the fear of responsibility prevailed. . . . Governmental action, already far too weak, was further diluted. It dribbled down until it was lost entirely in the appalling bottlenecks of administrative perplexity. The executive no longer executed: it slumbered in interminable deliberations.'[1]

The army and its High Command were just as rigidly bureaucratic as the civil service. The commander-in-chief, General Gamelin, regarded himself not as a military leader but, above all, as a co-ordinator: 'Having fallen to the moral level of an office holder, he created round him, in his image, an hierarchy of office holders.'[2] Perhaps the only man who combined a realistic judgment of the defects of the army with a clear vision of the means of curing them was a general of an unusual kind who tried in vain to convince his Chief of the need for political action: '. . . the military organism, because of the inherent traditionalism of its very nature, will not reform itself of its own accord. It is a matter for the State, it is a matter which takes precedence over all others. A statesman is necessary for the task. In France the great leader of this war will be a Carnot, or there will be no great leader.'[3]

[1] Pertinax, *The Gravediggers of France* (New York, 1944), p. 115.

[2] *Ibid.*, p. 35.

[3] Letter from General de Gaulle to M. Reynaud, May 3, 1940. Paul Reynaud, *In the Thick of the Fight* (Eng. trans., 1955), p. 286.

Prime Minister Paul Reynaud was no Carnot. Against the forces of decay which had sapped the energies of a huge administration left far too long to its own devices, he tried to appeal to a more successful tradition in the persons of its most famous relics, Field Marshal Pétain and General Weygand. They did not save a doomed regime but supplied suitable agents for its liquidation.

Vichy—Interlude or Portent?

The situation at the end of the Third Republic was the exact counterpart of that at its birth. It had inherited an invaded and defeated France from the second Empire—it collapsed under the impact of military defeat at the hands of Hitler's Germany. However conservative its spirit and institutions, its very creation on the ruins of the second Empire was a sharp move to the Left—its replacement by Vichy an even sharper one to the Right.

In political terms, the creation of the Vichy regime was a victory for the extreme lunatic fringe of the anti-republican Right. Marshal Pétain's closest advisers were steeped in the ideas of the *Action Francaise*, while Laval was a bitter enemy of parliamentary democracy and an admirer of Hitler who preached unreserved collaboration with the Germans. In practice, the so-called 'national revolution' of Pétain and his backers remained a pitiful pretence, and the attempt to steer an independent course between resistance and collaboration ended in complete surrender: from 1942 onwards, Pétain was little more than the unwilling figurehead for Laval whose government in its turn was simply the tool of the occupying forces and was engulfed in Germany's defeat.

The Vichy regime destroyed the Chamber, the Senate and the modest institutions of local self-government. The disappearance of elected representatives in some respects emancipated the bureaucracy from the last remnants of outside control and to this extent the French State of Marshal Pétain may be described as a pure bureaucracy: 'Under this unbelievable regime, the boldest laws can be passed, and are in fact passed, by the stroke of a pen. The editors of an absurdly overgrown *Official Gazette* enjoy to the full their pleasure in making laws, apparently forgetting the presence of the occupying forces and the fact that, if their power is absolute, it is only the shadow of power.'[1] However, it was not only the ruthless interference by the Nazis which made conditions unsuitable for a purely bureaucratic regime. In many ways, political direction of the bureaucracy was, in fact, much stronger than during the last decades of the Third Republic. One of the first measures of the Vichy government was the abolition of the virtual security of bureaucratic tenure by a law which permitted the suspension of all officials by simple ministerial decree. During the first six months of the regime, over two thousand officials were purged, above all amongst the higher ranks, including half the prefectoral corps. A curious feature of the new system was the use of a large number of officers of the immobilized French navy, from Darlan downwards, in administrative key appointments for which their Catholicism and their anti-British sentiments made them particularly suitable.

The hammer blows of defeat, occupation and reactionary *coup d'état* loosened the bonds which in more normal circumstances united the bureaucracy against all outsiders. Deeper loyalties than those to the administrative system determined the attitude of many officials as well as those of other Frenchmen, and drove them into opposite camps. At first they may have thought that allegiance to the grand-father figure of Marshal Pétain would dispense them from making this invidious decision, but with the rising tide of conflict closing in on them, political neutrality became less and less possible. The four years of Vichy were, therefore, on the whole not a time of purely bureaucratic consolidation and rule.

In one important respect the Vichy regime introduced an administrative reform which was at least in principle sound and in step with the needs of the time. The Napoleonic system of government by prefects controlled directly from the Ministry of the Interior in Paris had long outlived its usefulness: instead of permitting the central government to control the life of the country through its direct contacts with ninety governing officials, it had transformed the prefects into 'small-scale emperors' within a Republic whose overgrown responsibilities were subject to little effective control. Although

[1] André Siegfried, *De la IIIe a la IVe République* (Paris, 1956), p. 86.

Pétain's criticism of this state of things was conditioned by his army background, it was pertinent and shrewd: 'In the army, a major commands only three or four companies, a colonel three or four battalions, a general two or three corps. But the Minister of the Interior is supposed to command eighty-six prefects. And between him and the prefects the parliamentarians interfere on whom the prefect depends as much as on the ministers. How could the government function in these conditions? . . . My plan is to divide France into twenty regions which will group three, four or five departments according to their geographical and political relationships.'[1] Though this plan may have been influenced by Pétain's counter-revolutionary preference for the provinces of the old monarchy and was designed as a means of effective political control, the institution of regional prefects and the regionalization of the administration had considerable intrinsic merits.

From De Gaulle to De Gaulle

While the Third Republic was conservative or nothing, the origins of the Fourth Republic were necessarily revolutionary. Popular reaction to Nazi occupation and Vichy authoritarianism drove the post-war electorate even further to the left than at the previous elections which had swept the Popular Front into ephemeral power in 1936.

At the end of the war, Communists and Socialists had a clear majority in parliament with half the popular vote against slightly over one-third in 1936, the Radicals were reduced from more than a fifth to just over one-tenth and the traditional Right, gravely compromised by the attitude of many of its members towards the Vichy regime, fell from more than two-fifths to only one-eighth, while a quarter of the vote went to the new Catholic left-of-centre party, the MRP. With the resignation of General De Gaulle as Prime Minister early in 1946 as a protest against the restoration of parliamentary government, the way seemed to be clear for a broad movement to the Left. In fact, the very opposite happened and the political centre of gravity shifted steadily to the Right, until the regime foundered in May-June 1958 and made room for a new De Gaulle era.

[1] Robert Aron, *Histoire de Vichy*, 1940-1944 (Paris, 1954), p. 214.

The short and pitiful history of the Fourth Republic was dominated by the interaction of a bureaucratized party system and a bureaucratic machine of government. The concentration of forces at the opposite ends of the political balance which had clogged the delicate mechanism of French politics during the last period of the Third Republic was even more in evidence after 1944, because it was accompanied by the rule of party machines which deprived it of the tolerance essential to its functioning.

At the time of the liberation and during the following year or two, the Communists, and to a lesser extent the Socialists, had an enormous advantage over most of their competitors, not only because they were favoured by the sentiment of the moment but, above all, because they possessed national party machines. The temporary disintegration of the Radicals and the discomfiture of the discredited Right threatened to deprive the enemies of 'socialism' in all its forms of the possibility of effective parliamentary action, and the need for a comprehensive party of the Right and Centre was the main cause of the phenomenal rise of the Christian Democrat MRP.

The chief organizational asset of the *Mouvement Republicain Populaire* was its alliance with the Catholic Church, with the introduction of women's suffrage more than ever the most important para-political body in the country. Its leadership was distinctly left of centre on social and economic issues and the party was a coalition of forces which in the past had more frequently opposed than supported each other. As soon as the MRP had succeeded in stemming the red tide by exploiting the mounting friction between Communists and Socialists this coaliton began to break down. The right wing of its supporters tended to follow more demagogic leaders who voiced the dissatisfaction of the urban lower middle classes more effectively —at first the Gaullist RPF, then the Poujadist movement of 1956 and finally the neo-Gaullist Union for the New Republic.

The domination of party politics by mass parties on a national scale was thus the distinctive feature of the Fourth Republic. The loose coalitions of local interests which constituted the largest part of the Chamber of Deputies and most of the Senate under the Third Republic formed only a small minority after the liberation. The old

Right was reduced to a fraction of its strength, but the Radicals recovered from the low ebb of their immediate post-war position, largely due to the energetic efforts of their progressive wing under Pierre Mendès-France to reorganize them on the lines of a modern mass party in order to reap some of the benefits accorded to strongly organized parties under the Constitution of 1946.

This Constitution embodied the principle of government by a democratically elected Assembly through national parties with strict discipline over their parliamentary representatives. This system ran with every passing year into more serious difficulties, to a large extent due to the failure of both wings of the Labour movement.

In the Communist Party, the supremacy of the party machine had become an article of faith, because it was the condition for the subordination of Communist policy to the interests of the Soviet government. With the development of the cold war between Russia and the West, this dependence of the French Communists on the Soviets was in any case bound to poison their relationship with the Socialists, but at the same time they exploited their now superior strength in the same clever but unscrupulous manner in which they had used their tactical advantages during the Popular Front period. This completely alienated the Socialists and threw them in sheer self-defence into the arms of the MRP.

In the conditions of the post-war era, this move implicated the Socialists in policies which were against their principles and the interests of their supporters and ultimately unsuccessful, largely because they involved responsibility for a series of disastrous colonial wars which were amongst the main causes of the downfall of the Fourth Republic. This policy could be forced on the Socialist rank-and-file only through the rigorous machine rule exercised by its General Secretary, Guy Mollet, at the time of his accession to this key position the spokesman of the party's left wing.

The opposite but complementary policies of Communists and Socialists, both dominated by their respective party machines, resulted in an alignment of forces which brought parliament into permanent conflict with the mood of the French people and thereby undermined the popular basis of the regime. The Communists were effectively isolated in the country and within the Chamber for all purposes except that of overthrowing governments, but throughout this period they managed to retain and even increase their popular support—a testimonial both to the strength of their organization and to the weakness of the policy pursued by their enemies. The Socialists were involved against their better judgment in policies which alienated a growing number of their supporters and thus contributed to the political sterilization of the Left. The massive strength of the ostracised Communists on the Left and the growing restiveness of the anti-republican Right narrowed the choice of governments and made the formation of parliamentary majorities more and more difficult, thus discrediting the parliamentary system as a whole.

Ever since the failure of the Communist-inspired strikes of 1947, the initiative had fallen to the anti-republican challengers on the extreme Right. Although the Socialists were officially the party of progress, they behaved in fact as the convinced upholders of the *status quo*. Although the Communists claimed to be the party of revolution, and were regarded as such by friend and foe, they remained for over a decade frozen in the same posture of ineffective defiance. They constituted, indeed, the supreme instance of that *immobilisme* which was also the hallmark of most governments of the fourth Republic and which the Communists, in painful contrast to their strident incantations, maintained even during the final crisis of the regime—its collapse under the pressure of the army and its co-conspirators on the extreme Right who were at last to prove by deeds that their hostility towards democracy had not changed between 1940 and 1958.

If the helplessness of the Left in this crisis and afterwards was largely the result of the bureaucratic degeneration of both wings of the Labour movement, the ease of transition to the semi-authoritarian Fifth Republic was mainly due to the extent to which the bureaucracy had in fact become an independent ruling power under the cloak of parliamentary democracy. For the second time in eighteen years the administrative machine failed the government in the hour of need, but while its breakdown in 1940 was primarily due to its inefficiency in the face of a supreme emergency, in 1958 its attitude towards the government was a mixture of indifference and hostility.

In 1940 it was an administrative system suffering from grave bureaucratic defects; by 1958 it had become an organization in a state of advanced bureaucratic degeneration.

Perhaps the crucial decision in the history of the Fourth Republic was taken at its very beginning in the restoration of the traditional bureaucratic State. The provisional government at Algiers prepared this step with great care, but at the time of the liberation its success was seriously threatened by the activities of the Resistance Movement which had established the nucleus of a revolutionary government in the south of the country. The prevention of a revolutionary solution of the crisis of French democracy had been Pétain's main preoccupation during the last phase of the Vichy regime, and although General De Gaulle could afford to ignore Pétain's advances, he needed the acqiescence of the Communist Party. This he received from its official leader, Maurice Thorez, immediately on the latter's return from Russia.

With the re-establishment of the old government machine the balance of power shifted decisively against the forces of revolution and towards the restoration of a system ostensibly similar to that of the Third Republic. However, parliament consisted no longer of loose groups of politicians whose temporary coalitions were sufficiently elastic to express the mood of the moment without obstructing the process of administration by a rigid bureaucracy, but was itself dominated by party bureaucracies, and hemmed in by large ostracized mass movements on the Left and Right.

This unstable balance of forces produced governments which were too short-lived and too weak to exercise effective control over their officials, although some key ministers turned up in cabinet after cabinet. While the rights and privileges of the lower grades of the bureaucracy were protected by the unions, its chiefs became more and more the real rulers of the country, though frustrated and increasingly antagonized by the sheer impossibility of getting measures accepted which required substantial new legislation. At the same time, in a period of rapid inflation salaries tended to lag behind prices and the material dissatisfaction of the bureaucracy contrasted dangerously with its effective power.

The independence of the officials from the political leadership was most complete in the French empire which was ruled by the bureaucracy with very little concern for the wishes of the home government and occasionally with flagrant disregard of official policy at critical moments. The most fateful case in point was North Africa, and particularly Algeria, where the authorities, including the resident ministers, came completely under the influence of the local settlers, with the result known characteristically as 'the thirteen conspiracies of the thirteenth of May'.[1]

Although on this occasion the army played the decisive part, the success of the conspiracy would have been inconceivable without the complete demoralization of the official defenders of law and order. In fact the police—which only a few weeks earlier had shown its complete disaffection in riotous demonstrations in the centre of Paris—was just as unreliable as the officer corps and the higher bureaucracy and the Fourth Republic fell without even a show of resistance, while its leaders were exclusively concerned with transferring power in legal form to the new rulers: General De Gaulle was backed by the army but even more strongly by the bureaucracy.

To say that the outstanding feature of the Fifth Republic is the undisputed rule of the bureaucracy is not to belittle De Gaulle's towering superiority over the leaders of the Fourth Republic nor to overlook the tenacious consistency of his political conceptions. But in the setting of French conditions the General's call for a strong Executive responsible to the nation but not subject to changes in political direction according to every whim of parliamentary chance majorities was bound to confirm and thereby to increase the enormous powers which the bureaucracy had accumulated almost by default. De Gaulle's dominant idea of an independent arbitrator between the contending classes and parties was, indeed, the clearest statement of the pretensions of any bureaucracy.

De Gaulle's recall to power took place within the framework of a successful *coup d'état* by the (military and political) anti-republican

---

[1] Merry et Serge Bromberger, *Les 13 complots du 13 mai* (Paris, 1959) give a remarkable picture of the extent to which the officer corps was linked to the extreme Right in politics and of the close contacts of the conspirators with many of the highest officials throughout the country.

Right. Its obvious result, politically as well as economically was the temporary eclipse of the Left, of the Labour movement in general and the Communists in particular. At the same time its most striking feature was the triumphant self-assertion of the bureaucracy, symbolized by the promotion of career officials to ministerial appointments: 'The high official is today minister and the politician "on holiday". With the former, the whole administration feels itself promoted; is it likely that it will easily step down again?'[1] The Prime Minister himself, M. Michel Debré, started his career as a civil servant, was De Gaulle's war-time expert on the reorganization of the bureaucracy and later on proved his mettle as organizer of the leading bureaucrats in favour of De Gaulle's return to power.

But the bureaucratic features of the new regime are not confined to personalities. One of De Gaulle's most important demands was the transfer of wide powers of legislation by decree during the transitional period, and the use made of these powers by the bureaucracy in virtually all spheres of administration was, if anything, even more unrestrained than the flood of decrees during the heyday of Pétain's 'National Revolution'. The frustration of years of administration by subterfuge due to the defects of the legislative machine was relieved by an orgy of radical changes in the organization and substance of French public life, and the crying need for many, though not necessarily all, of them is the strongest condemnation of the defunct regime, though not for this reason an adequate justification of its successor.

4. THE MEANING OF FRENCH POLITICS

The progress of bureaucratic rule in France is the residuary product of the great social and political conflicts which mark the historical epochs of modern French society from the overthrow of the absolute monarchy by the Great Revolution to the overthrow of the Fourth Republic by General De Gaulle. In these conflicts, the problem of administration appeared at first only implicitly as part of the great

[1] Léo Hamon, *De Gaulle dans la République* (Préface de René Capitant), Paris, 1958, p. 95.

issue of the relationship between the 'Executive' and the 'Legislature'.

In French political thought, theories about the different 'powers' in the State have played a dominant part from the days of Montesquieu and Rousseau. Such theories were invariably the expression of definite interests, in the former case those of the semi-feudal officers and their aristocratic allies, in the latter those of the revolutionary third Estate, and their conception of the 'Executive' (which they viewed from the outside) was correspondingly crude. During the ancien regime the Executive was naturally envisaged in terms of the royal absolutism, although in practice its power over the machinery of government was severely limited by the quasi-independence of the entrenched 'officer' class.

The radical reorganization of the government in the Great Revolution therefore had the paradoxical result osf ubordinating the 'Executive' to the 'Legislature' in the political field, while delivering the administration from the limitations previously imposed by the special interests of the 'officers' and particularly by the judiciary. The survival of the new system thus depended entirely on the ability of the Legislature to control the Executive, and through it the administration. The sharp clash of interests between the beneficiaries of the new order and their enemies fatefully weakened the power of the Legislature and discredited the political regime in the eyes of the former. The result was a military and bureaucratic dictatorship under Napoleon I which provided France with a modern administrative machine capable of carrying out the policies of the government throughout the country.

The rise of the bureaucracy as an independent power was clearly seen by Napoleon's accomplice in the overthrow of the Republic, the Abbé Sieyès who made a theoretical distinction between 'Government' and 'Executive', though in a deplorably abstract way characteristic of his mediocrity as a thinker. The 'Executive' in this limited sense, which virtually coincides with that of administration, included the ministers who were as a rule without corporate existence as a Cabinet and functioned purely and simply as the servants of the real rulers, whether the king and his Privy Council or the Emperor and his ruling clique. This applied even to semi-parliamentary regimes like that of Louis Philippe, and the principle survived the July Monarchy: the Constituent Assembly of the Republic of 1848 did not choose a Ministry but an Executive Commission of Five which in turn appointed the government. This power was later on transferred to the President who proceeded to demonstrate its reality by dispersing the Legislature and establishing his personal dictatorship which, like that of his uncle, was based on the army and the bureaucracy.

Up to 1870 the outstanding problem of French political life was, therefore, not the weakness of the government but its strength and the difficulty of preventing it from using its command of a strictly centralized administration for the purpose of making itself independent of the forces of French society. The ultimate cause of this unstable balance of power between 'society' and the 'State' was the virtually unredeemed state of internal social tension at every critical stage since the eighteenth century.

The First Republic established the rule of the middle class and removed the feudal burdens of the peasantry while giving at least some of them additional land; but their conflicts with the Jacobins within the frontiers of France and the Royalists outside were so intense that they gladly accepted the dictatorship of a ruler of genius who broadened this conflict, until it reached world-wide dimensions and brought about his overthrow. The dominant interests after the Restoration were far too narrow to rule France except through a strong executive in charge of an even stronger bureaucracy. The result was two revolutions in less than eighteen years, while the Second Republic was rent by civil war and sought refuge from revolution in the arms of a saviour of society whose principal aim was to make himself and his disreputable associates its master.

The essence of the revolution in constitutional practice during the Third Republic was the virtual abolition of the Executive as an independent power through the determined action of parliament, and particularly the Chamber of Deputies, which transformed the President of the Republic from a weaker replica of the monarch into a figurehead for ceremonial occasions. Though the Prime Minister gained in importance as a result of the emasculation of the Presidency, the Cabinet was deprived of effective sanctions against the Legislature and became the simple agent of the parliamentary majority, where previously it had been the agent of the Chief of State.

This change could not have been accomplished without a temporary slackening in internal social tension following the massive bloodletting inflicted on the workers of Paris, and on the Labour movement as a whole, through the suppression of the Commune. The mock-heroic antics of Royalists and Republicans resulted in one of the periodic changes in the leading personnel of the bureaucracy and added some spice to the game of ins-and-outs. Apart from this they did little to interfere with the comfortable conviction of the middle classes that they had discovered the secret of squaring the political circle which had eluded their ancestors during the First and Second Republic: how to combine political democracy with their own rule. Their recipe was very simple: to use the bureaucracy for the actual job of government, while ensuring its operation in their own interests by judicious interference with its activities at every level—nationally through the political government which was kept in office (or overthrown) by the parliamentary majority of the day, locally through the pull of the deputy and senator over the prefect and his staff.

Though hardly a model of clean and efficient government at the best of times, this system worked well enough as long as its premises remained unchallenged. The revival of the labour movement was, in the long run, the most dangerous challenge to its existence, but for the time being the revelation of the strength and bitterness of feelings between Dreyfusists and anti-Dreyfusists loomed even larger in the public mind and contributed not a little to the transfer of power from 'Opportunists' to 'Radicals'.

With the first World War the golden age of the third Republic came to an end and the crisis of French democracy began. Instead of a gradual (and largely verbal) electoral shift to the Left, a progressive polarization of politics set in which weakened its middle-class centre and endangered the comfortable division of labour between politicians and bureaucrats for the common purpose of striking dramatic attitudes while leaving things unchanged. At the same time, the expansion of State activities increased the numbers and powers of the

bureaucracy and raised difficult structural problems in an obsolescent administrative system. New conditions called for more efficient
political control over the activities of the bureaucracy, but in effect
the opposite happened with the inevitable result that bureaucratic
defects were rife throughout the administration of the State, including its armed forces. Though not the main cause of the debacle of
1940, the helplessness and inefficiency of the civil and military
bureaucracy were just as much in evidence then as they had been in
1870.

Although the Third Republic was doomed, its collapse would not
have put the extreme Right Wing into the saddle, if the labour movement, both in its Communist and its Socialist forms, had not borne
an uncomfortably large share of responsibility for its downfall. Pétain
and his anti-Republican allies benefited from the revulsion of feeling
against the 'militants' of democracy without acquiring a genuine mass
basis of their own. Thus they relied entirely on the administrative
machine for the maintenance of their shadowy power exercised by
permission of the Nazi invaders.

With the Liberation the outlawed forces of democracy emerged
from their temporary hiding place in the Maquis and seemed to
sweep everything before them—except the machine of government
which remained essentially the same as under the Third Republic and
benefited considerably from reforms of detail regarding the recruitment of civil servants and safeguards for their position. The political
impetus to the Left found expression in substantial measures of
nationalization, long overdue reforms and improvements in the social
services, before it was lost in the quagmire of *immobilisme* which discredited the Fourth Republic long before its overthow by the
Algerian revolt and its backers.

Although every stage in this process except the short interlude of
the post-Liberation regime approached more closely to the reality
of bureaucratic rule, the bureaucracy itself played only a minor part
in bringing about this result, which was in the final analysis a product
of social tension for which it was not responsible. This tension, and
its political reflection in the polarization of politics, had deeper
causes.

The difficulty of reconciling conflicting social forces within a political democracy caused the decay of the Third Republic and the destruction of the Fourth. The dominant economic interests were too weak to obtain the voluntary support of the masses through the medium of well-organized mass parties, while the labour movement created impressive mass organizations only to see them transformed into mutually exclusive and hostile party machines pursuing self-contradictory and equally disastrous policies. Their failure created the political conditions in which the business classes could appeal to the State to put an end to an intolerable position and run the country on sound business principles—De Gaulle at the Elysée, Pinay at the Ministry of Finances. But the destruction of the Fourth Republic did not put an end to the conflicts which had proved fatal to it, and every new clash of interests has been reflected in the composition of the French Cabinet. The result has been a steady decline in its limited representative character. Politicians such as M. Pinay have been replaced by officials such as M. Baumgartner, and former bureaucrats hold virtually all key positions, including the Ministries of the Interior and Foreign Affairs as well as the Armed Forces, Finance and Education, in addition to the secondary but important Ministries of Housing and Public Health.

In the historic duel between democracy and bureaucracy the victory of the latter has never been more than temporary, because it has always proved to be lacking in the political sense needed for avoiding the Scylla of revolution and the Charybdis of external defeat, even under the leadership of a man of genius, be his name Napoleon Bonaparte or Charles de Gaulle.

CHAPTER TEN

CONDITIONS AND LIMITS
OF BRITISH DEMOCRACY

I. THE TRADITION OF OLIGARCHIC SELF-GOVERNMENT

The adherence to outdated forms and ceremonies of so many British institutions contrasts oddly with their modern character. Though the Norman-English State was rooted more directly in naked conquest than the French monarchy, or even than the empire of the Tsars, the British political system has proved capable of radical changes without losing its links with the past. Thus it has survived into a completely different world and has served as a model for more or less successful imitations in countries with widely different histories and alien social structures.

The ultimate reason for the elasticity and vitality of this system is probably the fact that English society has been recognizably modern for much longer than that of any other country. Serfdom died out early, the old feudal aristocracy exhausted itself in the civil and foreign wars of the fifteenth century and the power of the Church was overthrown by Henry VIII. The new class of landowners who made their fortunes on the ruins of the old order belonged to a society, and pursued interests, resembling much more closely those of the present day than those of their feudal predecessors, while the merchant adventurers abroad and their no less determined and rapacious domestic counterparts were from the start part and parcel of the new era.

Crown, Parliament and People

The strong monarchy of the Tudors owed many of its leading statesmen to these classes and most of its drive and resolution to the pressure of their interests. Yet the forces which supported the Tudor rulers in their vigorous nationalism and resolutely upheld the Reformation were unwilling to leave the effective government of the country entirely in the hands of the Crown and its Council. In full possession of local power as landowners and Justices of the Peace, they found their most effective political platform in the House of Commons whose influence and 'privileges' steadily increased, at first in harmony but soon in growing friction with the monarchy.

The change in political temper was unmistakable long before the death of Elizabeth I, but assumed a dangerous momentum only after the accession of James I whose experience as King of Scotland was a grave handicap for his task of governing England. In the developing struggle, the House of Commons was essentially the aggressor, because it represented the most powerful and dynamic groups of English society. The dependence of the Crown on these classes took the form of humiliating and largely unsuccessful demands for money, due partly to the effects of inflation on the king's finances but to a large extent to James's mismanagement and the extravagance of his unsavoury favourites. The stratagems and subterfuges of the Crown in its attempts to by-pass parliament poisoned the political atmosphere and forced the king to violate the constitutional conventions, until under Charles I the Scottish revolt against the extension of the episcopalian system unleashed the events which were to overthrow the monarchy and to transform England temporarily into a Commonwealth.

This upheaval raised previously submerged social groups to the political surface and threatened to turn into a social revolution—a challenge to the established order made possible only by the rift between different sections of the upper classes. In the course of the struggle, parliament lost its representative character and effective power shifted to the army, the stronghold of the most determined 'fanatics' whose religious convictions were in step with their social radicalism. Yet it was not the levelling and anabaptist privates who grasped and kept power but their officers under Cromwell and Ireton, though their rule remained uneasy to the end. The uncertainty of their position was caused by the same split within the governing classes which had been responsible for the fall of the monarchy. Hence the collapse of the system after Cromwell's death and the remarkable ease of the Restoration which was accepted by all sections of the propertied minority as a necessary safeguard of its permanent interests against the levelling tendencies of the masses.

The king on his part recognized the new distribution of property and the limitations on the royal power enacted by the Long Parliament in its pre-revolutionary phase. Otherwise the Restoration visualized a simple return to the *status quo*, with the king in full control of policy, particularly abroad, and of the machinery of government. But the Stuarts were, in the long run, incapable of adhering to a compromise policy acceptable to their own supporters: the new 'Whigs' were mortally offended in the persons of their most prominent leaders and through the wholesale purge of urban corporations, while the Tory gentry in control of the House of Commons was driven into reluctant opposition. During the last years of Charles II a new era of conflict began which reached its climax a few years later in the Glorious Revolution which was confirmed and completed by the establishment of the Hanoverian monarchy in 1714.

The new dynasty did not owe its position to its tenuous link with the person of James I and did not rule by the Grace of God but by that of a parliament determined to ensure that the still large powers of the Crown should be entrusted to reliable Protestants weak enough to respect the established order and to co-operate with its leading representatives: the age of the parliamentary monarchy had set in. The essence of the eighteenth-century constitution was not the 'separation of powers' which Voltaire and Montesquieu professed to find in it but a loose division of functions between the monarchy and the landed proprietors. The king's government remained in charge of the central administration with the agreement, and under the broad control, of the ruling oligarchy entrenched in parliament which also kept effective charge of local affairs through its hold on all official functions and its influence over most urban corporations.

The ruling oligarchy did not form a solid block. There was a social and political rift between the Tory squirearchy and the Whig magnates and financiers, and despite its fondness for feudal titles and traditions it was far from feudal in its social and economic basis. The foundation of its wealth was an agricultural system unique in a mainly feudal Europe. In addition there was a close, though not always harmonious, connection between the landed interest and the City of London, and the numbers of the gentry were steadily reinforced by rich merchants who rounded off a successful career of money-making in banking, trade or the colonies by buying land and having their sons educated as gentlemen. The elasticity of the system which distinguished it to its advantage from contemporary European society thus made the predominance of the landowners even more effective and practically complete.

The chief political instrument of the ruling oligarchy was parliament, but the House of Commons was far from being a rational representation of its various sections, though its property qualifications were a rough-and-ready attempt to restrict membership to landed proprietors. The right to vote was frequently vested in a small number of electors and constituted a valuable property and the same applied to a seat in the House: 'The ideas of the time closely connected franchise and representation with property, and gradually the vote and seat themselves tended to become realty, like an advowson, sublime in its ultimate significance, beneficial in practice to its owner.'[1]

The system facilitated the domination of parliament by a small number of powerful men, but despite the growing constitutional strength of the House of Commons it permitted the Crown to retain the essence of independent power through the art of political management. The use of official patronage for the purpose of making parliament accept the policy of the government assumed growing proportions with every change of regime, from Danby's administration under Charles II through Godolphin's organization of the queen's servants under Queen Anne to the perfection of the new technique under Walpole and its excesses under Lord North and his legion of the 'King's friends'. Harmony between Crown and parliament was ensured by the corruption of sitting members through titles, places and pensions, by the use of the government's resources

[1] Sir Lewis Namier, *The Structure of Politics at the Accession of George III* (1957 edn.), p. 126.

at elections and by the elevation of large numbers of 'placemen' to the seats of power. For more than three quarters of a century the government of the day was thus sure of returning a majority of its supporters at the next election.

The first twenty years of George III's long official reign showed the monarchy and its government in full possession of executive power and in an almost impregnable parliamentary position, but the external culmination of the system coincided with its internal decay. The idyllic 'classical' age of the British Constitution came to an end under the impact of military defeat: the Court Government of Lord North was unequal to the political task of preventing the American Revolution and revealed in its course the rottenness of the whole system.

Shortly after this grave defeat, and the additional shock of having to bow to the Irish demand for legislative independence, England had to meet the challenge of a revolutionary France, whose military and economic power had been multiplied through the replacement of a corrupt absolutism by an efficient and rationally organized military dictatorship. Britain found an invaluable, if involuntary, ally in the person of Napoleon whose policies were alien to French interests and doomed to failure, but it was a thoroughly exhausted and dangerously overstrained nation which had to deal with the aftermath of a great war—a serious economic depression and a tremendous debt burden.

In the long run, the forces of social and economic change at work within English society since the middle of the eighteenth century were even more dangerous enemies to the rule of the old oligarchy than military emergencies. The industrial revolution radically transformed the structure of the nation, while its political system remained basically unchanged, until it had become a patent anachronism. The ruling oligarchy no longer adequately represented the decisive social interests and was technically unfit for the solution of the pressing problems caused by the progress of power-driven machinery and the mushroom growth of new industrial towns. In the spiritual sphere, the era was marked by the development of dissent, the emancipation of large sections of the lower classes from a relationship devoid of genuine religious meaning; in politics, no such negative solutions were possible, because political power was essential for the realization of the purposes of the rising industrial middle classes.

As so often in modern British history, the battle between the forces of the old order and their enemies was joined for the first time not in England but in Ireland, where the nation-wide movement for Catholic emancipation under Daniel O'Connell threatened the established political order in its most vital part by breaking the power of the landlords over the miserable forty-shilling 'freeholders' who had previously been compelled to return their worst enemies to the House of Commons. Wellington and Peel partially surrendered to this agitation by accepting the demands of the respectable middle-class leaders of the Catholics at the price of disfranchising their peasant followers, and this model was not without its influence on English politics.

The great agitation preceding the Reform Bill of 1832 ended with the peaceful solution of one of the gravest crises in British constitutional history by a temporary compromise which had the effect of separating the middle classes from the artisans and the unskilled workers. Though open to logical criticism, this compromise had the advantage of offering a basis for further advance within the framework of traditional institutions. In important respects it also set a pattern for the settlement of future conflicts between the political representatives of discordant social interests within the existing political system.

The Old Administrative Order

During the eighteenth century, the local institutions throughout the country were almost exclusively in the hands of the landowners themselves and practically independent of the central authorities. After the Restoration the Crown occasionally interfered with the urban corporations, e.g. in Charles II's attacks on the charters of London and a number of boroughs, but the power of the Justice of the Peace as head of the local government, acting alone or with his colleagues, grew steadily and reached its peak towards the end of the eighteenth century. Although the most prominent task of the Justices was the administration of poor relief under the Old Poor Law, they also dealt with wages and food prices, trade and taxes, vagrants, prisoners and lunatics.

Within their narrow geographical limits, the powers of the Justices of the Peace might be compared with those of the intendants of the French monarchy, without some of the checks to which the latter were subject. The crucial difference was, of course, that in France the country was governed by officials of the central government, while in England the ruling oligarchy of local landowners acted on its own account. Within the limits of the system, self-government was practised by the assemblies of rate-payers in the vestry, the representative body of the parish which discharged many of the administrative functions of the Justices and whose few wholetime officials were controlled by them.

The dark side of this type of local self-government was the lack of rights of the rural population. It was also dependent on the largely static social order of which it formed a part and the rise of modern industry undermined the authority of the Justices by destroying the isolation of their petty empires. The most patently absurd expression of the antiquated system was the attempt to regulate poor relief by the borders of individual parishes. In course of time, a number of new functional bodies were set up in unspoken competition with the Justices of the Peace, but the new boards resembled them in maintaining their independence of the authority of the central administration.

The central government was thus limited to the Capital and to a few narrowly-defined national functions such as foreign relations, defence, the collection of revenue, the post office and a strictly-limited power over the judiciary. In theory, the Crown remained independent of parliament in its traditional role as head of the administration, but in practice the existence of a widespread spoils system ensured the ruling oligarchy of a dominant influence on its working. The huge number of sinecures in the public service provided the ideal soil for the luxuriant growth of such a system.

The maintenance of feudal forms was one of the causes of the survival of offices which had outlived their usefulness, and the royal household was particularly rich in feudal relics. Burke's famous demand for 'economical reform' was preceded by an onslaught on the administration of his day and particularly on the existence of separate administrations and judiciaries for once remote areas like Cornwall, Wales, Lancashire, etc. 'But since the central government was everywhere within the exclusive control of the Crown, the same characteristics were reproduced to a greater or less degree in every department. Nothing, indeed, could be more remarkable than the contrast between the classical ideals of order and proportion beloved by the England of that age and the Gothic eccentricity of its administration.'[1]

The lucrative shells of old functional offices were by their very nature sinecures, but other offices still serving more or less functional purposes could easily become sinecures by the appointment of deputies at low salaries—and it was characteristic of Burke's innate conservatism that this potentially much graver abuse was largely excluded from his strictures. The prevalence of sinecures was the outstanding feature of British central government throughout its length and breadth—in Exchequer and Customs, Privy Seal and Signet Office as well as in the royal household and in the Law Courts.

This exploitation of the administration of the State by the aristocracy and its retainers was the very opposite of bureaucracy. Given the social and political balance of power, the Government had to ensure the concurrence of the House of Commons by influencing voters and electors—and this meant that it had to employ all its resources, including the personnel of its administration, for political purposes. In the eyes of contemporaries the pressure of the authorities on elections was regarded as overwhelming, and the most usual form of this pressure was through government officials, '. . . the vast body of persons employed in the collection of the revenue in every part of the kingdom; the inconceivable number of placemen, and candidates for places in the customs, in the excise, in the post office, in the dock yards, in the ordnance, in the salt office, in the stamps, in the navy and victualling offices, and in a variety of other departments'.[2] One

[1] Sir David Lindsay Keir, *The Constitutional History of Modern Britain* (1947 edn.), pp. 300 f.
[2] John Douglas, *Seasonable Hints from an Honest Man*, etc., quoted by Namier, op. cit., p. 209.

of the effects of political management was an increase in the number of officials as a means of having more places to offer, but such a system was incompatible with the growth of independent bureaucratic power, however detrimental to the efficiency of the administration it was in other respects.

The same applies to the use of 'placemen' by the government in its parliamentary majority which depended on the co-operation of some of the 111 patrons who disposed of 205 seats in England alone in the middle of the century.[1] Part of the consideration which had to be given for this co-operation consisted of places and pensions for members of parliament and their dependants, usually in the most lucrative offices and sinecures. 'The price of this system of indirect subsidies was enormous but incalculable, for it is obviously impossible to estimate how much of the salary paid to a placeman was remuneration for work done, and how much was a poltical sinecure; or how much the public interest suffered by men being preferred for political reasons where personal qualifications and merit should have decided.'[2]

The political consequences of the spoils system on this truly magnificent scale were most damaging in the government of the colonies where aristocratic self-government in the British sense was difficult or impossible, while its inevitable effects—favouritism, inefficiency and corruption—were only too prevalent. Even the government of the American colonies was not genuine self-government by the population, although in many cases the colonists opposed the Governors and their officials with some success. The system showed British administration at its worst, and the large, if subordinate, share of personal ineptitude and crass inefficiency in the loss of the American colonies is notorious.

The country where the inherent defects of the aristocratic spoils system were combined with genuine bureaucratic power and degeneration on a serious scale was, however, Ireland: 'The colonial government of Ireland was a composite mechanism established for the double purpose of ensuring the maintenance of English power over the subject country and the "ascendancy" of the landlords over

[1] Namier, op. cit., p. 150.　　[2] Namier, op. cit., p. 205.

their subject classes. . . . The exploitation of the resources of the Irish State for the purposes of the British ruling classes was effected through three main channels: the appointment of incompetent Englishmen to responsible posts in Ireland; the transformation of great offices of State into sinecures by their grant to absentees; and the burdening of the Irish establishment with pensions which had no relationship to services rendered to or in Ireland. . . . The exploitation of the Irish Government and revenue by the English aristocracy was merely the spectacular climax of the pettier but even more thorough exploitation of their privileged position by the men on top of the Irish administration itself. . . . The subordination of all other interests but their own to their duty as servants of the British Government made the leaders of the bureaucracy the absolute masters of Ireland. It was, as Henry Grattan bitterly called it, "a monarchy of clerks, a government carried on by post and under the dominion of spies".[1]

The Social Basis of Civil Service Reform

Although the unreformed House of Commons survived the breakdown of Court Government by half a century, the technical inefficiency of the administrative system which had contributed its share to the loss of the Old Empire was a serious threat to Britain's success as a great power in the struggle with post-revolutionary France. Though parliamentary reform remained impossible for the time being, the younger Pitt carried out an energetic programme of economic and fiscal renovation. These reforms involved a gradual reduction in the number of sinecures, but on the whole they were less concerned with the personnel of the administration than with its machinery, and particularly with its archaic fiscal organization. The process was continued by Pitt's Tory successors until the end of their long rule and extended to other spheres badly in need of it, particularly the law courts, the prisons and the police.

The accession of a Whig Government in 1830 speeded up the reform of the financial system and of the armed forces. Perhaps even more important, it extended the influence of the central government

---

[1] E. Strauss, *Irish Nationalism and British Democracy* (1951), pp. 29 ff.

and laid the basis for a reform of local administration, thereby further reducing the area of aristocratic self-government at a time when the Reform Act gave the middle classes a chance of increasing their influence on the Government.

Immediately after the reform of parliament one of the most important Factory Acts was put on the Statute Book (1833). These Acts were the sign of a new era in legislation and administration. They created an independent Factory Inspectorate which tried to limit the excesses of the early industrial system and had a strong influence on the advance of social legislation. Even more important was the New Poor Law of 1834, like the Factory Act a consequence of the social problems caused by the industrialization of the country but very unlike it in its effects on the moral and material position of the working classes. Its outstanding administrative feature was the establishment of a central Poor Law Board under powerful Commissioners in pointed contrast to the local anarchy of the Old Poor Law. The municipal corporations of England followed suit a year later, the reorganization of the police and prison system was completed and the first Public Health Act, providing for another central Board, was enacted in 1848.

These new Boards were from the outset different from the traditional mould of British public authorities. They extended the responsibilities of the State to new spheres, experts replaced amateurs and specialization became the watchword of the day. This change was intimately connected with the growing friction between the squirearchy and the modern business classes. The social legislation of the 1830s and 1840s was to a large extent conditioned by the political situation, though this aspect may not always have been so clear to the leaders as to comparative outsiders such as Benjamin Disraeli.

The criticism of the condition of the country by the rising middle classes was not limited to its institutions but included the traditional methods of administration and, above all, its personnel. A substantial part of the civil service consisted of retainers of the old gentry to whose patronage officials owed their jobs and whose interests were normally far removed from the ungenteel affairs of modern industrial business. The robust attitude of the impatient middle-class reformers inspired Dickens' satire of the traditional bureaucracy in *Little Dorrit*, characteristically with a mechanical inventor as the victim of bureaucratic arrogance and imbecility. The ultimate stronghold of the old order was, of course, the Foreign Office—according to John Bright the outdoor relief department of the British aristocracy—which clung to patronage as the principle of staff selection long after its abandonment in the Home Civil Service.

The personnel of the great departments of State thus consisted of clerks who owed their appointments to the patronage of the heads of department or other influential patrons and who 'progressed upwards by seniority alone, as death made room'.[1] Such abuse of manpower was rapidly becoming obsolete with the growth in the number and size of public offices. Patronage as the general principle of selection is possible only in conditions where the governing classes form an enlarged family circle and Government is a small-scale industry. A hundred years ago, the Home Office had fewer than one hundred officials and the Foreign Service about twice that number. Patronage might have furnished a sufficient number of socially reliable and not too inefficient recruits willing to waste their time on routine duties until their superiors had exercised their privilege of dying in harness. But the demands of a vigorously expanding industrial society imposed new duties on the machine of government which made a complete overhaul of the system of staff recruitment and staff organization imperative.

Technical needs were reinforced by social and political interests. With the shift of the centre of power from the landowners to the business classes a new test of fitness for public office had to be found: personal recommendation had to give way to impersonal methods of selection which ensured the choice of candidates of intellectual ability as well as suitable social background. From the point of view of the new rulers, the problem was the replacement, or at least the neutralization, of the aristocratic nonentities so vehemently attacked by the Radicals through capable members of the middle classes in key positions of the public service. As the growth of public administration proceeded apace and the number of suitable candidates was

[1] Sir John Craig, *A History of Red Tape* (1955), p. 85.

limited, a better division of functions within the service had to be devised and the new recruits were to be placed almost immediately in positions of authority instead of wasting valuable years in subordinate positions.

Both purposes were realized in the conception of the famous civil service reform which began with the Northcote-Trevelyan report of 1854. Although fear of the revolutionary movement of the 'mad year' 1848 may have influenced progressive Tories such as Sir Stafford Northcote it was, at the most, a secondary motive. More directly contributory was the reform of the universities—governed by comparable considerations—and the introduction of competitive examination in the Indian Service by the Charter Act of 1853. The success of the Report was by no means immediate: although a Civil Service Commission was set up, for the time being 'presentation' was not abolished but combined with a qualifying examination. Provided the favoured candidate passed the minimum tests required for the efficient performance of his duties—which consisted largely of spelling and arithmetic—he was appointed irrespective of the claims of abler competitors.

The social strategy of the civil service reform was clearly formulated by Gladstone, at that time still a Peelite Conservative, in a letter to Lord John Russell which advocated open competition as a reliable way of ensuring the appointment of 'gentlemen' to the leading posts in the government service: 'I have the strong impression that the aristocracy of this country are even superior in natural gifts, on the average, to the mass; but it is plain that with their acquired advantages, their *insensible education*, irrespective of book learning, they have an immense superiority. This applies in its degree to all those who may be called gentlemen by birth and training.' The pointed antithesis between 'gentlemen' and 'the mass' looked far beyond the carefully limited political arena of the mid-nineteenth century to the battlefield of modern democracy.

Gladstone's perspicacity also fastened on another crucial feature of the Report. The implication of the separation of routine work from administration and the establishment of separate channels of recruitment for different grades was the conception of an army of clerks officered by the academic *élite* of the middle classes: '. . . it is to be remembered that an essential part of any such plan as now under discussion is the separation of *work*, wherever it can be made, into mechanical and intellectual, a separation which will open to the highly educated classes a career, and give them command over all the higher parts of the civil service, which up to this time they have never enjoyed.'[1] However, on this occasion Gladstone did not convince the veteran fighter for Reform and Liberty, and Civil Service reorganization remained largely on paper. It was only after a series of steps that Gladstone, no longer a Peelite chrysalis but a brilliant Liberal butterfly, introduced in 1870 open competition as the general, though not universal, rule of entry into the Civil Service. As the Cabinet was divided on the measure, each minister was left free to introduce the new system in his department; historically this was the cause of the fifty years' delay in the acceptance of competitive examination by the Foreign Office.

The new organization of the Civil Service was a 'class' system in the literal sense, particularly after the replacement of the distinction between the first and the second 'division' by the current arrangement of three main classes (administrative, executive and clerical). In the original conception these classes were strictly separate, without any provision for promotion from the second division to the first. Although pressure from below, and the gradual change in the climate of British public life, caused a relaxation of the promotion bar after 1890, this hardly affected the narrow class basis of the higher Civil Service before the first World War. Between 1890 and 1911 only eighty-four promotions occurred and these were 'concentrated on Customs and Excise, Admiralty, Inland Revenue, Works, Post Office, Local Government Board and Board of Trade'[2]—virtually to the exclusion of the policy-making ministries.

At the outbreak of the first World War, new entrants to the top branch of the Civil Service belonged almost without exception to the upper and middle classes, candidates for the second division were divided about equally between the middle classes and the lower

---

[1] John Morley's *Life of Gladstone* (1st edn.) I. 649 (Appendix).
[2] Kelsall, op. cit., p. 41.

classes and the diminishing category of 'boy clerks' was recruited to a rather larger extent from amongst the lower classes.[1] During the first half-century of its existence, the reformed Civil Service thus completely bore out Gladstone's estimate of the social effects of the reform. The overwhelming majority of successful candidates for the higher grades of the service formed part and parcel of the dominant social groups, and it was one of the great merits of the new system that changes in the composition of these groups were adequately reflected in the direction of the administration: by 1912, some of the key positions in the Service were for the first time held by the sons of tradesmen, 'the direct result of replacing patronage by open competition; it was no longer necessary to have influence in order to gain a foothold in the Service. Nor was it necessary at this time to satisfy an interviewing Board as to your manners and general bearing.'[2]

2. FROM TORIES AND WHIGS TO CONSERVATIVES AND LABOUR

In the heyday of the political supremacy of the great landowners and the unreformed House of Commons, the conflict between the two political parties, though by no means without its social basis, was hardly more than a struggle between two coteries. The limited extension of the vote to the wealthier sections of the middle classes in 1832 made the House of Commons, for the first time in its long history, virtually independent of the Executive without subjecting it to close party discipline.

The parliamentary cliques were not changed overnight by a revolutionary convulsion but slowly broken up or gradually transformed by the pressure of outside forces. The split within the Whig Party after 1832, and the much more important schism within the Tory Party during and after the abolition of the Corn Laws in 1846, produced the greatest measure of re-alignment possible within the existing framework. The years between 1832 and 1867 were a time of

[1] Kelsall, op. cit., p. 26.
[2] *Ibid.*, p. 166.

small parliamentary majorities and shifting party lines; they witnessed the accession of an ex-Whig aristocrat and an ex-Radical man of letters to the leadership of the Tories, and in the evolution of William Ewart Gladstone the first part of the most astounding parliamentary career of the century, and perhaps of British parliamentarism as a whole.

Forward to Liberalism

In terms of party organization, the effects of the Reform Act of 1832 were at first far from revolutionary. The increase in the number of voters, though substantial, was not large enough to require elaborate party machines, but the enfranchisement of a numerous social group threatened the political monopoly of the traditional cliques and thereby stimulated them to greater organizational efforts in which the Whips' offices played an important part. The 'registration societies' of the period were mainly concerned with the new electoral regulations, and for the greater part of the period before 1867 their political significance was small. Of greater immediate importance was the creation of the two famous political clubs—the Tory Carlton in 1831 and the Liberal Reform in 1836—which formed an ideal background for the operations of the Whips and party managers in their attempts to control members of parliament in the interests of their respective parties. But the comparative ease with which the parliamentary phalanx of country gentlemen on the Tory side could be disciplined in normal circumstances did not prevent the breakup of the party on the issue of agricultural protection, with Peel and Graham heading the progressive seceders and Lord George Bentinck and Disraeli maintaining the traditional policy.

The ultimate cause of this internal crisis of the Tory Party was the change in the structure of British society into a modern industrial nation. This change was only a little less unwelcome to the Whig leaders than to their counterparts on the Tory side, and it was only after the disappearance of Palmerston and Lord John Russell that the new men under Gladstone's leadership rose to power. By then the party had been substantially permeated by the rising middle classes who were no longer disposed to tolerate the tutelage of the old oligarchy in government and politics, particularly since the collapse of the Chartist movement in 1848 had removed the threat of an aggressive working-class movement from their rear.

In this process party organization played an indispensable part. After the Whig leaders had resisted the pressure of the middle classes through the registration societies for a considerable time, they were compelled in 1861 to accept the establishment of the Liberal Registration Association which was the precursor, though not the parent, of the famous Liberal party organization of the next decade. The household franchise Act of 1867 created a large new urban electorate, and the introduction of inwieldy three-member constituencies called for a disciplined and intelligently led mass organization which became the ideal popular basis for the hard-headed leaders of the new Radicalism. Many of them combined advanced political views with remarkable business acumen and organizing ability, and their efforts to obtain a bigger share in political power inevitably took the form of organized attempts to use the new democracy of the industrial towns of England and Scotland for this purpose.

The history of this new departure in British politics is bound up with Birmingham, which had once before been the cradle of a radical political movement, and with the early career of Joseph Chamberlain. The Birmingham Liberal organization, which its enemies denounced as 'the Caucus', was the New Model whose extension to the whole country became the aim of the Radicals in their struggle with the aristocratic parliamentary clique: 'The opponents of the Caucus are not to be convinced—they hate it for its virtues and because it puts aside and utterly confounds all that club management and Pall Mall selection which has been going on for so long and which has made the Liberal Party the molluscous, boneless, nerveless thing it is.'[1]

Chamberlain's first attempt to capture the Liberal Party by organizing the masses of its supporters against the traditional leadership through the National Education League had not come off. He soon came to the conclusion that 'Education for the Ignorant cannot have the meaning that belonged to Bread for the Starving . . . the assis-

[1] J. L. Garvin, *The Life of Joseph Chamberlain* (1932), I, p. 262.

tance of the working classes is not to be looked for without much extension of the argument'.[1] Hence his search for a more effective point of political leverage which he hoped to find in a reunion between the dissenters and the working class, and particularly the agricultural labourers: 'Free Church and Free Land are the best available wedges for forcing the gates of Conservative obstruction.'[2]

The success of the new, and formally democratic, Liberal party organization was due to the temporary co-operation of two essentially separate interests: the need of the business classes for mass support against the outmoded parliamentary cliques, and the need of the workers for respectable allies in their efforts to obtain political influence after the failure of their independent radical movement in the defeat of Chartism.

The Radicals could not succeed without harnessing the forces of democracy to their wagon, but they always intended to treat the masses as junior partners and to reserve policy decisions for themselves. They did not regard the reformed Liberal Party as an instrument of democratic self-determination for the unprivileged majority but as a political weapon for the realization of their own purposes. The politically active elements of the lower midddle and working classes of the towns were ripe for these Radical advances, because they were eager to use their newly gained political rights in order to transform the 'poor man's purgatory' in which they lived into a modern democracy conscious of its duty towards its underprivileged and uneducated 'masters'. But a moment was bound to come when the interests of the Liberal 'wirepullers' and those of their enthusiastic and hard-working working-class supporters pulled into opposite directions.

The friction between Whigs and Radicals intensified during Gladstone's second ministry, but the final conflict split the party on completely unexpected lines, because it was fought on the issue of Home Rule for Ireland. The Home Rule crisis deprived the Liberal Party not only of nearly all the Whig aristocrats but also of most of the solid business men who followed the creator of the Caucus, Joseph

[1] J. L. Garvin, *The Life of Joseph Chamberlain* (1932), I., p. 146.
[2] *Ibid.*, pp. 218 f.

Chamberlain, into the Unionist camp. It also demonstrated the limits of machine rule over the Liberal party organization.

If the 'Caucus' had really been a party machine in the American sense, a party bureaucracy dominated by a handful of clever manipulators in their own interests, it would have adopted their change of front; in fact, the party workers rallied enthusiastically behind Gladstone and inflicted a crushing defeat on the creators of the organization, Chamberlain and Harris, who were driven into the wilderness. Although in Birmingham itself Chamberlain managed to get a vote of confidence from the 'Two Thousands', the delegates of the local party members, he found after long and careful manoeuvres that his new policy was irreconcilable with leadership of the Birmingham Liberals. After his final break with the Liberals he got the better of his old organization with the help of the Conservatives who had meanwhile set up a party machine of their own: the era of 'Conservative and Unionist' organization was dawning.

Tory Democracy

Modern democracy in Britain began with the Reform Act of 1867 which was the work of a Conservative government, but the Tories had good reason to fear its effect on their parliamentary position. The success of the Radicals in organizing mass support for the Liberals had to be countered by similar methods, if a permanent Liberal majority in the House of Commons was to be avoided. As early as 1868 the constituency associations of the Conservative Party were united into a National Union which proved its electoral value at the elections of 1874, but it was not until the 1880s that it absorbed something of the spirit of modern mass organizations.

The problem of the Tory leaders was the converse of that exercising the mind of Chamberlain and his Radical associates. Instead of obtaining mass support for 'progressive' business men by appealing to the common interests of the workers and the middle classes against the old governing groups, the Tories went back to the ideas of the young Disraeli who had dreamed of exploiting the conflict of interests between capital and labour in the service of aristocratic privilege. During the hungry forties Disraeli claimed that the lower classes were conservative by nature and opposed to the Liberal representatives of their capitalist oppressors. But this contention had never been fully convincing and with the passage of time it lost most of the force it may have had in its day. The natural handicap of the Tories in wooing the masses had, therefore, to be balanced by appeals to the rising tide of imperialist sentiment and by rank demagogy.

The reorganization of the Conservative Party organization by such means, and admittedly in imitation of the Liberal organization, was even more closely bound up with the erratic career of Lord Randolph Churchill than the foundation of the Caucus with Joseph Chamberlain. At the same time, Lord Randolph was sincerely convinced of the need for far-reaching social changes and paid the penalty of his convictions in full measure.

'Tory democracy', like the 'Tory Radicalism' of the previous generation, may have been—in Gladstone's words—'demagogism . . . living upon the fomentation of angry passions, and still in secret as obstinately attached as ever to the evil principle of class interests',[1] but its success under a colourful popular leader was a fact which the leaders of the Parliamentary Tory Party in both Houses could not ignore. Lord Randolph Churchill quickly rose to political eminence and high office, and seemed to be destined to realize the political dreams of the young Disraeli whose handicaps did not exist for the scion of the Dukes of Marlborough. The new 'Conservative Parliament' was a serious challenge to the 'aristocratic cliques' entrenched in parliament, and Lord Salisbury had to negotiate with Churchill as one power with another, though he 'never showed the slightest disposition to grant the National Union effective control over policy, finance or candidatures'.[2]

It is impossible to decide whether the hope of transforming the Tories into a modern democratic mass party was at any time more than a pipe dream, for the political earthquake of the first Home Rule crisis radically altered the balance of power in favour of the official leadership. The split within the Liberal ranks between Home Rulers and Unionists brought the majority of business interests over to the

[1] Morley's *Life*, II., 413 (1905 edn.).
[2] R. T. Mackenzie, *British Political Parties* (1955), p. 173.

Conservatives, or made them dependent on Conservative support. Gladstone and his followers were severely beaten at the elections of 1886 and the Conservative leaders were soon able to turn the tables on the over-confident idol of the Tory democrats who eliminated himself by resigning once too often. When Lord Randolph Churchill 'forgot Goschen', Salisbury was only too glad to get rid of a dangerous critic whose usefulness was at an end and who could no longer seriously injure his opponents. The Conservative Party organization was reshaped on lines which made it a safe adjunct and instrument of the party leadership, and this position it has maintained ever since.

1886 was thus a critical date in British party history. The Tories settled permanently their organizational relations with the near-democratic electorate and attracted a large contingent of the upper and middle classes from the Liberals. The Liberal Unionists, Whigs and Radicals alike, maintained for some time a precarious independence between the main parties, and their absorption by the Tories was retarded by the Free Trade controversy in the opening years of the twentieth century. However they, no less than later recruits from the Liberal ranks, were ultimately integrated into the Conservative Party which became increasingly the bulwark of all sections of the governing classes, with a leadership which effectively reflected the continuing shift from the landed interest to the rule of modern big business.

The Growth of the Labour Movement

The Liberal Party had a splendid tradition, an elaborate and efficient organization, a gifted leadership and the support of a large section of the electorate, but its abandonment by the majority of the business interests decisively weakened its political position. In the last resort, it destroyed its *raison d'être* as a coalition between one section of the privileged minority and the majority of the lower classes, although its most brilliant performance as a progressive alliance of these elements took place as late as 1906-14, when the Free Trade dispute within the Tory ranks rallied an important section of the business classes around the old Liberal slogans.

The latent conflict between the Liberal leaders and their working-class supporters was not allayed, and may have been intensified, by the change of front of Joseph Chamberlain and his associates. Within the Caucus, the rank-and-file proved its political independence of the managers of the organization, but the split strengthened the hands of the parliamentarians under Gladstone who were fundamentally much less in sympathy with the social aspirations of the masses than the Radicals. Of the twin pillars of Chamberlain's edifice—the Dissenters and the workers—it was the former whose influence on Liberal policy became paramount, and the 'non-conformist conscience' produced disastrous effects on the fortunes of the Liberal Party in the Parnell crisis which Chamberlain engineered through Captain O'Shea. The spokesmen of the industrial workers, on the other hand, had reason to regard the framework of Liberal policy and organization as a strait waistcoat which they ultimately threw off through the formation of an independent political party of their own.

This process was speeded up by the reluctance of the local leaders of the Liberal Party caucuses to accept working-class candidates in constituencies where they would have stood a good chance of success. This was not surprising, because the dominant personalities and financial backers of the local Liberal organizations were as a rule recruited from the industrial middle class. The highly respectable trade union officials who found themselves thus cold-shouldered by Liberalism would have dearly wished to retain their allegiance to the party of Gladstone and progress and to enter parliament as 'Lib.-Labs.', but the hostility of the local Liberals put them on the political defensive, while their socialist antagonists steadily gained ground amongst the workers.

The minute socialist organizations thrown up by the long economic depression of the 1880s were far from indifferent to the needs of the workers and played their part in the success of the 'new unionism', the extension of trade union organization to the unskilled workers. But in order to gain an effective mass basis they had to forge an alliance with the official union movement which was little interested in independent political action and far from favourably inclined towards socialism. In the foundation of the Independent Labour Party (1893), the socialists established a potential bridge to the unions, though the new departure soon came under criticism from the Fabians on the Right and the Social Democratic Federation on the Left. The inability of the Liberals to protect the unions by parliamentary action from the effects of adverse judicial decisions finally convinced the leaders of the trade union movement of the need for an independent working-class party, however sceptical they may have been about other aspects of socialist propaganda.

The ILP was a genuine political party with a nucleus of party workers whose activities were directed simultaneously towards the winning of elections and towards influence on the trade unions as their indispensable link with the working masses: 'The greatest achievement of Keir Hardie and his ILP lay in the capture of Trade Union support as early as 1900. The whole strategy of the party from its foundation in 1893 was based on the conception of collaboration with trade unionists with the ultimate object of tapping trade union funds for the attainment of Parliamentary power.'[1] This coalition character of the Labour movement on its political side became even more strongly marked with the establishment of the Labour Representation Committee in 1900 and its transformation into the Labour Party after the electoral victory of 1906.

The small but dynamic body of socialist propagandists thus managed to 'permeate' the trade union movement but not without changing its own character in the process. This change was accomplished very quickly, for the Liberals regarded an understanding with the new Labour movement as vitally important for the purpose of dislodging the disunited Conservatives and Unionists from the government. For this reason the Liberal Central Office under Herbert Gladstone employed its influence in order to ensure the success of Labour members in constituencies where they stood the best chance of ejecting the Conservatives. The inevitable consequence of the close comradeship of this period, ably supported on the Labour side by Ramsay MacDonald, was the intimate alliance of the Labour Party with the Liberal government after 1906. Until the outbreak of the first

[1] H. Pelling, *The Origins of the Labour Party, 1880-1900* (1954), p. 233.

World War the parliamentary Labour Party was, in fact, little more than the extreme left wing of the government majority—a striking example of the growth of a new political force carved out of the body of another party without a split in its ranks and with the active assistance of its leadership.

The Liberal Party rendered perhaps its greatest historical service to the established order by leading the great majority of the British people united into war, but in so doing it not only split the official Labour movement but prepared its own demise as an effective political force. The feud between Lloyd George Liberals and Asquithian Liberals completed the process begun by Joseph Chamberlain in 1886: it drove the business classes almost to a man into the Conservative camp and permanently destroyed the chances of the Liberals of regaining power. Despite their large following they were thenceforth incapable of overcoming the handicap of a third party under the British electoral system, against which the Labour Party triumphantly asserted itself as the political rallying point of the opponents of big business rule. As if to leave no doubt about this claim it accepted a definitely socialist programme at the end of the first World War.

3. DEMOCRACY AND THE PARTY SYSTEM

Since the disintegration of the Liberals after 1918, British politics have increasingly reverted to the classical two-party system, with the Conservatives championing all sections of the property owning minority and the Labour Party basing itself mainly on the organized manual workers.

Form and Contents of the Conservative Party

In a political democracy, the Conservatives could not have retained the allegiance of half the electorate without widening their appeal well beyond the primary beneficiaries of their policies; in fact, the major proportion of the black-coated workers and a substantial section of the industrial working classes are normally content to accept their rule either from choice or from a much stronger antagonism towards the Labour Party. The social realities of the situation are clearly reflected in the Conservative Party organization. It is dominated by an outside power, the Leader elected by the parliamentarians; even when the election follows elevation to the Premiership this is no real exception to the rule, for the first qualification of a potential Prime Minister is his ability to command the support of the party in parliament.

Once installed, the Leader appoints the chairman of the party organization who directs its administration through the Conservative Central Office and its branches. The voluntary party workers in charge of the constituency parties are united in the National Union of Conservative and Unionist Associations which acts 'as an electoral machine and channel of communication between the parliamentary leaders and their followers in the country'[1] but has no direct influence on 'the determination of policy, the raising of funds and the selection of candidates'[2] which are the preserve of the official leadership. Although democratic neither in theory nor in practice, the system ensures that the primary social forces behind the Conservative Party maintain their position as the pivot of party policy and keep effective charge of the administrative system created for the purpose of influencing, directing and controlling the masses of their supporters.

A party of this character is inevitably exposed to the direct pressure of powerful vested interests but its political centre of gravity lies in parliament, and the Parliamentary Party is a reasonably accurate reflection of its primary social forces. The record of the Conservative Party in parliament does not bear out the frequent claim that it is the mere creature of the party Whips and managers. This was not true even during its most questionable era, the years immediately preceding the second World War, when the authority of the Whips was used relatively freely in order to ensure compliance with a disastrous policy culminating in a state of scandalous national unpreparedness at the outbreak of war.

[1] Mackenzie, op. cit., p. 180.
[2] *Ibid.*, p. 210.

By and large, the party machine acted under heavy provocation and showed remarkable restraint. Almost from the beginning of the 'National Government', the official leadership was incessantly under fire from an organized group of brilliant *frondeurs* inspired by the dominant personality of the party who disagreed with its approach to the most important questions of imperial and foreign policy—India and Ireland, rearmament and the relations with Nazi Germany and Fascist Italy. Nevertheless, Mr Churchill and Mr Chamberlain, Mr Eden and Sir Samuel Hoare, Lord Cranborne and Lord London-derry continued to belong to the same party and some of them, at times, even to the same Government.

The party machine did little, if anything, to falsify the true current of opinion within the Conservative Party, and even the balance of power between the leaders and their critics may not have been changed appreciably by its activities. The lack of bureaucratic rigidity of the party was fairly demonstrated by its metamorphosis between the spring of 1938 and the spring of 1940. Although it took an earthquake to replace the high priest of appeasement by the organizer of victory, the allegiance of the—largely unchanged—Conservative Party to Mr Churchill was no less enthusiastic and sincere than the new leader's devotion to its essential interests. The Conservative party's post-war record of recovery from the unexpected debacle of 1945 again proved its powers of recuperation and its ability to attract new talent to its service. The chequered history of the Conservative governments of the 1950s, and above all the dangerous Suez crisis, revealed the same elasticity in the central direction of the party, though not amongst its local supporters who stubbornly refused to put up with the services of 'left deviationists', while the party leaders were willing and eager to forgive and forget in the interest of a common front against the real enemy.

Organization and Policies in the Labour Party

Compared with the simplicity of the Conservatives, the Labour Party is a complex and problematical body. The original coalition between the small socialist propaganda societies and the Unions underwent its first important change with the reconstitution of the Labour

Party after the first World War. Previously it had been a kind of standing committee of its constituent bodies for the specific purpose of independent Labour representation in the House of Commons; henceforth it was to be a fully-fledged political party with a national organization of its own and with group association supplemented by individual membership.

The inevitable victim of this new conception was the originator of the party, the ILP, which lost its position as the political arm of the whole movement and tended to be regarded as an interloper on its home ground of local political organization. Its old leaders, Mac-Donald and Snowden, by-passed or abandoned it, because they were out of sympathy with its loyalty to the ideas of a by-gone era and out-raged by its opposition to the policy of the first two Labour governments. It was, however, characteristic that the final break occurred over an organizational issue, the acceptance of the standing orders of the Parliamentary Labour Party by the ILP.

The stalwarts of the ILP, like other British socialists, were thus confronted with the choice between accepting the organization and policy of the Labour Party or cutting themselves off from the main-stream of British working-class politics. But if they could not do without the Labour Party, the latter could not do without local 'militants', if it wanted to keep its organization and electoral machine alive throughout the country.

The local party leaders and officials in charge of the constituency parties are, with rare exceptions, not political 'extremists' out to ex-ploit their positions for the purpose of undermining the party leader-ship. They are on the contrary firmly loyal to the organization of the Labour Party which gives them the opportunity of using abilities which frequently do not find adequate use in their daily lives. They find their most important arena of political self-expression in local politics, and particularly in the representative institutions of local government in borough and county councils. In this field they are no more and no less activated by 'idealistic' or 'realistic' motives than other parts of the Labour movement, and are far from enthusiastic about radical innovations.

Their distinctive characteristic in national affairs and in their attitude towards the policy of the official Labour movement is neither high-flying enthusiasm nor sympathy with the views of the extreme Left, but their relative freedom from immediate involvement. For this reason they tend to regard the Labour movement—outside their own local affairs—much more as an instrument for the realization of its socialist aspirations than is compatible with the facts of the general situation. Their relatively independent status, much more than a consistent and reasoned approach towards the political problems of the day, thus creates the possibility of friction between the local constituency parties and the vested interests in possession of the power centres of the Labour movement—the trade unions in control of the party's finances and the Parliamentary Party in effective charge of its policies.

The structural problems of the trade unions, their effectiveness and their relations with their members, are outside the scope of the present analysis. They are commonly criticized as being too large and too remote from the mass of their members, and there is a fair amount of *prima facie* evidence for this criticism though such broad generalizations do not do justice to the variety of union size and type. In the political field there is a similar range of views, but in their passage through Union Conferences, the Trades Union Congress and the Labour Party Conference these tend to assume the colour of the dominant machine. In spectacular cases this may involve a reversal of previous decisions on cardinal political issues, or even a radical change in the general political attitude of a large union following changes in its key officials. The powerful hold of the unions on the Labour Party is concentrated in the hands of the central union bureaucracies and maintained by means of the majority of union nominees on the National Executive Committee of the Labour Party and of the financial dependence of the central party organization on union funds.

This duality of the party organization which normally takes the form of an underground tug-of-war but sometimes flares up into open conflict is one of the main causes of tension within the Labour Party. It has resulted in the establishment of a strong and bureaucratic central party machine which asserts itself against the radical-

ism of the local party workers by means ranging from negative control of the selection of candidates to the lavish use of disciplinary
measures culminating in the expulsion of individuals from the party
and the disaffiliation of whole branches. But while the central party
administration has some of the characteristics of a ruling bureaucracy in its relations with the rank-and-file membership, it remains
broadly dependent on its primary force, the official leadership of the
trade unions, and has become increasingly amenable to the influence
of the parliamentary leadership. However, this dependence is more
a matter of the last resort than of day-to-day control and may not be
an adequate safeguard against bureaucratic defects such as an inclin-
ation towards routine and a lack of creative imagination. It is, therefore, not due to chance that 'Transport House' has recurrent bouts
of weakness which tend to make it an uninspired and insufficiently
forward-looking organization with a corresponding decline in its usefulness as an instrument of political action.

The lack of coherence and common purpose of the party's organization is reflected in its nominally supreme organ, the Annual Conference. This is a composite body consisting of representatives of
the unions, of the individual membership of the constituency parties
and of a few socialist societies. The voting strength of the unions
is based on their membership paying the 'political levy' and therefore a multiple of that of the individual party members and the small
affiliated societies; it is further reinforced by the device of the 'block
vote' which throws the support of all delegates from each Union behind their majority, thus putting a disproportionate premium on
strength in the same way in which the electoral system deprives the
minority vote in each constituency of effective representation. Up
to 1937, there was in addition a union veto on the constituency representatives on the National Executive. The acceptance of the constituency parties as a separate section for the purpose of electing
their representatives on the National Executive Committee acknowledged their indispensable part in running the electoral machine
without amounting to more than an annual popularity poll amongst
the leading figures of the Parliamentary Labour Party. The Conference in its present form thus has the dual function of permitting

R   257

the organized democratic self-expression of the party membership and of providing the ultimate sanction for the predominant position of the unions.

The Labour Party as an organization is firmly ruled by the trade unions through their majority both at the Conference and on its executive, as well as through their hold on the central party machine. But the party organization in all its branches has only a relatively limited say in determining the policy of the Parliamentary Labour Party, which is in principle governed by the policy decisions of the party's Annual Conference but in practice determined by the Parliamentary Party itself.

Socialism and the Parliamentary System

The coalition character of the British Labour movement has been reflected from the start in the composition of its Parliamentary Party. The majority consisted of trade unionists many of whom owed their seats to Liberal assistance and retained strong Liberal sympathies; the leadership contained a strong element of ILP men such as Keir Hardie, MacDonald and Snowden, or Fabians such as Sidney Webb. With the rise of the party to the dignity of the official parliamentary opposition, the parliamentary leadership became an alternative government and tended to assert its independence. The personnel of the first Labour Government was settled by the traditional process of free choice by the party 'leader' within the limits of the internal balance of power, and the majority of the party regarded its performance mainly as a test of its ability to manage the machinery of government in the traditional way.

The party leaders fiercely resented the radical (ILP) criticism that a minority Labour administration ought to use its position mainly for the purpose of demonstrating its socialist convictions, and rejected demands for a greater measure of rank-and-file influence on the personnel and policy of a future Labour Government. MacDonald scorned the ideas of H. N. Brailsford, an editor 'with no executive responsibility' who claimed to know 'how he would act if he were King, Lords and Commons combined, the head of every Department of State and all the Under Secretaries as well', thus clearly indicating the point of cleavage between a mass organization and a 'responsible' parliamentary group forming part and parcel of the British political system. He condemned just as strongly the 'schemes and proposals' passed at party conferences 'by the votes of delegates who will never have to explain or defend them' and warned that 'no Parliamentary Party worth its salt will allow its work to be settled for it by bodies who will not have to face Parliamentary attack'.[1]

MacDonald's doctrines were discredited in the eyes of the Labour movement by the practice of the second Labour Government and by his defection, and during the 1930s the balance of power shifted from the small and ineffective parliamentary party back to the union leaders whose influence determined the rejection of Lord Morrison as party leader and the selection of Lord Attlee as compromise candidate. During this period the political direction of the Labour movement was largely centred in the National Council of Labour which was securely dominated by the unions. With the entry of the Labour party into the war-time coalition government, the virtual cessation of elections and the recognition of the unions as an Estate of the Realm, the dividing lines between the political and the industrial wing of the movement became less distinct than at any time before or since, a process symbolized by the translation of Ernest Bevin from Transport House to Westminster and the War Cabinet.

The landslide victory of the Labour Party at the elections of 1945 owed comparatively little to the efforts of local party workers and almost everything to the course of history. The first majority Labour Government was the result of a mass revulsion from the rule of the Conservatives as the party responsible for British pre-war policy and an expression of widely held hopes for a different and better future. The solid achievements of the Labour Government of 1945-50 may not have fulfilled these high-pitched expectations, but they riveted the loyalty of its supporters to the Labour Party, while inducing its enemies to strain every nerve to oust Labour from office.

The steady retreat from—real or imagined—radical socialism, which was already evident at the elections of 1950 and 1951 and

[1] Fenner Brockway, *Socialism Over Sixty Years* (*The Life of Jowett of Bradford*) (1946), pp. 229 f.

gathered speed throughout the 1950s, was accompanied by a steady decline in the electoral fortunes of the Labour Party; it is probably more than a coincidence that this process was paralleled by a steady shift in the balance of power within the Labour movement which established the supremacy of the parliamentary group over the party and that of the ministerial caucus, whether in office or in opposition, over the Parliamentary Party: 'The Parliamentary Party for the most part receives the advice it wants to hear from the National Executive Committee and the Party conference, first, because the Parliamentary Labour Party normally dominates the National Executive Committee by the system of overlapping membership, and second because the Parliamentary Labour Party leaders are usually in effective control of the conference since the block votes of the big Trade Unions are almost invariably cast on the side of the parliamentary leaders of the Party. And on those rare occasions when the National Executive Committee of the conference (despite these safeguards) tells the Parliamentary Labour Party what it does not want to hear, it is by no means inevitable that the Parliamentary Labour Party will accept the advice or "instructions" tendered to it.'[1]

This emergence of the Parliamentary Labour Party as the true centre of power and that of its leader as party leader with powers comparable to those of the Prime Minister on the government side has introduced an important new factor into the Labour movement. From the parliamentary point of view, the function of the Labour movement outside the House is entirely that of an electoral auxiliary with the task of ensuring the election of the largest possible number of members of parliament. Extra-curricular activities by the rank and file of the constituency parties, such as the expression of opinions on the political issues of the day, are at best superfluous and generally positively dangerous, because they are likely to frighten off potential supporters. Although the power of the unions is too great to make it possible to look at them in the same way, their support may be more of a necessary evil than a boon at times when public impatience with strikes and other labour disputes may make close identification with the trade unions an electoral liability.

[1] Mackenzie, op. cit., p. 424.

The supreme deity of the parliamentary mythology is the 'floating voter' whose support or defection may make all the difference between victory and defeat—provided that the enthusiastic loyalty of the traditional supporters of the party remains unimpaired. In its natural preoccupation with election results, the parliamentary leadership tends to visualize politics in the light of a game of skill with the aim of detaching marginal government supporters from their precarious allegiance and tempting them to the side of the opposition. Despite its apparent realism, this policy suffers from incurable defects for a party of the character and in the position of the Labour Party.

This is due to its natural handicap as an alternative government within the British party system, because the business classes as a whole do not regard it as an acceptable, if inferior, substitue for the Conservatives, and in the words of the late Professor H. J. Laski, 'in a capitalist society, the possession of confidence from those who own and operate the instruments of production is pivotal to successful government'.[1] Only when the Conservative rulers of the country fail to convince a majority of the effective electorate, within the limits of the electoral system, that a business administration is preferable to an anti-business administration does this handicap turn into an electoral asset. This is unlikely to happen in times of economic prosperity. The policy of wooing the marginal voter at the expense of the Labour Party's socialist programme is thus unlikely to be successful except at a time when he might well regard these principles in a favourable light. It is essentially based on the requirements of a parliamentary party within the British party system rather than on the long-term interests of a popular movement—but this does not alter the fact that within the limits of the British political system a movement cannot operate effectively except through a parliamentary party.

The labour movement is thus in danger of becoming immobilized by a frustrating balance of its elements, the coalition of voluntary workers in the constituencies, the trade-union financed central party organization with an Executive representing the union majority and

[1] H. J. Laski, *Parliamentary Government in England* (1938), p. 198.

the constituency minority at the Annual Conference, and the Parliamentary Party. The unions agree with the parliamentarians on the need for close control over the constituency parties and with the latter on the working-class character of the movement. The constituency parties disagree with the desire of the unions and the parliamentary leadership to confine them to the subordinate role of a local party machine for the fighting of elections on programmes determined by the central leaders. They, as well as the unions, disagree with the limitation of the party's policy to measures likely to appeal to all non-Conservatives in the hope of catching enough marginal voters to obtain office.

This complex system of conflicting forces bears witness to the fact that the British Labour movement remains a living social organism and has not been transformed into a bureaucratic party machine. It is, however, essentially unstable and liable to be upset by a change in the internal balance of power. The history of the Labour Party and the logic of the British party system as a whole suggest that the most likely change is in the direction of a further increase in the weight of the parliamentary leadership. Such a development would almost certainly involve the growing use of the party organization for the purpose of crushing internal opposition. In this it would probably be successful, though at the price of reducing the efficiency of voluntary party work—and therefore the electoral chances of the party.

The ascendancy of the parliamentary leadership, which is the normal and healthy state of affairs on the Conservative side, thus constitutes a pathological symptom for a Labour movement with socialist aims and confronts it with an almost insoluble dilemma. It is, perhaps, for this reason that its opponents have always done their best to promote this process by denouncing every sign of self-assertion by the rank and file of the party as a departure from the traditions of the parliamentary system. As the latter has been created in response to pre-democratic conditions, this may not be untrue—but the price which the Labour Party would have to pay for this conformity might well be not only failure in its primary function but, paradoxically enough, default on its essential part in the parliamentary game—the provision of an alternative government.

Parties and Government

Despite the justified pride of the British people in its democratic tradition, the basic fact about British politics is the priority, both in time and importance, of the parliamentary system over democracy. During the eighteenth and early nineteenth centuries, the system of oligarchic self-government was based on the absence of democracy in the modern sense, and although there was no lack of extra-parliamentary movements before 1867, the organization of political power did not start, as a rule, with the voters and reach upwards to parliament and the government. Organized political parties were created, on the contrary, by the conscious efforts of the forces represented in parliament and reached downwards to the electors for the purpose of supplying those forces with a mass basis, when the course of social evolution made this necessary for the maintenance of their political power. The only exception to this rule, the Labour Party, remains in a somewhat anomalous position, because it has not succeeded in conforming completely to this type, though with increasing proximity to the exercise of political power it has made great strides in this direction.

If, therefore, in Walter Bagehot's phrase, 'party government is the vital principle of representative government', this is in the last analysis due to the fact that the British party system has always been moulded by the needs of the system of government. Its main purpose is that of a valuable, even indispensable, auxiliary in the task of settling which group should be given control of the Executive: 'The real business of a political party in Great Britain is to get a Government of its own leaders into office, and, if possible, keep it there.'[1] It depends on the point of view from which the process is observed whether it is described as a method of ensuring the parliamentary majority of possession of the Government or one of providing the Executive with a parliamentary majority.

Although British parliamentary democracy is undeniably successful in practice, some of its outstanding features are difficult to reconcile with democratic principles. In the first place there is an electoral system which cheerfully ignores the fundamental democratic

[1] H. J. Laski, *Parliamentary Government in England* (1938), p. 71.

demand of effective minority representation, because this may clash
with the primary purpose of supplying the Government of the day
with a clear-cut parliamentary majority. The arguments in favour of
a more equitable system are mainly sponsored by the Liberals, because single-member simple-majority voting has helped to destroy
them as an effective political factor. These arguments have never
made any impression on the front benches of the two main parties,
the actual and the potential government, which find the present system greatly to their liking, although its operation is by no means fair
between them and in practice tends to favour the Conservatives.

Another important effect of the domination of the party system by
the system of government is the elevation of the party leader to a
position of almost dictatorial power. This is a simple reflection of
the towering position of the Prime Minister in the government which
tends to give to general elections the character of plebiscites between rivals for the premiership: '. . . the leader of each of the great
parties is either Prime Minister or potential Prime Minister and it is
this fact, not the internal mechanisms of the party, which is the
governing influence in determining the role the leader plays in the
affairs of his party.'[1] The choice of the leader has become the politically most significant act in the life of a party, and neither the Conservatives nor Labour give the rank-and-file membership a chance of
influencing the result, because the election is reserved exclusively to
the parliamentarians.

The members of parliament, on their part, are necessarily subject
to varying degrees of party discipline which is administered in the
first place by the whips. Party discipline is, in the final analysis, the
means of ensuring that every member plays his part in defending or
attacking the government of the day which consists, as the case may
be, of the leaders of his own party or its opponents. As the existence
of the two-party system is incompatible with the election of 'independent' members of parliament, 'bolting' is either equivalent to
political extinction or a step towards a complete change in party
allegiance.

The behaviour of the parties in parliament is that of a Government

[1] Mackenzie, op. cit., p. 300.

and an anti-Government with their respective supporters, and this conception fashions parliamentary procedure and most parliamentary processes. The Opposition is an essential part of the system, and this is suitably expressed in its title and in the recognition of its official leader as a dignitary of State—as well as by the sluggishness of parliamentary life during periods of all-party government in a national emergency. If it is the function of the Opposition to oppose, it is that of the majority to defend the Government of the day in all its actions. Whatever its admirable qualities, an assembly organized in this manner is bound to become a shield for the Administration. When two disciplined but numerically unequal groups engage in this contest day after day, and session after session, with the outcome of the voting certain on virtually every issue before it has been joined, the parliamentary struggle inevitably becomes somewhat unreal, and the very need to contrive a difference between the parties on every item of the parliamentary agenda tends to create the impression that there is, in fact, no real difference between them.

For this reason many critics of the British party system have fastened on the apparent similarity of the political opponents in their relations with each other and with the government. Sarcastic references to the basically hollow and artificially inflated differences between Tweedledum and Tweedledee date back a long time. More than a century and a quarter ago, Tom Moore observed that:

> 'The Whigs, when in Office a short year or two,
> By a *lusus naturae* are turned into Tories.'

Some years earlier, and much more profoundly, William Hazlitt described the Whig of his day as 'but the fag-end of a Tory . . . the Opposition have pressed so long against the Ministry without effect that, being the softer substance, and made of more yielding materials, they have been moulded into their image and superscription, spelt backwards.'

From this brilliant 'conceit' it was only a short step to the denunciation of party strife in the House of Commons as a sham-fight with wooden swords: 'A Tory is the indispensable prop to the doubtful sense of self-importance and peevish inevitability of negative success which mark the life of a Whig leader or underling. . . . To overturn the one is to trip up the heels of the other. Their hostility is not directed against things at all, nor to effectual and decisive opposition to men, but to that sort of petty warfare and parliamentary *tracasserie*, of which there is neither end nor use. . . . Soft words and hard blows are a losing game to play at: and this, one would think, the Opposition, if they are sincere, must have found out long ago. But they rather wish to screen the Ministry, as their *locum tenens* in the receipt of the perquisites of office, and the abuse of power of which they themselves expect the reversion.' And the moral of this deadly analysis was driven home by a famous metaphor summing up his opinion of both parties: they reminded him 'of Opposition coaches, that raise a great dust or spatter one another with mud, but both travel the same road and arrive at the same destination'.[1]

Much of Hazlitt's invective remains as apt now as it was then, because there has been relatively little change in the relations between the political parties and the Executive. However, although Hazlitt has found many modern followers, in one important respect his analysis is no less out-of-date than the means of transport of the early nineteenth century. To regard 'the perquisites of office and the abuse of power' as the real object of political warfare is characteristic of an age in which the parties were little more than parliamentary cliques, because the great social problems of the time were prevented from entering parliament. With the establishment of political democracy, the House of Commons became the battle ground of wider interests than the 'Ins and Outs'—provided that these interests conformed to the rules of the parliamentary game.

By making parliament the effective link between the mass democracy and the real government of the country, democracy has been limited to a form where popular participation in the direction of public affairs consists in the casting of a vote at election times in carefully circumscribed conditions. These conditions admirably suit the Conservatives but tend to deprive the Labour Party of much of its political effectiveness, while making the struggle of third parties for parliamentary recognition an almost hopeless enterprise.

[1] W. Hazlitt, Preface to *Political Essays*, Collected Works (1902 edn.), III, 43 f.

The reverse of this successful insulation of parliament from much of the rough and tumble of a modern mass democracy is the serious limitation of its powers of control over the Government and its decline *vis-à-vis* the Executive during the democratic twentieth century.

4. THE PROSPECTS OF BUREAUCRACY IN GOVERNMENT

The power of the Executive in the British political system has always been great and in certain respects paramount. In its original shape as the royal prerogative it was carefully hemmed in by statutory limitations and made subject to parliamentary control through the doctrine of ministerial responsibility; on the administrative plane it has survived in the remarkable measure of discretion of the civil service over an extensive field, and, therefore, remains a very important fact.

The Real Power of the Civil Service

The gradual shift of the political centre of gravity from representative institutions towards the professional service of the State has subtly changed the content of traditional relationships while maintaining their forms. The outstanding instance is the changed character of that very ministerial responsibility which at one time was the embodiment of parliamentary supremacy and which is frequently still regarded in this light. With the domination of parliament by disciplined party groups, the resignation of ministers in response to parliamentary criticism has become virtually confined to occasions when they are being thrown to the wolves by their own leaders, as in the memorable cases of the Hoare-Laval agreement and Dr Dalton's budget leak. As a rule, ministers are covered by the solidarity of the whole government and its hold over the majority of the House of Commons. Their responsibility to parliament thus assumes mainly an administrative character and, viewed from this angle, it is the political expression of the lack of effective responsibility of the civil service. Its real result is to remove the actions of the civil service from the sphere of parliamentary criticism.

Similarly, the 'sound rule which requires Members of Parliament

267

to communicate with the Minister in charge of a department and not to make a direct approach to his officials' may have been designed to safeguard 'the status of Ministers in Parliament', but its most important consequence is the protection of his officials from political pressure of a kind not unusual in the United States and, at least before the fall of the Fourth Republic, in France: 'A civil servant might be deflected by the political influence of an MP or a group of MPs. He might be made to feel that his own future depended to some extent on the favour or disfavour in which he stood with members of the Legislature.'[1]

However, in everyday political life ministerial responsibility is much less important as the—problematical—ultimate sanction of the House of Commons against the Government than in the practice of parliamentary questions which allow members of parliament to voice criticism of administrative detail as well as of high policy. The great value of 'question time' as a check on bureaucratic abuses is undeniable, but circumstances have conspired to make it much less effective than in the past. The first reason for this deterioration is simply the huge increase in administration which makes it impossible to ventilate more than a minute fraction of the problems to which it gives rise, while increasing the number of questions so much as to depreciate their value. Another, and potentially even more important, reason is the growing disparity of knowledge between the questioner without access to the records of the department and the civil servants in full possession of the facts.

In many cases, answers may be bluntly refused as not in the public interest, but on the whole the civil service prefers the rapier to the bludgeon. The art of framing replies disarming criticism by formal denials, the technique of throwing off an awkward pursuer by feints and subterfuges and the subordination of the nominal purpose of supplying straightforward information to the real aim of protecting the minister from 'supplementaries' have reached a high pitch of perfection and are no doubt satisfying intellectual pastimes. At the same time such developments have set rather narrow limits to the

[1] William A. Robson, 'Bureaucracy and Democracy' in *The Civil Service in Britain and France* (1956), p. 10.

usefulness of this method of controlling the administration, not because of any inherent weakness of the system but as the result of a shift in the balance of power between questioners and respondents.

Perhaps the greatest institutional weakness of parliament as a means of controlling the administration is the fundamental conception of the parliamentary system as the scene of a continuous contest between defenders and attackers of the Government. This conception identifies the civil service, as the assumed tool and servant of the political government, with the political self-interest of the majority and compels the minority to formulate every issue in party-political terms. Criticism and justification of administrative actions alike thus inevitably assume a political character, and all too frequently cancel each other out without penetrating to the administrative reality behind the parliamentary contest. This deep-seated feature of British parliamentarism may also be the ultimate reason for the absence of a specialized committee system which is mistrusted alike by the parliamentary opposition, by the Government and, of course, by its official advisers as an encroachment on the rights of the Executive.

The civil service is, therefore, effectively cushioned against parliamentary control, though it has to put up with a certain amount of interference from this quarter. This independence is matched by its strong position in relation to its nominal superiors, the political government. The minister in charge of a department of State is normally assisted by one or more parliamentary secretaries and a parliamentary private secretary whose actual functions may be rather wider than their names imply but which relate primarily to the parliamentary aspect of the minister's duties, the representation and defence of his department in parliament.

As the head of a large administrative government office, however, the minister is entirely surrounded by 'his' permanent officials and must rely exclusively on them for the preparation and execution of policy. The higher civil servants are, therefore, 'permanent politicians' who do not 'so much work under the direction of the Minister as work with him',[1] and whose share in this co-operative effort has

[1] Kingsley, *Representative Bureaucracy*, p. 269.

inevitably grown with the enormous expansion in government activities during the last generation. At the same time they are the effective masters of the administrative machine of the Government, and
only the strongest minister would think of challenging them on their
home ground. As he spends a large part of his time as spokesman for
his department, and with briefs prepared for him by his officials, he is,
indeed, the last man capable of exercising independent outside control over its administration.

Even the minister's influence over his personnel is very limited,
for the appointment of the most senior officials in every department
is not in his hands but in those of the Prime Minister. This may be
rather more than a mere formality, but the arrangement greatly
strengthens the *de facto* powers of the Treasury, one of whose
permanent secretaries is the head of the Civil Service responsible for
advising the Prime Minister on the abilities and the suitability of
candidates for promotion to the highest posts.

This is, perhaps, the most spectacular manifestation of the 'managerial autonomy' achieved by the British Civil Service: 'In general,
the civil service is governed, not by Acts of Parliament, but by a series
of rules issued under the prerogative powers of the Crown . . . in
that process, the permanent officials in the Establishment Branch of
the Treasury emerge as the masters of the civil service. The constitutional responsibility of the Minister for the conduct of his own department remains, but the civil service is ruled from Whitehall rather
than Westminster.'[1] The fact that this development, so far from
being peculiar to Great Britain, is practically universal or at least
widespread only adds to its significance: 'This drift towards a syn-
dical State machine is one of the unnoticed oddities of the last fifty
years.'[2] In traditionally bureaucratic regimes this feature may simply
be the logical completion of a recognized process, but in a parliamentary democracy such as the British it contrasts strikingly with
the popular idea of an omnipotent House of Commons and a system
of public administration proud and content with its role of being
the humble servant of the elected representatives of the people.

[1] Kingsley, op. cit., pp. 188 f.
[2] Brian Chapman, *The Profession of Government* (1959), p. 297.

This conception must be revised in another sphere of great political and practical importance, that of local self-government which is, perhaps, the most characteristic institution of British democracy. The heyday of local autonomy passed with the power of the country squire, and during the nineteenth century the central government encroached again and again on the powers of the local authorities which gradually became more democratic but less independent. At present, the elected councils of counties, county boroughs, boroughs and urban and rural districts play a prominent part in the day-to-day administration of the country, but their initiative is ham-strung by their growing dependence on the national Government in the exercise of their most important functions, from the—rather in-complete—supervision of the local police by their watch committees to the stringent government control of their investment policy: 'The increase of official control over local government has weakened the responsibility and authority of the local laymen. Too often commit-tees are screens behind which official decisions are taken in the capital. . . . In some degree and in certain spheres of local government administration, laymen on councils have been relegated to the status of lay figures by the powers of control and supervision conferred upon central Government departments and exercised in practice for the most part by officials.'[1]

Considered in relation to parliament, to the political government and to the local authorities, the British Civil Service thus represents a powerful and largely autonomous force which must figure promin-ently in any realistic interpretation of the British system of govern-ment. In a very real sense, its independent position is both the con-dition of modern mass democracy and one of its most important limitations, because it ensures that, whatever the party in power, the actual government of the country remains firmly in the hands of its civil servants; and in contrast to the legally trained and legalistic bureaucrats of many European countries, the higher civil servants in Britain have retained to a remarkable extent the tradition of amateur gentlemen acting in the name of the law according to their corporate discretion.

[1] (Sir) K. C. Wheare, *Government by Committee* (1955), p. 250.

A Bureaucratic Britain?

It remains to be seen whether this position of tremendous influence and considerable power has transformed the British civil service into a 'triumphant bureaucracy' or a 'new despotism' as its critics claimed more than thirty years ago and continue to claim today. The expansion of the range of public administration through the Welfare State compels recourse to administrative tribunals and the use of delegated legislation, two of the features regarded as most objectionably bureaucratic by writers such as Sir Carleton Allen and Lord Hewart. In a political system which entrusts the Executive and its officials with a wide measure of discretionary power, the growth of these methods of government may justly give rise to alarm. However, not only are both of them indispensable, but neither of them raises insoluble problems of control, and the systematic attention to statutory instruments by a special parliamentary committee has produced little evidence of abuse. With the necessary vigilance and improvements in the provisions for an impartial review of official acts, these institutions are perfectly compatible with the highest standards of a modern democracy. Though evidence of the growing strength of public administration, their existence is no indication of bureaucracy in any but a very loose and vulgar sense: whether administrative power is legitimate authority or bureaucratic abuse depends less on its scale than on the conditions in which it is being employed.

The British Civil Service seems to be more vulnerable to charges of growing bureaucratic defects as an instrument of government. During the last half-century it has undergone two periods of massive war-time expansion followed by only partial post-war contraction, not perhaps an ideal background for the promotion of technical efficiency. After 1918, the wish for a return to normal 'peace-time' conditions was very much in evidence and may have contributed to a policy of recruitment and promotion which restricted the personnel of the highest grades to a narrow social class.

At the same time, there was a determined attempt 'to break down barriers between Departments'[1] and to strengthen the dominance of the Treasury, though there is not much reason to believe that the

---

[1] Sir Edward Bridges, *Portrait of a Profession* (Cambridge, 1950), p. 12.

main cause of this trend was a desire to raise the efficiency of the service. On the contrary, in the bald words of the Select Committee on National Expenditure, 'as far as the Treasury is concerned, the period from 1919 to 1939 was marked by an almost complete failure to foster the systematic study of organization as applied to Government Departments'. It was, on the whole, a time of stagnation and even reaction, which encouraged the growth of bureaucratic defects. 'Charges of congestion, duplication, insufficiency of delegation and slowness in reaching decisions' were frequently brought 'against the organization at the highest Departmental level'.[1]

The permanent Civil Service naturally and inevitably formed the backbone of the expanding government departments in existence at the outbreak of the second World War and the *cadres* of the new Ministries formed in its course, but the characteristic feature of the time was the outstanding contribution made to the success of the huge machinery of war-time administration by temporary civil servants from other walks of life. The two great reservoirs of recruitment for many of the most responsible posts were the universities and big business. At the highest level they were represented by Lord Keynes and Lord Woolton, both of whom soon occupied diplomatic and political key positions well above the ranks of the Civil Service. However, a large number of young Dons achieved prominence as administrators and policy makers, while business men were as a rule employed in mobilising and controlling their own and other industries, where their very presence assured the business community that its co-operation in war-time schemes of rationalization and concentration would not prejudice its long-term interests.

The general impression left by the performance of the Civil Service in war time is that war administration was not only too big but also too important to be left to professional civil servants, just as strategy was too important to be left to the generals. The relative ease with which the system of administration absorbed large numbers of outsiders for the duration of the war indicates, however, that the professional civil service was comparatively free from the caste spirit which distinguishes a ruling bureaucracy.

[1] 16th Report (HC 120, 1941-2), paras. 56, 85.

An opinion on the post-war performance of the Civil Service must largely be based on the indirect evidence of the successes and failures of the policies pursued by succeeding British Governments. In the absence of authentic information it is impossible to answer the question put by Lord Woolton in 1951 to the leading Treasury officials, 'whether the financial trouble into which the country had fallen was due to the advice that the civil servants had given to the previous Chancellor, or due to the fact that the Ministers had not taken their advice'.[1] Whether fair in the circumstances or not, the answer to questions such as this is fundamental to the issue of the efficiency of the administration on the highest level, that of the preparation and execution of top-level policy.

There obviously is a sphere where the advice of the civil servants is either not asked for or not accepted by the political government. It is, to say the least, unlikely that the Labour Government decided to nationalize the steel industry on the advice of its senior civil servants, though their influence may have affected the half-hearted way in which this decision was carried out. Similarly, the Conservative leaders decided on the Suez expedition of 1956 almost certainly without—or against—the advice of the Civil Service. On the other extreme, many Government departments, such as the Home Office or the Ministry of Agriculture, have a supply of 'departmental' measures of legislation which are conceived, prepared and executed by their staffs without the initiative of their political chiefs. The normal run of Government policy probably falls between these extremes, with the politicians likely to get their way on measures important to them in their capacity of politicians and the officials advising in favour of the policy favoured by the department and emphasizing the dangers and difficulties of the opposite course of action.

The fact that the Conservatives in opposition were in favour of a policy of much closer relation with the Continent of Europe, while their policy in office was virtually indistinguishable from that of their Labour predecessors or that the Labour Government initiated the policy of Central African Federation which was almost diametrically opposed to the principles of its colonial policy in general, strongly

[1] Lord Woolton, *Memoirs* (1959), p. 372.

suggests the existence of official policies which remained virtually unchanged by changes of Government. It may, indeed, be true that 'there has been a tragic monotony of failure to appreciate the meaning of changes, social and political, to measure the strength of nascent national feeling, to gauge the impact on Britain, to devise policies to strengthen the country's diplomatic, political and economic strength to cope with it'[1]—and that all this was the fault of the Civil Service, though at the moment this cannot be supported by convincing evidence.

The rare occasions when the detailed workings of the government machine have been exposed to light were, of course, largely connected with failures such as Crichel Down and may, therefore, not be representative, but they conform to the general impression of a system reacting to the pressure of outside events and always one step behind them. This is strikingly confirmed by the expert description of the 'greatest of all current problems in the Foreign Service' by Lord Strang whose words may well be applicable to other spheres of administration confronted by a 'process of every-growing complexity': 'Expansion of staff, though sometimes inevitable, is no more than a partial solution to this problem. For it cannot relieve those at the top of the organization in their problem of delegated responsibility: on the contrary, it augments the weight of it. The analogy of the pyramid, so serviceable hitherto, begins unaccountably to fail us here: for the fact is that the apex of a pyramidal structure of the administrative kind becomes the more uncomfortable to occupy, the more gently the sides of the pyramid slope. Also, the force of gravity appears to slope upwards. Certain it is that the burden for those of the top increases with every new Department . . . that is added in order to meet some fresh need.'[2]

These necessarily disjointed impressions point to the existence of serious weaknesses in the structure and operations of the civil service, particularly at its highest level, though opinions may differ as to their gravity and their share in the responsibility for political failures.

[1] T. Balogh, 'The Apotheosis of the Dilettante' in *The Establishment* (ed. Hugh Thomas), (1959), p. 100.

[2] Lord Strang (and other members of the Foreign Service), *The Foreign Office* (1955), p. 198.

These defects are not of the kind characteristic of the growth of a ruling bureaucratic *élite* but rather indicate a gap between the performance of the administration and its present-day needs.

If the Civil Service has achieved much greater independence than the conventional view of the British Constitution admits, there is little reason to claim that it is on the way towards becoming a ruling bureaucracy in the Russian, or even in the less alien French, sense. Such a view grossly exaggerates the actual position to the point of travesty by mistaking distant trends and embryonic developments for accomplished facts. Above all, it ignores the fundamental truth that bureaucratic rule can arise only on the basis of a permanent near-balance of opposing social forces, which in Great Britain has not been reached or even approached.

The British business classes with their allies have never been in serious danger of losing their dominant position, and the degree of social tension between their interests and those of the rest of the community has generally remained fairly moderate. The inept economic policy of the inter-war years, with its subordination of the productive capacity of the nation to the supposed needs of financial orthodoxy, caused a temporary rise in tension which later on merged in the great popular revulsion against the effects of the policy of appeasement and led to the election of the post-war majority Labour Governments of 1945 and 1950.

It would be a mistake to identify directly the variations in the political fortunes of the main political parties with changes in social tension, though they are undoubtedly closely related. The rise of the Labour Party reflected widespread dissatisfaction with the rule of the business interests under Conservative Governments, but with rare exceptions the Labour Party has remained a minority, though a very large one in terms of votes, and its most influential leaders as well as its trade-union backers have consistently deprecated any radical challenge to the traditional social and political order. The resulting tension within the Labour Party between its Right and Left wings may best be interpreted as a kind of shock absorber preventing the tension between the great parties themselves from reaching a point where the political system as a whole would be in danger. This multi-tier structure, together with the operation of a two-party system operating in conditions designed to prevent a stalemate, generally at the expense of the minority, gives British parliamentary politics a strongly conservative bias which can only be overcome by a very definite shift of the electorate towards the Left.

On the few occasions when this shift has been strong enough to instal Labour Governments in office, the outcry against the growth of bureaucracy has greatly increased in volume and intensity, but it may be suspected that it has mistaken the symptom for the cause. State action limiting the freedom of movement of the business classes undeniably increased in such periods, because the social purposes of a Labour Government, however modest in themselves, can only be carried out by such action. As far as they are practicable within the existing social system, they modify its operations through government regulation and control enforced by the Civil Service. This certainly makes the latter more prominent, and it is probably also true that the Civil Service has enjoyed rather more independence under Labour and that Labour ministers have been inclined to accept the advice of their officials rather more meekly than their Conservative counterparts. This may have applied particularly to ministers who began their careers in the lower or middle ranks of the Civil Service, such as Philip Snowden and Sidney Webb under Ramsay MacDonald, and the promotion of temporary war-time civil servants to government rank in the Attlee governments of 1945–51 may supply more recent parallels.

It is not at all unlikely that the higher Civil Service has played a considerable part in neutralizing the professed political intentions of the post-war Labour Governments, and the glowing testimonials to its impartiality by ex-ministers, so far from being evidence to the contrary, might be taken as pointing in this direction. The general influence of the Civil Service in favour of the 'middle course' has probably become even stronger since Mid-Victorian times, when it was shrewdly described by Walter Bagehot: 'Ministers have to make good their promises, and they find a difficulty in so doing. They have said the state of things is so and so, and if you give us the power we will do thus and thus. But if they come to handle official documents, and converse with the permanent under-secretary—familiar with disagreeable facts, and though in manner respectful, yet most imperturbable in opinion—very soon doubts intervene . . . the new Minister says to the permanent under-secretary, "Could you not suggest a middle course . . ." and the end is always that a middle course is devised that *looks* as much as possible like what was suggested in opposition, but which *is* as much as possible what patent facts—facts that seem to live in the office, so teasing and unceasing are they—prove ought to be done.'[1]

In the special conditions of 1945 this dependence on the Civil Service was particularly important, because the situation was marked by a much more radical break with the past than is usual on changes of Government in more normal times: 'The new Government found themselves pledged to an almost revolutionary programme, but entirely dependent upon the civil servants to work out for them the highly complicated commercial details that were involved.'[2] This judgment may overstate the revolutionary implications of the Labour programme but it hits the nail on the head in emphasizing the limitations imposed on the Government by its complete reliance on normal Civil Service advice and procedure. The peculiar position of the British civil servant as 'permanent politican' under a two party system makes him naturally disinclined to irreversible changes which might involve the administration in serious trouble on a change of government, whatever his personal or political opinions. This aversion may well have left its imprint on much of the legislation of the post-war Labour Governments and still more on their administration; future historians in full possession of the facts may come to regard it as one of the more prominent reasons for the wide gap between their aims and their achievements.

If the hostility of the business classes towards the rule of the 'bureaucracy' under Labour thus tended to mistake the eminently conservative function of the higher Civil Service in the post-war era, it was nevertheless of considerable political importance through its effect on the policy of the Conservatives during the 1950s. The aim

[1] *The English Constitution*, pp. 144 f.
[2] *The Memoirs of Lord Woolton*, p. 358.

of 'setting the people free' involved a definite reduction in official powers, particularly in relation to the use of private property. In this context, the famous Crichel Down case was of more than symptomatic significance. The ferocity with which it was prosecuted to the point of the resignation of a popular minister fulfilled its purpose by serving notice on the Civil Service that the business community had no intention of abdicating in favour of the 'bureaucracy' and expected to be obeyed in matters where its individual and collective interests were at stake.

It may, however, be doubted whether the dominant classes of British society would be equally determined and effective, should circumstances require changes involving the collective interests of the Civil Service—and its recent performance has not been so convincing as to make this a purely hypothetical case. In the reform era of the nineteenth century, from the Northcote-Trevelyan Report of 1854 to Gladstone's Order in Council of 1870, this question never really arose. The obstacles in the path of reform were straightforward political difficulties, and the attitude of the officials themselves towards the contemplated changes counted for comparatively little. At present the Civil Service is a mammoth organization whose movements are controlled much more effectively by its own chiefs than by the political government. Formally, parliament may enact any law it pleases about the status, composition and operations of the civil service, but in practice such measures would either be regarded as encroachments on the powers of the Executive or submitted by the Government—and prepared and executed by the Civil Service, and particularly by the Treasury. The present balance of power between administrators and politicians is such that in matters deeply affecting the Civil Service the administrators themselves have the last, as well as the first, word.

This state of things is the necessary starting point for a brief look into the future. Although Britain has successfully avoided a serious bureaucratic degeneration of its public administration, the power of the Civil Service has waxed while that of the House of Commons has waned. It is not that the Civil Service has encroached on the preserves of the House of Commons but that parliament has failed to keep pace with the changing balance of power between different sectors of government. By subordinating virtually all other considerations to the needs of a clear-cut majority as the basis of stable government, British parliamentarism has steadily narrowed the scope of effective control over the activities of the Government, and still more over those of its permanent officials.

Whatever measures may be designed to adjust this balance, it is unlikely that it can be radically altered without a complete overhaul of the procedure and activities of the House of Commons. Without a grave convulsion of British society which there is no reason to anticipate, the same tendencies are, therefore, likely to operate in future, with a clear-cut division of functions between parliament and the administration, and the political government as their only link.

The inevitable consequence of this system is the careful protection of all vested interests, roughly in proportion to their effective power, and the determination of policy as the result of forces pulling in different directions. In such a system the Civil Service has little chance of becoming a ruling bureaucracy, but it has an excellent chance of staking and consolidating its claim as the vested interest specially concerned with public policy. The characteristic danger of such a development is neither revolution through the clash between a corrupt State and the outraged forces of society as in Tsarist Russia, nor dictatorship resulting from the stalemate between equally strong opposed interests as in France, but stagnation through habitual compromise at the expense of the future. This political myopia may be a hereditary reflex acquired at a time when a hand-to-mouth policy was reasonable and natural, because the mouth was hardly able to swallow all the plums within reach of the hands. Its perils in a different world were tragically brought home to the British people during the inter-war years, and the more hopeful but more dynamic post-war era may probe the adequacy of the traditional British political system even more deeply.

CHAPTER ELEVEN

BUREAUCRACY: CAUSE OR SYMPTOM?

1. COMING TO TERMS WITH LEVIATHAN

Bureaucratic rule is an evil which, once established, is almost ineradicable. It distorts the play of social forces by suppressing its enemies and stimulating its sycophants. Either way it makes gradual reform difficult or even impossible and invites violent revolution, as a rule at a high cost in human lives and material resources. But its overthrow by hostile forces rarely disposes of its historical consequences. Although discredited and defeated, it has created an ineluctable pattern for the succeeding regime which may at first merely try to adapt the organs and methods of the old system to its own purposes, only to end by re-establishing its substance while denouncing its forms.

The examples of Russia and France, however different in social background, economic structure and political history, both illustrate the extreme difficulty of repudiating the legacy of a fully-fledged bureaucratic system. In Russia, almost immediately after the Revolution a bureaucratic dictatorship was restored which differed from its predeccessor in many important respects but nevertheless remained a bureaucracy of even greater thoroughness, with the addition of a supplementary system of control through the bureaucratized Communist Party. In less than a generation its excesses had become a clear threat to its survival and, though reprieved by Stalin's death and the emergence of a reformer as his successor, there has been no change in the essentials of the power structure which would justify the expectation that good intentions will ultimately prevail over the bureaucratic tradition of centuries.

In France, the remodelling of the despotic monarchy of the *ancien régime* by Napoleon I remained the central factor in the changing political scene until the downfall of the Second Empire. The parcelling-out of power between politicians and bureaucrats under the Third Republic might at one time have encouraged the hope that the absolute State had been deprived of its taste for supremacy and turned into a complacent bourgeois. But the stresses of the transition to a more or less modern industrial society and the emergencies of 1914 and 1939, followed by a series of colonial wars for the maintenance of a crumbling empire, were too severe to be accommodated within the framework of parliamentary democracy; and the bureaucratic State took over as the natural receiver in bankruptcy of the democratic hopes of *la grande nation.*

To avoid the rut of bureaucratic rule and degeneration is thus no mean gain for a political system. The English-speaking world and the smaller continental democracies have, therefore, every reason to praise their political good fortune, and they may be pardoned the weakness of ascribing it to their superior political wisdom. Nevertheless, the universal expansion of governmental power and official influence makes the control of bureaucratic tendencies of the public administration a problem of much more than academic interest in all modern countries.

If bigness itself were sufficient to cause bureaucracy and ultimately bureaucratic government, the battle would be lost before it is even joined, for the giant State—and mass organization in party politics —has come to stay and may well continue to grow. But although the enormous size of modern organizations is a source of more or less serious bureaucratic defects, it does not necessarily produce bureaucratic degeneration. This happens only when the almost inevitable shift in the balance of power between an administration and its primary force is aided and abetted by outside factors.

With the loss of accuracy inseparable from such generalizations, this fundamental 'law' of modern organization may be condensed into a simple statement: *Large-scale administration tends to develop substantial symptoms of bureaucratic degeneration only when it functions within a field of sharply opposed social forces; it tends to change into bureaucratic rule only when these forces are nearly equal in absolute strength so that their conflict creates an equilibrium of power. In the State with its monopoly of legal power, such an equilibrium must em-*

brace all the dominant power factors: in political parties it is normally limited to the underlying organization.

The key questions of the problem of bureaucracy are thus not technical but social and political. Formulated in a loose but convenient way, they resolve themselves into estimates of the probable trend of social tension in modern society and, more specifically, in individual societies organized as separate political units. Such estimates lack the precision and reliability of technical calculations and they are also liable to a bias which may affect not only their accuracy but their very basis. The extension of government action in the Welfare State has been assailed by many critics as an intolerable bureaucratic excess; but if it results in a lowering of social tension—as it manifestly has done in every industrial nation which has made a serious effort in its direction—the ultimate effect should be the very opposite. If the power of a bureaucratic administration is bound to grow with a rise in social tension, it may confidently be expected to fall with a decline in the strength of the factor responsible for its growth. Differences in political outlook may thus lead to diametrically opposed conclusions on this subject, as on most others in social affairs, but this need not affect agreement on the need to avoid bureaucratic degeneration and rule.

The most insidious danger of the businessman's phobia of bureaucracy in the sense of government action is precisely to confuse this issue by making it a party matter; it is also utopian in its aims and faulty in its analysis of the facts. This vocal and popular *laissez faire* criticism of bureaucracy is in the last resort a reaction to government interference with private enterprise and the rights of private property; it is primarily a form of propaganda against the public control of economic life which adds very little to the understanding of the real problems of bureaucracy in which it is, in fact, not much interested. On the contrary, it has no real objection to bureaucratic methods within the 'legitimate' sphere of government where it regards them as innocuous or even meritorious; it is only when government impinges on the interests of the business community that it becomes an intolerable menace to liberty through the growth of official agencies for the regulation of the economy.

The practical prescriptions of the business critics of bureaucracy are just as sterile as their diagnosis of the evil. Let the State and its officials leave business men free to run their own affairs within the limits of the law (which are drawn as narrowly as possible), and bureaucracy will look after itself or at any rate not reach dangerous proportions. Let government itself be controlled by business men employing sound business principles, and bureaucracy will be stamped out root and branch.

Such ideas are inadequate to the point of caricature and have been shown up by the experience of many business men in government during and after the last war. The running of large administrative departments on 'business principles' is little more than a myth. The enormous growth of the theory and practice of modern management specially adapted to the organization of big business clearly demonstrates this fact. The technique of public administration is no doubt frequently antiquated and never perfect, but the same is only slightly less true of many old-established and prosperous business concerns. The difference is not one between administrative methods and business methods but between good administration and bad administration.

The *laissez faire* criticism of bureaucracy is a crude rationalization of powerful interests which has little relevance to the facts of life in advanced industrial society in the second half of the twentieth century, where about one-third of the national income passes through the hands of public authorities, where public investment for peace or war may make all the difference between boom and slump and where the maintenance of full employment and mass purchasing power has become an article of faith for all political parties, both for political and for economic reasons. Modern man must live with modern Leviathan, and the question is not how to kill it but how to tame it.

For if, at the most fundamental level, the future of bureaucracy in the real sense may well depend on the operation of broad historical forces defying purely technical devices, this is no reason for passive fatalism in face of an urgent topical problem. The real difficulty is, of course, the fact that part of this problem consists in a gradual shift in the balance of power between a nominally subordinate but organized and expanding system of administration and a theoretically sovereign primary organization which finds increasing difficulty in controlling it, partly because it is insufficiently prepared for this task and partly because it is rent by conflicting interests. If the administration functions within a field of social tension, control is bound to be defective, for no technical device, however well designed, can offset the effects of a social and political stalemate.

If it is true that the progress of bureaucracy is not tied to specific institutions but operates mainly through a change in the balance of power between them, the case for deliberate experimentation with new institutions becomes very strong; not because they are necessarily superior to the existing system but because this system, and the institutions which form part of it, has been subjected to the eroding effect of a progressive change in the balance of power. The fact that a certain proposal does not fit into the traditions of the existing system, far from being its final condemnation, may thus be a strong *prima facie* argument in favour of employing its principles, though not in favour of slavish imitation.

It is not at all impossible that an institution which is transplanted to a new environment may exert a stronger and even more salutary influence at least temporarily than in its original soil. The supremely British institution of parliamentary question time has lost much of its cutting edge in its old environment, because the civil service has learned by long experience how to cope with it, but it might be a very valuable addition to the armoury of control of the administration in other systems. In Britain, the operations of the Restrictive Practices Court provide an outstanding example of a successful innovation which has produced something of a revolution in the formal *mores* of the business community within a few years, and this example may not be without relevance for political institutions.

With this consideration in mind, the practical steps available may be divided, somewhat arbitrarily, into measures for strengthening the control of the administration through representative bodies and new measures for giving the public better protection against administrative decisions.

Parliamentary Control

Amongst the time-honoured ideas made obsolescent or obsolete by the advance of administrative power is the clear-cut division between parliament and Executive. Not only has parliamentary control of the Executive declined virtually everywhere, and not least that of the mother of parliaments, but also the Executive, regarded as a political body, has lost much of its control of the administrative machine of government. To strengthen the power of parliament thus appears the obvious way of ensuring that the dominant political forces maintain effective control of the civil service through representative political institutions: 'Parliamentary control of the Executive is inseparably linked to the Minister's own problem of how to control his own Ministry.'[1] If in Great Britain the issue of bureaucracy has so far remained relatively subordinate, this has not been due to the effectiveness of parliamentary control but to the fact that the business classes have, on the whole, remained in control of British society. On the other hand, the quantity and quality of informed and unfavourable criticism of parliamentary methods and procedure is equalled only by the complacency with which it has been rejected time and again by the powers that be.

The issue of parliamentary reform in general is a large subject in itself, but one of its aspects has a direct bearing on the improvement of measures against the growth of a bureaucracy. This is the question of specialized parliamentary committees as a device for bringing parliament closely to grips with the administrative process. In Britain the use of such standing committees is limited mainly to the financial aspect of control, and bodies such as the Public Accounts Committee or the war-time Committee on National Expenditure have proved their value within these limits. However, proposals for the systematic extension of this device to the setting up of specialized permanent standing committees in close touch with individual government departments have been repeatedly rejected.

The potential implications of such proposals in their most sweeping form are, indeed, incompatible with the function of the British parliamentary system, as was clearly shown more than fifty years

[1] Bernard Crick, *Reform of the House of Commons* (Fabian Tract 319, 1959), p. 35.

ago in a bold and consistent critique of this system as a whole which included the creation of such committees as its centre piece. F. W. Jowett ('of Bradford'), one of the pioneers of the Independent Labour Party, denied the effectiveness of parliamentary control of the Executive and claimed that ministerial control was, in fact, merely a cloak for the independent power of the permanent officials. His remedy consisted in 'the overthrow of the present system of single Ministerial control, supported as it is by joint Cabinet responsibility, and the substitution in its place of a system of committee government similar to the system which prevails in county and local government. . . . For those who are now Ministers, they might be chairmen of committees, but the powers they now wield should be vested in the committees over which they preside.'[1]

These proposals are a historical curiosity, for they were far too radical for the Government or even for the parliamentary leaders of the Labour Party, because they struck at the heart of the two party system. But the much more moderate suggestions supported by such undoubted admirers of the traditional British political system as Earl Lloyd George and L. S. Amery met exactly the same fate, and the same applies to a whole host of similar proposals made from time to time. All of them aim at the creation of a number of specialized standing committees, consisting of members specially interested in their subjects and keeping in close touch with the respective departments of State without, however, interfering with the exclusive responsibilities of the minister for executive action.

Although usually rejected as incompatible with the British parliamentary system and as having been discredited by the experience of France and the United States, such committees play an important part in many countries and might well do the same in Britain, particularly for the purpose of strengthening parliamentary control of the administration. The fact that they would have to be grafted on to a system with different traditions, so far from being an argument against them, may well be regarded as a further strong recommendation, because it might prevent the growth of the kind of defects which have been justly criticized in some other countries: 'Ministers

---

[1] *What is the Use of Parliament?* (1908), pp. 28, 29.

with us, unlike French or American Ministers, are unquestioned masters of the House and supported in their position of authority by a solid majority there which is naturally reflected in the composition of its committees.'[1]

The activities of such specialized committees might well become the focal point of detailed control of the civil service. Thus they might deal with some of the more technical questions asked at present in the House of Commons, thereby reducing not only the excessive strain on Question Time but also the opportunity for ambiguous or otherwise unsatisfactory answers which would have less chance of passing an audience familiar with their subject matter. They might, as recently suggested,[2] take over the work of the Committee on Estimates and might develop a technique of efficiency audits or adapt the Hearings of American Congress committees to British conditions, though there is no need for the wholesale adaptation of foreign models: with a virile political system, experience and the logic of developments would determine the precise form and scope of the institution, once it comes into being against the resistance of the beneficiaries of the *status quo*.

Parliamentary committees have an authority all their own which cannot be equalled by any other body, but there seems to be room for independent consultative committees representing outside interests and particularly any organs of local government affected by the operation of central government departments. Such committees should have the right, or rather the duty, of submitting matters of importance to the corresponding parliamentary standing committees and might limit the encroachments on the sphere of local self-government by the central authorities.

MP and Ombudsman

The parliamentary representative is a man of considerable influence in all democracies, though his prestige may vary from country to country. It is, therefore, natural and inevitable that he should be ap-

---

[1] L. S. Amery, *Thoughts on the Constitution* (1953), p. 54. The reference to France relates to the Fourth Republic.

[2] Crick, op. cit., p. 36.

proached by his constituents when they may want to obtain a favour from the authorities—which may obviously give rise to grave abuses —or when they think that they have been badly treated by a public body and want protection against abuses. With the growing volume and complexity of government activities this part of a representative's duties is bound to grow and it is, therefore, closely linked with the problem of bureaucracy in the widest sense: 'The public, when confronted with the bewildering diversity and, at times, remoteness of officialdom, needs to feel that it has an intermediary to whom it can turn for advice and help.'[1]

This help may take the form of a letter to a Minister, either to ensure the applicant of proper attention to his case or, in some instances, in order to question or challenge the action taken by a government department. Such a challenge is unlikely to be ignored, because the representative is either a government backbencher able to make his voice heard in the counsels of the ruling party, or he is a member of the Opposition eager to raise the matter in public for the purpose of embarrassing the Government.

The value of such an intervention with a government department is, therefore, considerable. As the member of parliament represents an independent and nominally superior power, it must be regarded as an important method of checking arbitrary administrative action. Its limitation lies in the fact that it is confined to a single case. It is, of course, possible that a letter from a member of parliament may induce the department to revise not only its course of action in a specific instance but also its procedure in all cases of a similar kind, but there is nothing in the relations between representative and administration to ensure this result. On the contrary, these relations, while courteous and respectful, are distinct and official, with the administration carefully weighing every word and giving away as little as possible, particularly when dealing with a member of the Opposition.

If the investigation of individual grievances is to be used as a generally effective method of controlling the administration, a more systematic device is required. The institution of the Ombudsman which

---

[1] Crick, op. cit., p. 10.

T   289

originated in Sweden but has 'colonised' other Scandinavian countries may well supply a model deserving of transplantation to new soil. It does not in any way weaken the position of the member of parliament as an honorary and honorific 'contact man' between the public and the government, but it permits the thorough probing of alleged administrative miscarriages in a way which would be impossible and, indeed, intolerable if it were carried out by the individual member of parliament.

The position of the Danish 'Parliamentary Commissioner for Civil and Military Government Administration' has been authoritatively described by the holder of this office.[1] He is a lawyer elected by parliament of which he must not be a member, and his jurisdiction comprises the public service as a whole, including Ministers but excluding the judiciary and local government. He is entitled to see official documents and records and may take action in case of official mistakes or acts of negligence, by ordering either prosecution before the ordinary courts or disciplinary proceedings; matters of major importance are to be reported directly to parliament.

These powers are substantial and the institution seems to meet the need for an impartial recipient of complaints against mistakes or abuses by the Civil Service. Many of them may be due to the public's ignorance of the way in which the government works, and in such cases the Commissioner may render a valuable public relations service both to the administration and to the public. The need for such an institution is shown by the fact that in a small and well-run democracy such as Denmark the number of complaints addressed to the Parliamentary Commissioner has risen from an annual rate of 750 in 1955 to 1,025 in 1957, about half of which qualified *prima facie* for investigation, while one in ten had some justification.[1]

However, the official purpose of the institution is rather more ambitious than so far described. The Commissioner is enjoined to 'keep himself informed' about cases of official mistakes and negligence and,

[1] Professor Stephan Hurwitz, *The Danish Parliamentary Commissioner* (*Public Law*, Autumn 1958, pp. 236-253). The article includes a translation of the Law No. 203 of June 11, 1958, setting up the Commissioner and of the parliamentary directions issued to him.

[2] *Ibid.*, p. 242.

even more comprehensively, 'on behalf of parliament keep himself informed of the civil and military government administration'.[1]

There is a world of difference between the useful task of independent investigation of individual grievances against specific official acts and a roving commission to act as watchdog of parliament in respect of the whole field of public administration. The former needs a small expert staff to sift complaints, explain to the complainant the reason for correct official decisions and institute further enquiries in case of need; the latter must supervise the administrative process as a whole in order to discover 'whether any person within his jurisdiction pursues unlawful ends, takes arbitrary or unreasonable decisions or otherwise commits mistakes or acts of negligence in the discharge of his or her duties'.[2] This is a task comparable in size and difficulty to the process of administration itself, which would require an enormous Inspectorate covering all branches of the Civil Service.

Without an organization of this kind—which would raise more problems than it can solve—such a task is clearly incapable of fulfilment, and the patent eagerness of parliament in handing over to the Commissioner the duty of supervising the administration as a whole smacks more of an elaborate pretence than of a serious will to wrestle with an intractable problem. Although the Parliamentary Commissioner is an excellent device for a limited purpose and in a position to carry out a task which neither parliament as a whole nor any individual member of parliament could tackle equally well, this institution does not in any way remove or reduce the need for parliament in its collective capacity to take adequate measures for controlling the administration.

Administrative Courts

Although the supervision of the executive branch of government is primarily a political matter, the redress of grievances suffered through the actions or omissions of administrative officials may well become a legal problem. If in Great Britain this aspect of the subject has at

[1] Section 5 of Law, and Article 1 of Directives, pp. 246, 249.
[2] Article 3 of Directives, p. 249.

times dominated the debate as a whole, this was only partly due to the interest taken in it by lawyers since Dicey's time. At least to some extent this fact reflects the remarkably wide privileges of the British Executive. The Government and its officials have retained more than a trace of the original status of the Crown as absolute legislator which has given it until recently quite unjustifiable advantages in litigation. In modern conditions, this has made it far too easy for the Civil Service to escape public accountability either by claiming privilege in order to prevent the disclosure of vital facts or by making ministerial decisions, as a rule taken by officials in the name of the minister, virtually unassailable by legal means.

There are good reasons for preventing private interests from upsetting the declared wishes of the legislature by protracted and costly litigation, but the critics have made a strong case for limiting the discretionary powers of the government which make a simple official statement, unsupported by any reasons, conclusive beyond the possibility of appeal. However, this might well be achieved by better means than the establishment of an elaborate system of administrative jurisdiction. Apart from the danger of putting the power of annulling political decisions into the hands of judges, such a system may well favour the growth of bureaucratic traits in administration; while making the operations of the Civil Service less arbitrary it tends to make them more rigid and may be used for the purpose of strengthening the corporate position of the bureaucracy *vis-à-vis* the political government even farther.

In this respect the institution of an administrative Court is similar to the organs of internal control and supervision of the administration which are a characteristic feature of typical bureaucracies such as those of Russia or China and which have invariably failed to achieve their purpose, because they are subject to the same forces which favour the bureaucratic degeneration of the system of government as a whole. In the last resort, the only effective check on the machine of government as a whole, ignoring normal methods of financial and disciplinary control, is that imposed by an independent outside power through political action. The ultimate limits of such action are determined by the balance of power within society and cannot be extended by purely technical arrangements, but there is ample room for improvements within these limits.

Political action for the better control of the administration must be based on the fact that outside control of administration is just as important as control of policy and that the traditional political system must be made fit for this purpose, without undue reverence for arrangements and institutions which are no longer in line with current needs. Although no panacea is in sight, the task can be tackled with a reasonable hope of at least partial success, provided that action is not hamstrung by excessive regard for vested interests whose stubborn defence of the *status quo* has proved only too effective in the past.

2. MASS ORGANIZATION AND POLITICAL ACTION

Modern Parties, and with them political mass organizations, have become an integral part of political life with the entry of the unprivileged masses on the political stage. In broad terms, the purpose of a party organization is that of concentrating the political strength of its supporters and of transforming it into effective political energy. The means adopted for this end depend largely on the framework within which the party operates. In a parliamentary regime such as the British, political energy is by and large effective in proportion to its influence on election results, and party organization is closely linked to the electoral system. In bureaucratic regimes, the State rules the population through its officials. The beneficiaries of the existing state of affairs thus have little use for well-organized parties, but their opponents set great store by their organization.

This different emphasis distorts the balance of the political system and weakens the political power of the conservative interests in times of crisis, when they cannot shelter successfully behind the bureaucracy. Under an absolute dictatorship like that of Tsarist Russia, the only effective parties were those whose aim was the overthrow of the regime, and when the Revolution withdrew the support of the State from their opponents, the most extreme and best organized party soon grasped supreme power, eliminated all others and has since maintained its dominant position as the true power centre of the Soviet State.

Even in a parliamentary bureaucracy like that of France during the Third Republic, the conservative parties rarely went beyond loose federations, and modern mass organizations were confined to the Left, and particularly to the Labour movement. Though the crisis of French society during and after the second World War was much less grave than the 1917 Revolution in Russia, it exposed the conservative classes almost unaided to the hostility of the masses under Communist and Socialist leadership, and their party organization was totally insufficient to enable them to withstand this onslaught. Throughout the Fourth Republic, various ephemeral groupings tried to rally the large potential support of the Right, and in the end its extreme anti-Republican wing in alliance with the army overthrew the regime.

Bureaucratic States thus inhibit the growth of a balanced party system and the absence of such a system may endanger the safety and survival of the regime in times of crisis, when the bureaucracy loses its normally powerful hold on the population. In democratic countries, on the other hand, the officials of the Government share the task of ruling the people with the political parties which are primarily responsible for ensuring the allegiance of the mass of the people to the established order. This division of functions is remarkably effective but quite informal and dependent on a low or moderate level of internal tension which is the condition of political democracy. As a rule, the most satisfactory arrangement for this purpose is a two-party system, though in favourable conditions such as those prevailing in most of the smaller European democracies more or less stable coalitions between groups of parties have also proved workable. Religious, regional and national pecularities embodied in history and tradition all play an important part in shaping the political institutions of each individual country which determine in their turn its party structure, but the normal state of affairs is the division into two parties (mainly in the English-speaking world) or at least into two camps.

In Western Europe, the main line of division between these two camps ran for a considerable time between the 'bourgeois' parties and the Labour movement. With the split between Social Democrats and Communists this division has become much more complex in countries where the Communists have gained a strong following amongst the workers, e.g. France and Italy, but in the smaller democracies and in Britain it remains the most important party political difference. The inherent problems of this situation are, perhaps, most apparent in Britain, because the two-party system emphasizes their ultimate results.

If the two parties are to ensure the political allegiance of the people to the existing regime, they must themselves accept it and they must be sufficiently strong to exclude political tendencies incompatible with it. A two-party system gives both parties a valuable stake in the *status quo* by giving the sweets of office to one of them and holding out to the other the hope of enjoying them at some future time. Hence both parties will develop broadly similar attitudes to the State and its administration. At the same time, the rival parties between them practically exhaust the possibilities of effective political action for all but a handful of highly-placed individuals: the two-party system makes them complementary in the sense of minimising the chances of other forces to break into the charmed circle of actual or potential party leaders. To all intents and purposes, the choice for the citizen with political interests lies between throwing in his lot either with one party or with the other—unless he wants to forgo the opportunity of effective political activity. As the parties are, almost by definition, agreed on maintaining the fundamentals of the existing system, their exclusive position safeguards the political stability of the system against any challenge except that of violent revolution.

From the point of view of the beneficiaries of the system, a political democracy with a two-party system (or an equivalent multi-party system under two permanent leaders) is greatly superior to a bureaucratic regime. There will always be a strong conservative party capable of rallying a large measure of mass support and therefore much less dependent on official help by the bureaucracy. On the other hand, in a political democracy the Labour movement will be opposed to any radical change in the political structure of the State and will accept the rules of the political game as binding in all circumstances. Provided the property-owning minority is willing and able to prevent a dangerous rise in social tension, even if this requires substantial concessions, enlightened self-interest suggests that such concessions are amply justified.

The effects of this state of affairs on the Labour movement are, of course, more far-reaching than on its conservative antagonist, which is normally dominated by a leading minority and uses its mass organization primarily as an electoral auxiliary. The Labour movement starts as a democratic mass party, generally with definite socialist aims which cannot be realized without radical social and economic changes. Its transformation into an alternative government within the existing political framework involves a growing divorce between the mass party and the parliamentary leadership in control of policy. The resulting internal tension creates the need for a strong party organization which is by definition not subject to the control of the mass party and which may tend to coalesce with the parliamentary leadership. Freedom from outside control promotes bureaucratic defects, and from a means serving the primary aims of the party the organization is transformed into a 'machine' intent on preserving its own position at almost any price.

The gradual rise of the party organization is paralleled by its growing professionalization. The power of the party machine and the sharpening division between leadership and rank-and-file weakens the idealistic incentive for voluntary party work and reduces the opportunities of service by the personally disinterested supporter, except at election times, though the value of voluntary political activity remains as great as ever for the aspiring politician.

A conservative party relies normally on a stream-lined organization of paid local representatives; its financial support is as a rule assured, and the management of its operations is a relatively simple matter. For the Labour movement, the transition to professional or semi-professional status is both more difficult and politically more important. Its financial resources are much more limited and the financing of a party machine of professional organizers presents a major problem, with the paradoxical result that its organizers spend much of their time in raising funds to pay their own salaries and acquire a disproportionately strong financial interest in the operations of the organization.

Though conditions vary from country to country, the concentration of policy decisions in the hands of a narrow circle of leaders and the professionalization of the party organization can be observed in the democratic Labour movement of practically every country outside the Soviet world where no independent Labour movement exists. The change from a 'movement' with broad social purposes and correspondingly radical political aims into the auxiliary of the parliamentary (and trade union) leadership creates the need for a strong central organization. The emergence of a semi-professional party machine closely allied with the leadership causes radical changes in the nature and internal balance of power of the party. Both forces expose a party of this kind to the danger of bureaucratic degeneration to which Conservative parties frequently remain immune. In the last resort, this is due to the fact that the Labour movement operates in a much more highly-charged field of hostile social forces. In favourable conditions, this has not prevented the working classes from improving their material conditions and social status, while integrating their political aspirations in a political party whose function is no longer that of changing the existing political system but, on the contrary, that of a breakwater against dangerous social currents; it acts in fact as a shock absorber preventing excessive disturbances from penetrating to the core of the social and political system and upsetting its balance.

During a long period of economic prosperity and rising mass standards of living, it may be expected that social conflicts will be muted, the political temperature will remain constantly tepid and the level of mass concern in politics will be relatively low; in such conditions it would be reasonable to assume a consolidation of the existing situation of complementary party machines operating the political government in alliance with one or the other of the strong vested interests of society—in other words, an Americanization of party politics matching similar developments in the economic and cultural field.

Such a system would be perfectly viable while these conditions are satisfied, but it would grow more and more rigid in important respects. The Labour movement would become less and less capable of fulfilling its historical function of leading the forces of opposition to the *status quo* with which it would become more and more closely identified. At the same time, the monopoly of political influence maintained by the complementary party machines would make it almost impossible for dissatisfaction to find another organized outlet within the existing system. Lastly, the bureaucratization of the parties and the concentration of power in the hands of the parliamentary leaders would make the system as a whole progressively less responsive to outside pressure for reforms—including the strong and growing need to reform the relations between the representative political bodies and the public administration. Bureaucratic parties may thus mean a more favourable soil for the growth of bureaucracy in the Civil Service.

The result of these trends might well be a comfortable equilibrium of vested interests, reducing political struggles to a civilized game of chess where the supremacy of the strongest player would always be ultimately recognized without complete disregard for the interests of the junior partners. Although not very exciting to watch, the system might be both sensible and profitable for the interests responsible for its operation, but its duration would depend not only on the permanence of domestic prosperity, or at least on the absence of severe economic upheavals, but also on international stability; and while such a Golden Age may not be impossible, it requires a good deal of hopefulness to gamble on this possibility in a game with the highest stakes.

In practice, conditions are likely to fall substantially short of this earthly paradise of the vested interests. Social tension may rise due to a depression, a change in economic climate or continuing international complications, and rising tension must find a political outlet. The more advanced the bureaucratization of the parties, the less likely are they to respond to this need. If tension rises only for a time, the system will take the strain and thereby add to its reputation for stability; if it rises permanently, the breakwater may be overwhelmed and political democracy itself might be endangered.

In critical circumstances, the ability of the Labour movement to attract the forces of change and to live up to their expectations may thus assume crucial importance not only for its own future but also for that of the advanced industrial nations of Western Europe. Freedom from bureaucratic tendencies and machine rule is perhaps the most important condition enabling it to play this part. It is, therefore, by no means encouraging that in this respect the Labour movement is the most problematical factor in the political life of modern society, though in other respects its most hopeful element.

INDEX

300

Index

THE END